THE SECOND ASSAULT

Recent Titles in
Contributions in Women's Studies

THE SECOND ASSAULT
ASSAULT Rape and Public Attitudes

Joyce E. Williams
&
Karen A. Holmes

Contributions in Women's Studies, Number 27

Greenwood Press
Westport, Connecticut • London, England

Library of Congress Cataloging in Publication Data

Williams, Joyce E
     The second assault.

     (Contributions in women's studies ; no. 27 ISSN
     0147-104X)
     Includes bibliographical references and index.
     1. Rape — United States. 2. Rape — United States —
     Public opinion. 3. Rape victims — United States —
     Attitudes. 4. Public opinion — United States.
     I. Holmes, Karen A., joint author. II. Title.
     III. Series.
     HV6561.W54   364.1'532'0973   81-339
     ISBN 0-313-22542-7 (lib. bdg.)   AACR1

Library of Congress Catalog Card Number: 81-339
ISBN: 0-313-22542-7
ISSN: 0147-104X

First published in 1981

Greenwood Press
A division of Congressional Information Service, Inc.
88 Post Road West
Westport, Connecticut 06881

Printed in the United States of America

10 9 8 7 6 5 4 3 2 1

CONTENTS

ILLUSTRATIONS

TABLES

PREFACE

Women who are raped experience more than the obvious effects of physical and sexual victimization. All too frequently a *second assault* is directed toward the victims of rape, an assault of judgments and attitudes which may be unwittingly perpetrated and yet is equally devastating in its impact. The second assault is not simply a reflection of the behavior or attitudes of any one individual or group toward specific victims. Rather, it reflects the wider social context of rape, the coming together of both historical and contemporary attitudes about men and women, their relationships and their "appropriate" behavior. For women who are raped, the essence of the second assault is skepticism, blame, and even condemnation, emanating from society at large, from one's own community, from one's own self-blame (an internalization of the attitudes of others), from family, and from significant others.

In this work, we conceptualize rape as a compounded phenomenon, and we seek to investigate its impact from the perspective of the victim. We simultaneously attempt to illuminate rape as it exists in the "public mind," and specifically at the level of the racial-ethnic community. Our theoretical perspective is that of racial-sexual stratification. However, our testing of the theory is limited not only by the methodological constraints of attempting to empirically assess such an emotional issue, but also by the fact that we have studied the subject in only one metropolitan area in the southwestern United States. We therefore advise the reader not to overgeneralize our findings as representing the ultimate reality of all rape victimization or of all public attitudes about rape. Rather, we present this research as a case study, as one "piece" of social reality which focuses on how rape was experienced by some victims in one geographic area as juxtaposed to their community's perception of rape.

Our interest and concern with the issue of rape date back to the mid-1970s when we both worked as volunteers with a community service-delivery program for rape victims. Early in that experience we began to talk and to exchange ideas about rape. Our discussions and the questions we formulated returned again and again to two observations: (1) that while rape is always a negative, traumatic experience, it seems to be differentiated by such structural variables as social class and race-ethnicity; and (2) that rape as a social phenomenon is more than the violent, idiosyncratic behavior of a rapist. This work is the result of our efforts to explore, to understand, and—to a degree—to explain the interplay between society and the experience of rape, the interaction between the victim and her social world. Our perspectives evolve from two traditions: humanistic sociology and social work advocacy.

From the theory of racial-sexual stratification which guided our research, rape is viewed as a convergence of racism and sexism in a social system where life chances (positive and negative) are determined largely by sex and/or race-ethnicity. Rape, as a social phenomenon, is examined in terms of the interplay of individual biography and the power of a White, male-dominated social structure. On another level, we suggest that in everyday life, individuals relate to rape in terms of how they perceive certain risks or threats associated with it, and that these are socially determined. Therefore, males and females, Whites, Blacks and Mexican Americans are related to these risks in different and unequal ways: by frequency of victimization, by frequency of being labeled the "alleged rapist," by societal reaction, by impact and consequences. To women, rape is a threat to life, safety, sexual autonomy, and personal control. Some women, by virtue of who they are, appear more vulnerable to victimization than others; some women are considered more "at fault" than others. To men, rape can also be a physical threat, although sexual assault on males is infrequent (except perhaps in jails and prisons) compared to the incidence against females. More than this, however, to men, rape represents a threat to property, to exclusive sexual privilege, and a threat as perpetrators of the crime—as suspects.

Few people are indifferent to the issue of rape because it does pose a threat, but more insidious than indifference is a self-protective denial of reality. The public manifests such denial in many ways: denial that a woman can be raped unless she "wants to be" or unless she "asked for it"; denial that all women are potential victims by virtue of their physical strength, anatomy, and socialization; and denial that all men are potential or suspected rapists for the very same reasons. The end result of pervasive threat and social uneasiness is a kind of defensive thinking which identifies rape as happening only to females who behave inappropriately or assume foolish risks, and/or that rape is perpetrated by sick, depraved males who hate women. The public must defend itself against rape and against the victims of rape in order to preserve a sense of well-being; the victim must, in turn, defend herself against public attitudes that assault her a second time.

This work was originally executed as two independent parts of one research project: a study of rape victims (under the direction of Holmes) and a study of public attitudes (under the direction of Williams). From inception of the initial research idea through final writing, however, the work has been a joint endeavor. Our conceptualization of the problem clearly suggests that rape has both intrinsic and extrinsic meaning, that while the victim's experience may be the more visible side of rape, the public's reaction becomes a significant part of her experience. With this approach, we hope that we have succeeded in integrating both the personal and public views of rape to provide a more holistic grasp of the problem. To neglect either, we believe, is to preclude an understanding of the interactive nature of rape and its consequences for us all. The organization of the book follows this dual conceptualization, moving from the victim's experience into the public view of rape.

Chapter 1 provides an overview of the "rape problem," tracing the development of knowledge through the contributions of psychiatry and psychology, sociology, and, most recently, the feminist literature. Chapter 2 develops our theoretical framework as a theory of racial-sexual stratification, while the research setting, design, and methodology are described in Chapter 3. Chapters 4 and 5 focus on the victim, first with a detailed qualitative description of the rape experience, followed by a quantitative analysis of variations in victim responses to rape and a systematic look at rape-as-crisis. A transition is provided by Chapter 6 where both victims and the public offer their opinions about rape, its cause and prevention. Chapters 7 and 8 examine public attitudes about rape, first by describing the complex social context of rape, and then by attempting to establish some causal, empirical linkages between attitudes about rape and certain sex and race-related beliefs and attitudes. Finally, Chapter 9 reflects what we see as some of the major implications of this work, particularly in terms of acknowledging rape as more than a social problem, but as part of a system of racial-sexual stratification.

As a final note, we acknowledge an obvious feminist perspective, but we have tried to achieve an overriding humanistic perspective in the work as a whole. While there is truth in Susan Brownmiller's assertion that rape is "a conscious process of intimidation by which *all men* keep *all women* in a state of fear," surely men also know fear or they would not need the intimidation and weaponry of rape. Rape is not just "the crime against women" or a "woman's nightmare." It is an assault against personhood which has its origin and maintenance in a system of social inequality that victimizes all, but some more than others.

Joyce E. Williams
Karen A. Holmes

ACKNOWLEDGMENTS

We would first like to acknowledge the National Center for the Control and Prevention of Rape (NCCPR) for providing grant support (RO1 MH27928) for the research project on which this book is based. That support allowed us to pursue a common interest from idea to fruition. We, of course, accept full responsibility for the final product. The ideas expressed are solely our own and those of the persons who participated in our research as we have understood them.

Many individuals have contributed their time and energies to this work over the past five years. In a sort of loose chronological order, and more briefly than we would like, we wish to express our appreciation to Ruth Galloway and Barbara Wilkinson of Galloway Field Service for recruiting and supervising interviewers for the public attitude survey; to the interviewers themselves for their tenacity and long hours of work; to Richard Santos and Yvonne Gonzales for translating the interview schedules into Spanish; to Oliver Heard, J.D., for legal assistance in developing the informed consent agreements; to John Lindquist for drawing the public attitude sample; and to Hubert Feild for his suggestions regarding statistical analysis. We would also like to acknowledge the past coordinators and members of the Alamo Area Volunteer Advocate Program, Inc. (AAVAP), for permission to engage in the victim research, and special thanks to Rory Rodriguez of AAVAP for help with interviewing Spanish-speaking victims; also, our thanks to Sylvia Calloway and the staff of the Austin Rape Crisis Center for their generous assistance with the victim research.

Most members of the research team learned first-hand about the multiplicity of roles involved in a project of this kind. As research assistants, Candace Foster, Glenda Smith-Hansen, and Dianne Martin worked laboriously on the coding of public attitude data; Carol Cockrell single-handedly carried responsibility for computer processing of all the data; our inimitable "contact person" in the victim research was Jackie Michalec who, along with Dianne Martin, conducted many of the victim interviews. Janna Taylor and Christy Visher diligently typed early and final drafts of both interview schedules, while Brenda Farmer-Atherton typed most of the final project report as submitted to the NCCPR. Finally, Barbara Starr took our initial drafts and skillfully transformed them into the illustrated figures which appear in this book. Our very sincere thanks to each of them for their many contributions.

While we obviously cannot acknowledge them by name, we offer a very special debt of gratitude to those women (victims) who, despite whatever apprehension they may have felt, granted us an interview. They discussed their experiences with a remarkable sense of resolve and with the frequently voiced hope that "maybe it will help others to understand." We share that hope and offer our thanks for the trust they placed in us. Finally, our appreciation is no less sincere for the 1,011 citizens of San Antonio, who comprised our public attitude sample and took time to think about the problem of rape and to share their thoughts with our interviewers.

We are grateful to all of those persons who, by their time and effort, supported the spirit and intent of this work. However, because "rape research" is still somewhat new and different, the *lack* of support we encountered should also be mentioned, particularly for the benefit of those about to embark on similar projects. "Rape research" is apparently not yet quite legitimate: the ubiquitous "man-on-the-street" wonders what there is to study ("Don't you think most of those women are just asking for it"?) and is already certain of the solution to the problem ("For them who really do rape, just hook up ol' 'Sparky'"). ("Sparky" is a term used locally to refer to the electric chair at the Texas Department of Corrections.) But perhaps even more revealing are the comments made within the "liberal" halls of academe where male colleagues (now former colleagues) tittered that they would like to "volunteer for the rape research," or inquired from time to time if they could "learn how to rape." To treat rape as an object of humor is, of course, a defensive response to a subject that creates considerable discomfort and that, ironically, is part of what our work has been about. Ultimately, we hope that this research not only makes a contribution to the legitimization of rape as a subject of scientific inquiry, but that it also moves us beyond discomfort, toward a more enlightened understanding of the complexities of "the rape problem."

THE SECOND ASSAULT

FROM PERSONAL TROUBLE TO SOCIAL ILL

1

The controlling, restrictive fear of rape is part of being a female. It is part of socialization to the feminine role. It is one of life's cruel ironies, however, that the experience of rape which a woman has been taught to fear and to resist to the point of death brings not a public show of support but a public display of skepticism and even blame. All too frequently, rape victims experience a second assault perhaps more cruel in its compounding effect than the first.

Until recently, rape was no more than "personal trouble" for any woman who happened to fall victim to this "heinous crime." And all too frequently the victim chose not to report her violation or to share her trouble outside of a few intimate friends and family members who guarded the secret to protect her from public embarrassment. The protective, silent shield of guilt and embarrassment has not disappeared, but at least for a significant number of women, it is gradually disintegrating—largely because of the women's movement and the growth of feminist ideology which have served to increase sensitivity to the women's issues that have accompanied it. Rape has become a *cause célèbre* for feminists; their interest is both symbolic and real. The rape issue is real in that rape is a serious threat and danger to today's woman. According to FBI crime statistics, in 1979, 67 out of every 100,000 females in this country were reported rape victims. That victim rate has increased steadily since the mid-1960s when it was 23 per 100,000. The number of unreported rapes is estimated conservatively to be at least four times the number of those reported. For feminists rape has a symbolic interest in that it is by definition a crime against woman, denying her the freedom to control her own body, to choose her own sexual partners, or to choose sexual abstinence. Thus, in one act, rape represents the violent filching of freedom, sexual objectification, male dominance, and force—all issues to which the women's movement has vigorously addressed itself. Clearly, the definement of rape as a social problem rather than as personal trouble to be borne in silent shame is a product of the women's movement

(Rose, 1977a). The issue of rape has provided feminists with credibility, and the anti-rape movement has given substance to feminist rhetoric.

Although not always positive, throughout the 1970s the issue of rape was before the public—on the printed page, on television talk shows, on television dramas, and in the press coverage of trials involving a woman's right to defend and/or avenge herself, as in the cases of Joanne Little and Inez Garcia. In 1978, the International Women's Year Conference debated and passed a resolution denouncing rape and advocating support for services to victims of rape. On a local level, community groups began work to secure and maintain adequate medical-counseling services for rape victims. Women's groups sponsored workshops on rape and self-defense and held speakouts to encourage women to talk about rape and to report it as they would any other crime. Advocacy groups began work to insure the rights of rape victims with the police and in the legal-judicial process. At least one judge was removed from office as a result of his blatantly sexist remarks about a rape case. In some cities, women organized against rape were known to publicly label a man as a rapist after the judicial process had acquitted him, and in a few cases, women even took justice into their own hands in dealing with rapists.

Rose traces what she terms the anti-rape movement to a stage of institutionalization which was preceded by and resulted from the earlier stages of incipiency and coalescence within the women's movement. According to Rose, institutionalization means acceptance of rape as a social problem by the formal organizations and institutions of society and the subsequent marshaling of resources and legal-judicial processes to alleviate the problem (1977b, pp. 179–85). Institutionalized response is evident in the fact that some states have revised their rape laws and others are in the process of doing so. Areas of change include deletion of the corroboration requirement, elimination of certain testimony about the victim's "character" (past sexual history), and expansion of the law to include husband-wife rape and sexual assault in general. Reform measures are also evident in police training and in the judicial process to insure that the victim is not on trial, and that "lack of consent" does not have to be proven by physical resistance which might, in fact, endanger the victim's life (BenDor, 1976).

A major result of institutional change has been the development of community services for victims of rape (Largen, 1976; and Gager and Schurr, 1976, pp. 257–78). Since the early 1970s, there has been a steady proliferation of programs, initiated in most cities in the form of a crisis line with volunteers offering telephone counseling and referrals. Largely because of the organized efforts of women's groups, most major cities (and many smaller ones) now have some form of counseling and medical services designed to meet the needs of rape victims. In many cases, these services are tax supported. The more progressive police departments have responded to the lobbying-educational efforts of the anti-rape movement by including in their officer training special instruction and sensitization about rape victims; some departments are now utilizing female officers to take statements from rape victims and to investigate rape cases. It should also be pointed out that not all institutional responses to the anti-rape movement have been local. The federal government made an early response to the needs of rape victims by funding a number of rape crisis centers across the country with Law Enforcement Assistance Administration (LEAA) funds.[1] A comprehensive manual of responses to rape (community, medical, and legal-judicial) was developed as a "prescriptive package" by the Center for Women Policy Studies, funded by LEAA (Brodyaga, et al., 1975). In the mid-1970s, the National Center for the Prevention and Control of Rape was added to the National Institute of Mental Health to provide funding for research into the causes and prevention of rape.

A good indicator of public and academic interest in a topic is the number of publications—both of a popular and a scholarly nature—which appear over a certain time period. Such publications, of course, then play a part in both defining a problem and resolving or alleviating it. One measure of interest in rape is the appearance—from the early to mid-1970s—of several bibliographies and edited collections of works on rape. A bibliography by Feild and Barnett (1977) is an update of an earlier work (Chappell, Geis, and Fogarty, 1974); it covers materials published since 1974 and cites 371 references. An annotated bibliography compiled by Kemmer (1977) covers the rape-related literature published in English from 1965 to 1976 and cites 348 references from professional journals, popular periodicals, and books. From 1975 to 1977, four edited collections of works on rape were published (Schultz, 1975; Walker and Brodsky, 1976; Nass, 1977; and Chappell, Geis, and Geis, 1977). In a very short time, the rape-related literature has proliferated, further contributing to public awareness and to the definition of rape as a social problem, and perhaps demonstrating some measure of success for the feminist anti-rape movement. This increased attention has redefined a victim's trouble, making it into a social problem. Unfortunately, however, as we stand ready to mobilize for combat and prevention, we are poorly equipped. We are looking for a "cure" when our causal assumptions have been reached more by default than by the accumulation of empirical evidence.

Rape and the Search for Cause

Some representative literature can be offered to document that the "cause" of rape has moved (somewhat chronologically) from micro, to meso, and to macro in perspective. The micro-level view of causation is represented by the clinical studies of rapists which accounted for most of the rape literature well into the 1960s; the meso-level view is represented by the sociological studies which began to appear in the 1960s; and finally, the macro-feminist literature came to the forefront in the early 1970s. Until the feminist perspective gained prominence, the focus was obviously on the offender, although, as some of the literature illustrates, when the victim was discussed, she was often seen as having "participated" in her own rape.

The Clinical Perspective

Clinical studies of rapists have largely been limited to incarcerated or institutionalized offenders. There are obvious problems with such populations: they cannot be assumed to be representative, and they generally provide only a small number of sample cases. Such studies have often categorized rapists into typologies based on motivation (Guttmacher and Weihofen, 1952; Kopp, 1962; and Gebhard, Gagnon, and Pomeroy, 1965); treatment classification (Pacht, Halleck, and Ehrmann, 1962); or "clinical classes" based on sexual and aggressive impulses as well as descriptive features of the rape itself (Cohen, et al., 1971). These studies have obviously treated the offense of rape as an isolated act of a deviant individual; rape is viewed as symptomatic of individual pathology or "character disorder." "Rapist" is not, in and of itself, a psychiatric classification, and clinicians have been unable to isolate personality characteristics which distinguish the rapist from other offenders. Neither can a consensus be found to explain what causes rape or even what constitutes "the psychology of rape." Since most clinical studies have reflected the assumption that the rapist is a deviant or pathological case, little attention has been given to the role society thrusts on males from their "blue blanket" beginning, nor has attention been given to the female role in general. Rather, females have been studied in male-related. roles (for example, the domineering mother, the teasing-seductress, the castigating female). The clinical portrait of a rapist is that of a male who feels "weak, inadequate and dependent" (Fisher and Rivlin, 1971): the act of rape is seen as an expression of hostility toward females who, knowingly or unknowingly, threaten the male ego. Very few clinicians have directed their analytic skills to society at large; instead, they have studied the aberrant behavior of individuals who somehow did not learn how to handle being masculine in a socially acceptable way. Perhaps the view of rape as sick, idiosyncratic behavior would not have survived so long had clinicians not been limited to studying only those rapists who got caught or confessed. They might have seen in "everyman" some of the same "symptoms." From infancy on, we teach a little boy to "be a man," a phrase that carries a frightening array of expectations.

A work by MacDonald (1971) recognizes rape as a multidimensional phenomenon and purports to "throw some light on the crime, the offenders and their victims" (p. vii). Ultimately, however, MacDonald is a clinician, turning a Freudian eye on both victims and offenders, and recounting an inordinate number of case examples describing rapes that are at best matters of subjective definition and at worst false accusation. MacDonald's concern for male victimization overshadows his concern for female victimization. He not only devotes a full chapter to false accusations of rape, but also has another on injustices in the courts (against males accused of rape). Still a third chapter is devoted to the judicial review of a rape case in which the victim "asked for it" and was tried for her reputation and behavior. Meanwhile, feminists have said what clinicians have failed to say, and apparently have not seen: that rape is the exacerbated act of "being a man." As Jean MacKellar put it: "The man who rapes does so because he lacks a better means for making his point, 'I am a man'" (1975, p. 135). A recent work by Groth and Burgess (1977) provides empirical support for the "I am a man" syndrome. Examining detailed data on 225 rapes (92 victim reports and 133 offender accounts), the authors identified two kinds of rape based on underlying psychological determinants: (1) *power rape*, which provides the offender with a sense of strength and power (65 percent of the 225 cases were so labeled); and (2) *anger rape*, characterized by violence and the use of unnecessary force (35 percent of their cases). However, Groth and Burgess still treat rapists as sick, labeling their behavior as symptomatic of internal or developmental crisis. These authors also ignore the underlying issue of sex-role socialization, acknowledging only indirectly the implications of their findings in this respect.

The Sociological Perspective

So strong was the clinician's territorial claim to rape as a problem of deviant sexual behavior that social psychologists and sociologists did little work in this area, except to take note of rape along with other violent crime, until the late 1960s and early 1970s. The first major sociological work was that of Menachem Amir, using the Durkheimian model "to find the relationship between the rates for the offense and the participants, and other various social facts to which they may be connected" (1971, p. 319). Amir's study of rapes reported to the police in Philadelphia over a two-year period (1958 and 1960) is primarily ecological and focuses on characteristics of offenders and victims. He has been criticized by feminists for devoting an entire chapter of his book to "victim-precipitated" forcible rape. However, Amir is simply following a tradition established by the well-known sociologist, Marvin Wolfgang, in his analytic treatment of victim-precipitated murders. Amir explains that victim-precipitation "consists of acts of commission (e.g. she agreed to drink or ride with a stranger) and omission (e.g. she failed to react strongly enough to sexual suggestions and overtures)" (p. 261). Amir then analyzes 122 cases (19 percent of his total population) which he labeled as victim-precipitated based on a description of the circumstances of the rape as recorded in the police offense report.

Amir's work has been frequently cited by feminists and by race scholars as a classic example of "victim-blaming." His analysis of victim-precipitated rape is, in reality, only part of his total work. His major focus is on the offender as he seeks out a causal explanation for rape, and he turns to a well-established and frequently used sociological theory: the subculture of violence. Two facts apparently led Amir to this explanation: 77 percent of the reported rapes in his study occurred intraracially between Blacks, and based on an analysis of occupation and place of address, the offenders were overwhelmingly poor. Therefore, he theorized that rape was an integral part of a lower class subculture of violence where "aggressive and exploitative behavior toward women become part of their [lower class boys] normative systems" (1971, pp. 325–26). As the first community-wide study of rape using social as opposed to psychological facts, there is a wealth of ecological analysis in Amir's work, and while much can be learned from it, his theoretical explanation is a double exercise in victim-blaming. He gives considerable attention to victim-precipitation and then moves to a subculture of violence explanation which places the blame for rape as a social problem not on society at large, but on a Black subculture of poverty and violence. There are several problems with this approach: (1) The subculture theory itself has been seriously questioned and criticized as largely the product of White sociologists; it is an "outsider's" explanation of poverty-related, Black behavior.[2] (2) The representation of Blacks in the incidence of rape in Philadelphia is not characteristic of all cities or of all time periods. (3) The theory may only fit those rapists about whom something is known (from police reports); it may not fit those where information on the rapist is sketchy, and it probably does not fit the majority of unreported rapists at all.

Amir's work has had considerable influence on the sociological study of rape. Researchers working with data from other cities have tended to compare their findings with the Philadelphia study, although they have frequently differed from it in important ways (Agopian, Chappell, and Geis, 1974; Chappell, Geis, Schafer, and Siegel, 1977; and Chappell and Singer, 1977). The work of Lynn Curtis is another example of meso-level theory as an explanation of rape. Curtis differs from Amir by attributing the cause of Black-Black rape to a contraculture as opposed to a subculture of violence. Although the characteristics of a contraculture are not made entirely clear, it is seemingly comprised largely of young, Black, urban males who are in overt conflict with the dominant culture. For example, Curtis explains that the subculture of violence includes some Black females, while the contraculture is primarily a male bastion. By definition then, males rape females (most of whom are also Black) outside the contraculture, and this is why "sizable numbers report to the predominantly white American police institution" (1976, p. 127). In Curtis' conceptualization, male members of the contraculture are "outsiders" in the Black community. He also implies, but offers no supporting evidence, that only "outsiders" are reported to the White police establishment. Given that the meso-level approach to the problem of rape has been soundly sociological, most writers have been careful to acknowledge the inequities (economic and racial) which spawned the so-called Black subculture or contraculture, though some have ignored the power stratification that maintains it. However, there may be insidious—though unintended—consequences of our present knowledge base with regard to rape, a knowledge base shaped largely by empirical sociological work (with data fitted to a subcultural model) and mixed with the ideology of the feminist anti-rape movement.

The Feminist Perspective and Some Unanticipated Consequences

The origin of the feminist, anti-rape campaign (at least in print) is frequently attributed to the publication of an article by Susan Griffin, "Rape: The All American Crime" (1971), where she described rape as a violent form of social control serving effectively to keep women in their "place." Other feminist literature is no less ideological, but much of it has been aimed at survival and self-help as well as consciousness-raising, encouraging women to report and prosecute rapists, and providing support and the rudimental guidelines for establishing service-delivery programs for rape victims (Connell and Wilson, 1974; Horos, 1974; and Medea and Thompson, 1974). Some early works were written primarily to destroy the common myths that surround rape (MacKellar, 1975) and to examine the institutional systems that victims encounter when they elect to report a rape (Gager and Schurr, 1976). Without doubt, the magnum opus of the anti-rape literature is Susan Brownmiller's *Against Our Will: Men, Women and Rape*. Nearly half the book is an historical chronology of rape as a tactic of war, as an outgrowth of mob violence, as an offensive weapon of racial oppression, and as a defensive minority reaction, all documented with over 400 source notes. It is not pleasant reading. It is disturbing because it lays bare the true meaning of rape: it is not sex; it is power, convoluted racial-sexual power.

One of the unanticipated consequences of the burgeoning feminist anti-rape campaign lies in the increasing incidence of rape. Apparently, this campaign has given more women the courage to report assaults since, statistically speaking, the number of known (reported) rapes has been increasing steadily for several years. However, there is really no way to determine what proportion of the increase is attributable to increased reporting, increased police acceptance of cases, and/or an increase in the crime itself. Apart from the possible spurious increase as a result of more reporting, the women's movement will likely produce another, more direct—albeit short-term—increase in rape: the rape of "liberated" women. The ideological posture of feminists on the issue of rape is unequivocal: rape is the product of a sexist society, emanating from the differential and unequal masculine-feminine sex roles to which we are socialized and subjected from birth. If the cause of rape is firmly rooted in the fact that males are socialized to be masculine-dominant and females are socialized to be feminine-submissive, it is then possible to generalize to the view that "men are conditioned to be rapists; women are conditioned to be victims. In the most dehumanizing sense, it is a 'perfect' pathological fit" (Gager and Shurr, 1976, p. 255).

It is in a sociological work by Weis and Borges (1973) that we find the most direct linkage between a predicted increase in the incidence of rape and the women's movement. Their reasoning is firmly rooted in the feminist explanation of rape as emanating from sex-stratification-socialization in our society. They contend that socialization (sex-role learning in particular) exploits both men and women and ultimately produces both offenders and victims. In their view, until society comes to accept the "liberated woman," she will be especially vulnerable to rape—by strangers and by acquaintances. The liberated woman will make choices in life-style, dress, language, work, leisure, friends, and sex partners on the basis of personal preference, not on the basis of traditional sex-role expectations. Realistically, until men develop some understanding of the new feminine behavior, the incidence of rape can be expected to increase. There are two reasons for this increase. First, the liberated life-style will be an open invitation to men who still cling to the stereotype of what "nice" women should and should not do. Consequently, the behavior of the liberated female is likely to increase sexual assaults by strangers (assailants unknown to the victim). As Weis and Borges point out: "Her appearance in behavior and dress, meant to convey only her anticonformity and striving for independence from male protection, may be misinterpreted as an indication of indiscriminate sexual availability" (1973, p. 96). Second, the liberated woman is often sexually active and will not rely on moral or virginal protestations to reject a sexual advance. As a result, situations in which unsuccessful seductions become rapes—"date rapes"—are likely to increase. If a woman says "no," it is likely a matter of personal choice, and as Weis and Borges note, "since both participants 'lose face' when the refusal is blunt and without the usual justifications, the rejected suitor may take it as a personal attack" and respond with physical force (1973, p. 97).

In the long run, the women's movement can be expected to contribute to more autonomy for both sexes and to sexual equality which will allow women to ask and be asked for sexual experience, but will also grant them credibility when they say "no"—all changes that should contribute to a reduction in the incidence of rape. In the short run, however, there are reasons to expect a continued increase in rape: (1) changes in female behavior—increased mobility apart from traditional male "protection," greater freedom in behavior, dress, and activity; (2) increased reporting of rape because of the educational and supportive functions of the anti-rape movement; and (3) reactionary rape by males who see liberated females as "asking for it" or by rejected would-be sex partners. While the feminist literature on rape contains one overriding theme—that rape is the product of a sexist, violent society—what is not explicitly acknowledged is the deduction that the incidence of rape will increase in the interim as society is radically reformed into a state of sexual equality. At the present time, women's liberation is a dialectical process containing both the problem and its solution.

The other significant unanticipated consequence is one that has been ignored or overlooked in the feminist perspective, perhaps because there is an obvious strain or even an antithesis. Given the existing racial-sexual stratification of society, to have raised rape to the level of a public issue (as the feminist anti-rape movement surely has) is to place yet another burden of responsibility (blame) on minorities—Blacks nationwide and, in some communities, Hispanics and/or Native Americans. As the anti-rape movement has gained momentum, considerable community pressure has been exerted on law enforcement personnel to treat cases more seriously and to apprehend rapists. Further pressure has been exerted on the judicial system to be less discriminating in terms of the cases that are finally tried. Clearly, if the legal-judicial system simply does *more of the same,* then minority males will be arrested and prosecuted in greater numbers. To date, the feminist anti-rape movement has overlooked this issue, and attempts at objective analysis have been hampered by indigenous problems: (1) Accurate statistics on rape are unknown and only estimates, or perhaps "guesstimates," are available as to reporting variations by intra- versus intergroup rape. (That is, do women report any more or less if their assailant is of their own race-ethnicity?) (2) Empirical study of rape has been limited by incomplete data (usually police or victim reports) and constrained first by a clinical or micro- (deviant case) approach and later by a meso-level sociological approach (the deviant or pathological subculture).

Gaps in the Knowledge Base

The feminist anti-rape perspective has contributed a first-rate interpretive history of rape and an accrual of work directed at the needs and problems of rape victims. In terms of linking rape with causal factors on the macro-level, however, feminists have apparently been content to run with the *a priori* assumption that rape is caused by sex-role stratification, despite the fact that no empirical evidence has been offered. Reflection on both societal stratification and available statistics clearly suggests that the feminist rationale is incomplete. Society is not only sex-stratified, but also color-stratified. It is not just male-dominated, but White male-dominated. While Curtis contends that the data available on rape support the contraculture theory, he goes further in acknowledging that the contraculture is a product of White male power. He criticizes feminists for being short-sighted in their rhetoric on "white male chauvinism," and he points out that, by all statistics, the majority of rapes are intraracial and disproportionately Black-Black. Curtis suggests that Black-on-Black rape is a pattern of behavior symbolic of the White male power structure: "White males are the power brokers who have erected the racial and economic barriers forcing black adaptations and who have set the sexual exploitation theme in motion— without being able to similarly prevent blacks from expanding on it" (1976, p. 131). Other writers offer cogent criticism of the subcultural explanation of rape, the limited data on which it is based, and the built-in cultural and class bias of such a perspective. Gager and Schurr, for example, point out that this so-called "subculture" cannot be considered "isolated and distinct from our general culture...violence, hostility toward females, and re-pressed anger are prevalent dynamics in American life" (1976, p. 211). This discussion has alluded to some representative works that have added to the knowledge about rape and have attempted to deal with its causation. There is, however, a dearth of empirical evidence with regard to two related aspects of the rape problem: the victim's experience and its impact, and public attitudes and their sources vis-à-vis rape. It is these two facets of the problem and their interrelatedness with which this work is concerned.

Rape Victims: Toward Empirical Understanding

To date, most of the victim-related literature has demonstrated a prag-matic concern for service-delivery and an increased level of understanding of the victim, her problems and needs (Abarbanel, 1976; Clark, 1976; Not-man and Nadelson, 1976; and Bode, 1978). While some efforts have been made to empirically examine the rape victim's experience, such work is a miniscule portion of that now in print, and it tends, by and large, to lack methodological sophistication. For obvious reasons, there has been and should be a hesitancy to impose empirical designs and measures on personal tragedy. It is not surprising, then, that much of what is known about the rape experience is subjective, based on a limited number of case studies and characterized by a great many unsupported assumptions, one of which is that rape constitutes or precipitates a crisis.[3]

Rape-As-Crisis: Rejecting the Myth of Rape Wish

Although crisis theory has been in existence for over thirty years, it has recently enjoyed renewed popularity as a viable perspective from which to understand and help persons experiencing a variety of stressful life events or circumstances.⁴ It is likely that the affinity for a crisis model for rape results largely from a feminist discomfort with the more traditional theoretical view on rape—namely, the psychoanalytic perspective that has tended to attribute a "rape wish" to women. In contrast, the crisis perspective is amenable to feminist ideology in that it is a nonpathological model. That is, the person in crisis is viewed as "normal," and whatever problematic behavior and feelings are in evidence are assumed to be time-limited, realistic responses to a given event or situation. Pragmatically, crisis intervention services can be effectively provided by trained volunteers or paraprofessionals as well as by degreed clinicians. To a great extent, services to victims have evolved from a rejection of the prejudicial view that women "want" to be raped and that they somehow "ask for it." The crisis model simply assumes that rape victims are in need of support systems to help them cope and regain their equilibrium. Thus, disenchantment with some professionals' views on rape and rape victims (or toward women in general) converged with the feminist anti-rape movement, resulting in the formation of new programs specifically designed to help rape victims. The advocacy, feminist stance of rape crisis centers also explicitly acknowledges that a rape victim's trouble is not just the personal trauma brought on by the rapist's assault; her trouble is also in the public's general attitude about rape. These attitudes will have an impact on her as significant and generalized others respond to her experience. Indeed, they will become a part of her experience.

At face value, the crisis model appears to be a viable and relatively value-free way of looking at the experience of rape. However, from a treatment perspective, it is important to ask whether rape does precipitate a crisis, and if so, whether it does so for all victims.⁵ The importance of these questions evolves from the view that, in order to be fully effective, the selected treatment model should be congruent with the client's presenting problem. The techniques of crisis intervention may well be effective in helping people in crisis, but are they of value for those not in crisis? As yet, none of the victim research has addressed the basic question of whether the rape victim's experience fits the theoretical definition of crisis. Nor has anyone yet dealt with the possibility that crisis may be a culture or class concept (evolving out of a White, middle-class need for equilibrium and congruence) which sets up certain prejudicial expectations about how all rape victims should respond. The dilemma of the *a priori* rape-as-crisis conceptualization remains just as it was when the following observation was made several years ago: "As the victim's reaction to rape has only recently begun to be studied, definitive statements regarding that process and stages of the woman's reaction are premature. *The most useful approach appears to be to view the rape as a crisis situation* in which the victim is faced with an extreme environmental trauma" (Calhoun, Selby, and King, 1976, p. 121). As the most influential examples of the victim research are reviewed, this conceptual dilemma will crystallize further, as will the need for an empirical assessment of rape-as-crisis.

The Present State of Victim Research

Research efforts involving the collection of data from victims have suffered from methodological limitations, some of which could have been avoided, although some are built-in constraints (sample size, representativeness, absence of control groups) which cannot be eliminated altogether. For example, many of the victim studies have been conducted under the auspices of service-delivery programs because they provide ready access to respondents. While the information collected from such research cannot be generalized to all victims, it is, in all fairness, a beginning in an area that until recent years was unexplored. The first attempt to identify and delineate victim responses to rape was made by Sutherland and Scherl (1970). Based on their work with thirteen victims, they were able to identify a three-phase pattern of response: the acute reaction, outward adjustment, and integration/resolution. All of the victims in this study were White, ages eighteen to twenty-four, and probably of above-average socioeconomic background. Most had been seen by the authors in a setting similar to a community mental health facility within forty-eight hours of the assault, and followup was over a one-year period. While the sample size is neither large nor representative, the findings helped to lay the foundation for subsequent research, including a followup by these same authors (Fox [formerly Sutherland] and Scherl, 1972). As a pioneering effort in victim studies, the impact of their research has been substantial; in particular, these articles represent the first specific linkage between rape and crisis in the literature. Consequently, they seem to be largely responsible for the assumption reflected in service-delivery efforts and in later theoretical works that rape is a crisis. The fact is, however, that neither of these articles discusses how crisis concepts relate to the rape experience. For example, while the authors state that "a clear pattern of responses to the assault emerged" (1970, p. 509), no attempt was made to link this pattern to the temporal framework which is integral to crisis theory. One is left with the impression that the resulting rape-as-crisis conceptualization may have evolved as a convenient assumption rather than as the result of careful theorizing.

By far the most prolific and influential writers in relation to victim research are Burgess and Holmstrom (sometimes published as Holmstrom and Burgess) who collected data from a sample of 146 victims. (In some cases that sample has been broken down into subgroups; for example, 109 adult females, 34 adolescents, and 3 children.) Their first book, *Rape: Victims of Crisis* (1974a), is based on what was learned during the first year of a victim counseling program at Boston City Hospital and deals primarily with the treatment of the victim following the assault. Special attention is given to analyzing and explaining the counseling approach they developed based on a crisis model. This work not only offers one of the first comprehensive descriptions of a professional rape crisis program, but also, as a first, the authors have explicated the theoretical base of their service-delivery in clearly linking crisis theory with their interventive efforts. In a later work using a somewhat different perspective, they present an analysis of the coping behavior of rape victims in which three distinct phases are identified: the threat of attack, the attack itself, and the period immediately thereafter (1976a, p. 413). In yet another article, they attempt to document the effects of rape on task performance for children, adolescents, and adults (1976b). In the latter work, a conceptual linkage is established by viewing rape as an external crisis that may be compounded by one's developmental stage in the life cycle (that is, a maturational or developmental crisis). What is of particular interest is that Burgess and Holmstrom move beyond the basic question of how rape is a crisis or how it precipitates a crisis. Their discussion of how a developmental crisis may interact with a situational crisis (rape) is highly theoretical and requires something of a "leap of faith" since there is no empirical evidence to support a causal linkage between rape and any kind of crisis. However, in earlier works they identify the "rape trauma syndrome" (1974 a, c) which includes two stages: the immediate or acute phase in which the victim's life-style is completely disrupted, and the long-term process during which the victim must reorganize her life. Here, the rape itself is viewed as a life-threatening situation with the syndrome viewed as the result.

Burgess and Holmstrom have no doubt influenced subsequent victim research and have made good use of their data, but two criticisms of their work must be made, one of which relates to semantic issues and the other to research methodology and presentation of findings. On the one hand, Burgess and Holmstrom have moved forward in developing a clearer conceptual linkage between victim responses to rape and the viability of crisis intervention services (the article attempting to link situational and developmental crises notwithstanding). Yet, the label of "rape trauma syndrome" used to identify and describe victim reactions creates some conceptual confusion. Specifically, is this label intended to qualitatively differentiate between victims in crisis from those manifesting the syndrome? If so, what variables differentiate them? If these terms are not, in fact, viewed as conceptually (or behaviorally) different, then this semantic juggling only serves to exacerbate an already complex phenomenon. The second area of criticism—regarding methodology and the presentation of findings—crystallizes only as one sequentially examines several of their works; the problem is simply one of a rather loosely designed methodology. Specifically, not until their second book (Holmstrom and Burgess, 1978) do they provide information regarding how data were collected (unstructured "interview guides," participant observation, and supplemental data gathered from a variety of outside sources). Since most of their works contain numerous, lengthy quotes from victims, there is a richness of detail that could not have otherwise been obtained, but it is also likely that some degree of built-in bias exists with the analysis and presentation of findings. It is also unfortunate that some of their works (the book on institutional reactions in particular) reflect a serious lack of clarity and specificity in the tabular presentation of findings, serving only to raise more questions. The criticisms of these works should not be interpreted as a denigration of their contribution, which is substantial, in the area of victim research. These criticisms do, however, reflect a concern for the state of the knowledge, and they suggest the need for greater methodological rigor.

Two other works frequently cited as pioneering efforts in rape victim research are those by Russell (1975) and Bart (1975)—polar opposites in terms of "sample" size. Russell's book consists of a compilation of interviews with 22 victims, while Bart's article is an analysis of data collected from 1,070 victims who responded to a questionnaire appearing in *Viva* magazine. Russell does not attempt to present her work as empirical, but rather, as an effort to educate people about rape from the victim's perspective. It is unfortunate, however, that some of the rape experiences that are described—usually in very graphic detail—may, in fact reinforce stereotyped negative perceptions of rape victims. Given the geographic setting (Berkeley, California), the social climate of the time (the 1960s), and the method by which respondents were obtained (advertising and word of mouth), these victims probably represent something of an atypical group, a fact Russell never acknowledges. Further, only 22 of the 90 women who were willing to be interviewed had their experiences included in this book, and no information is provided as to the decision-making criteria for inclusion/exclusion of cases. The actual contribution of this work lies less in the verbatim accounts of selected rape incidents than in the author's brief sociological analyses; the accounts themselves come across as much too sensationalistic to be educational. The data compiled and analyzed by Bart, while clearly nonrepresentative in a methodological sense, are more effective in terms of educating people about rape. The large number of respondents gives the work credibility, and Bart's writing style clearly communicates the impact of the rape experience.

More recent works show promise that rape victim research is moving toward a more objective, empirically oriented perspective. For example, McCombie (1976) presents a descriptive profile of victims seen through the Beth Israel Crisis Intervention Program in Boston, a profile that also includes some assessment of victim responses. Perhaps the most sophisticated empirical work on rape victims to date is that by Canadian social scientists

Clark and Lewis (1977), who analyzed all reported rapes in Toronto for the year 1970. The authors make an important contribution to the victim data base with their systematic, comparative analysis of "founded" versus "unfounded" (both labels resulting from police investigation) rapes and in their development of a property theory of rape. In all fairness, however, this research cannot be compared with other victim studies because it is based on secondary data (General Occurrence Reports, comparable to the police offense report in the United States).

In the largest research study yet published, McCahill, Meyer, and Fischman (1979) have attempted to investigate the consequences of rape. This is the first longitudinal study of victims' adjustment; the total sample consisted of 1,401 women of all ages who reported a rape (including attempted and statutory rapes) at Philadelphia General Hospital from 1973 to 1975. From this sample, 790 victim interviews were conducted shortly after the rape, and 213 victims were again interviewed eleven months later. The amount of data collected is massive and probably accounts for some of the inconsistencies and confusion in the presentation of findings. Equally problematic, however, is the absence of a theoretical framework with which to "make sense" of the findings. While the study is empirical as well as descriptive, the findings are left hanging as discrete pieces of information. Unfortunately, this failure to integrate the findings into a meaningful theoretical framework seriously limits the potential contribution of the research. Finally, Katz and Mazur (1979) have attempted to review and synthesize the existing data on rape victims. The work is encyclopedic but leaves the careful reader unsatisfied with its often simplistic synthesis and its juxtaposing of very complex data with some global statements ascribed simply to "the feminists." Their conclusions are hardly new, but they are reinforcing: (1) rape is similar to all other crimes against the person *except* for society's attitude toward the victim (she is held responsible); (2) most victims develop psychiatric symptoms following a rape, and crisis intervention (with short-term followup) is touted as the most viable form of therapy.

The empirical data, although limited, are largely characterized by the untested assumption that rape is a crisis or that it precipitates a crisis. As yet, there is scant evidence in the existing victim literature of efforts to systematically document the impact of the rape experience—that is, to describe and attempt to measure the substance of this experience, and to expose its intrinsic meaning from the victim perspective. Finally, there are no data that offer a reasonable explanation of why (as Katz and Mazur conclude, and as others before them have concluded) rape victims differ in the minds of the public from the victims of other crimes of violence. Why are rape victims suspect? An answer to this question apparently lies with public or community attitudes about rape, an area that remains almost totally unresearched, despite the fact that it is the "other side," the extrinsic meaning of rape.

Public Attitudes and Rape

It is the community which provides, or fails to provide, support for victims of rape, and it is the community where victims must return, and community attitudes with which they must cope. It is also the community to which, ostensibly, police, prosecutors, and judges are accountable and from which juries are drawn. Yet, we have only vague notions of community attitudes and how they vary—if they do—by age, race-ethnicity, and sex. A search of the rape-related literature reveals very little of a systematic nature dealing with public attitudes about rape. This is problematic, not simply in terms of an academic "need to know" but because assertions are freely made with regard to what the public thinks and/or what it will tolerate. The authors, for example, have heard prosecutors state publicly that they cannot take rape cases to court because they are not "good cases" (meaning that the victim's behavior and/or reputation are not above reproach) and juries will not convict. Such assertions from prosecutors would lead one to conclude that the public must have a rather narrow and inflexible definition of rape. Both the police and various women's groups—while coming from very different perspectives—have advocated public education as a part of their anti-rape activity (the former for prevention, the latter for consciousness-raising). Yet, the attitudes, knowledge, and working definitions of the public they propose to educate are a vast unknown. In fact, the empirical data on public attitudes about rape are scant and often contradictory, perhaps because they derive from such diverse sources as public opinion polls and attribution theory in social psychology.

In the early 1970s, a group of social scientists sampled the city of Baltimore and conducted a public attitude rating of the seriousness of specific acts of crime (Rossi, et al., 1974). A sample of 200 adults ranked 140 crimes ranging from murder to various kinds of property offenses. The list included four specific acts of rape, all of which were ranked in the top half; however, this means very little since most of the less serious offenses were property or white collar crimes.[6] What emerges from these findings is that the public considers it more serious to rape a stranger than a neighbor or former spouse. There have also been several simulation-type studies conducted among college students to test attitudes about rape victims by means of attribution theory (Calhoun, Selby, and Warring, 1976; and Selby, Calhoun, and Brock, 1977).[7] The findings show that males are more likely than females to see rape victims as having contributed to their own rape. It has been theorized that females are less likely than males to attribute victim-blame because as potential victims themselves they identify with victims. Other works, however, suggest just the opposite—that is, potential victims (females in this case) tend to blame the victim as a defensive tactic; to avoid seeing themselves as victims, they rationalize that the victim is responsible for her own rape (Walster, 1966). The work of Jones and Aronson (1973) testing the "just world" notion found that "respectable" persons (for example, married women and virgins) were seen as having "caused" their own rape. Because they did not deserve their misfortune in terms of intrinsic characteristics, they must have "done something" to deserve it. The findings reflected no differences between males and females.

Klemmack and Klemmack (1976) interviewed over 200 females in Tuscaloosa, Alabama, to explore the congruency between legal and social definitions of rape, looking at respondents' tendency to define various situations as rape in relation to the circumstances of the assault, their own socioeconomic characteristics, and their own attitudes about women. Based on the findings, the authors concluded that: (1) respondents were willing to acknowledge a situation as rape, provided there were fairly clear indications that the victims had no control over the event; (2) the prosecutor interested in obtaining a conviction should search for educated women who have fewer stereotypically traditional views of women's role in society; and (3) current normative definitions of rape are inconsistent, both internally and in relation to the legal codes (p. 146). Unfortunately, the Klemmack research has restricted generalizability because of the geographic location of the sample, the restriction by sex (females only), and the fact that respondents are not identified by race.

In 1977, two cases involving judicial attitudes toward rape came to public attention. In Wisconsin, a judge dismissed the case of a fifteen-year-old boy accused of raping a high school classmate, saying the boy reacted "normally" to prevalent sexual permissiveness and to the provocative way women dress. The other case involved a California judge who commented that women hitchhikers are looking for trouble because it would not be unreasonable for a male driver to assume that such females would consent to sexual relations. Following these two incidents, and a public furor by women's groups, the Harris Survey asked a national cross-section of more than 1,500 adults some questions about rape. The majority of respondents saw rape as a violent crime that should be dealt with as such; they disapproved of the actions of the judges and approved of the recall vote against the Wisconsin judge. The findings also indicated that females were slightly more pro-feminist in their attitudes than males (Harris, 1977). Of further interest are findings from a study of judicial attitudes toward rape victims conducted by Carol Bohmer (1977). Interviews with thirty-eight judges in the Philadelphia court system indicated that they categorized rape cases as one of three types: (1) Genuine Victims: those who are attacked by "a stranger leaping out of the shadows of a dark alley;" (2) Consensual Victims: the complainant was seen as "asking for it," regardless of whether the assault was consistent with a legal definition of rape (a bar pickup was used as a stereotypic example); (3) Vindictive Females: the alleged rape was seen as totally consensual sex or as fabricated for the woman's own idiosyncratic, vindictive purposes.

The work of Hubert Feild (1978) is, to date, the most comprehensive effort to measure public attitudes about rape. His survey includes a random sample not only of over 1,000 adult citizens of a "medium-sized community" in the South, but also of 254 police patrol officers, 20 incarcerated rapists, and 118 female counselors from rape crisis centers in twelve major metropolitan areas across the country. Feild's work is exploratory in attempting to devise a multidimensional "Attitudes Toward Rape" instrument and to determine demographic and attitudinal correlates. His work seems to confirm that attitudes toward rape are multidimensional (comprised of such factors as perceived victim-precipitation, motivation for rape, and punishment for rapists) and are linked with attitudes about women and their role in society—that is, people who view women in traditional roles are likely to see rape as being a woman's "fault." The demographic characteristics of sex and race were also associated with attitudes toward rape. Women, by and large, had a more feminist view of rape than men; Blacks (except for those with nontraditional attitudes toward women) were found to be more nonfeminist toward rape than Whites. Feild's work provides some support for the feminist macro-level approach to rape and also breaks ground in quantifying public attitudes about rape.

Given the magnitude of the problem, these limited data are unsatisfactory. They do, however, confirm the need to develop descriptive public attitude data and to attempt to isolate significant predictors of such attitudes within a meaningful social or community context. Since some racial-ethnic lines are historically clear demarcation boundaries for sexual activity (voluntary and involuntary), the community broadly defined by race-ethnicity provides a meaningful structure for such investigation. Because society is not only sex-stratified, but also race- *and* sex-stratified, attitudes related to sex roles and to sexuality and racism are suggested as the possible loci of forces that shape or determine community attitudes about rape.

Rape as an Empirical Problem

While the feminists have raised rape to the level of a social problem, there are strains in the anti-rape movement and gaps in the existent rape-related literature, both of which provide the rationale for the present research. The behavioral manifestation of feminist attitudes about rape is the anti-rape movement which promises to increase reported and legally processed rapes. Meanwhile, feminist ideology promises to increase "women's liberation" which, in turn, could increase the actual incidence of rape. It has been asserted *a priori* by feminists that rape is an insidious manifestation of sex-role stratification-socialization; yet, empirical evidence is very limited. Public education efforts, though well-intended, suffer from a lack of data with which to counter long-standing stereotypes which still dichotomize victims into those who were "really raped" versus those who "asked for it."

The sociological literature on rape has taken the problem beyond the clinical, micro approach by focusing on rape rates and group characteristics of offenders and victims, thus establishing some ecological and demographic patterns for rapes known to police or reported in victim surveys. By and large, sociologists studying rape have linked its cause to a subculture of violence or a contraculture, both phenomena identified with poverty-stricken young Blacks. When this causal explanation is added to the anti-rape movement, the unanticipated results—barring significant changes in the reporting and processing of rape cases—are (1) that minority males will bear the brunt of the anti-rape, law-and-order activity; (2) that minority communities will become more skeptical of rape—seeing it as a means of racial oppression—and less supportive of minority females who are victims of rape; and (3) that as rape is increasingly identified as a "minority problem"—a crime perpetrated by minority males against minority females and/or majority females—it will contribute to a renewal of racism and prejudice in the dominant community.

The predominant diagnostic and treatment model—crisis and crisis intervention—applied to rape victims is also based on untested assumptions. At the present time, service-delivery efforts remain at an intuitive level, guided by good intentions but lacking in empirical support. While there is no reason to quarrel with the conceptualization of rape-as-crisis, there are potential dangers that the model may be too simplistic, too time-limited, too culture-bound. If these fears have any foundation in fact, then minority females—already disproportionately victims of rape and systematic discrimination in service-delivery and criminal justice—will benefit less from the treatment model than will White middle-class victims. Furthermore, the model may create expectations as to how victims should react to rape and how rapidly they should "recover" with negative repercussions for all women as potential victims.

The issue of rape is complex and intricately interrelated with racism and minority-majority intergroup relations. To fundamentally attack the issues involved, it is imperative to understand rape as an individual experience which is compounded by the reactions of significant and generalized others who respond to the victim. Rape is thus conceptualized as comprised of interwoven intrinsic (personal) and extrinsic (public) dimensions. It is this compounded phenomenon which this work attempts to explore and explicate. With regard to the personal, intrinsic dimension of rape, the authors have three objectives: (1) to develop a descriptive profile of the rape experience; (2) to assess (on the basis of empirical evidence) the impact of the rape experience in relation to crisis theory; and (3) to assess victims' perceptions of service-delivery in view of their needs. With regard to the public or extrinsic dimension of rape, there are also three objectives: (1) to provide a definitive description of cross-cultural attitudes toward rape, comparing Anglo, Black, and Mexican-American samples;[8] (2) to investigate the degree to which attitudes about rape are linked (for each group) with sex-role attitudes and expectations; and (3) to examine some of the interrelated aspects of sexual inequality and racial-ethnic inequality. By combining these two sets of objectives, the authors hope to temper the emotionalism of rape by rigorous investigation—to offer a rational, empirical basis for understanding the individual trauma of rape within the context of its social origin—a racially-sexually stratified society.

Notes

1. Two such programs originally established with LEAA funds have been designated as Exemplary Projects (EP) by the National Institute of Law Enforcement and Criminal Justice. The Rape/Sexual Assault Care Center of Des Moines, Iowa, earned the EP designation in 1976, and the Stop Rape Crisis Center in Baton Rouge, Louisiana, was recognized as an EP in 1979.

2. For a critical analysis of the poverty subculture theory and the culture of poverty literature, see Charles A. Valentine, *Culture and Poverty* (Chicago: University of Chicago Press, 1968). For more recent works, see L. Richard Della Fave, "The Culture of Poverty Revisited: A Strategy for Research," *Social Problems* 21 (1974): 609–21; and Barbara E. Coward, Joe R. Feagin, and J. Allen Williams, Jr., "The Culture of Poverty Debate: Some Additional Data," *Social Problems* 21 (1974): 621–34.

3. As this manuscript was in the final stages of revision before going to press, we discovered an article describing research conducted in Hawaii which, in some respects, closely parallels our victim study. No doubt, there may be other similar studies in progress; suffice it to say that we could not revise the manuscript to accommodate all "new discoveries." However, the reader may wish to see Libby O. Ruch and Susan M. Chandler, "Ethnicity and Rape Impact: The Responses of Women from Different Ethnic Backgrounds to Rape and to Rape Crisis Treatment Services in Hawaii," *Social Process in Hawaii* 27 (1979): 52–67.

4. The "birth" of crisis theory is usually traced to the work of Erich Lindemann who published a study based on research with the survivors of the Coconut Grove nightclub fire; see "Symptomatology and the Management of Acute Grief," *American Journal of Psychiatry* 101 (1944): 141–48. Contemporary works which provide excellent overviews of the theory are: Naomi Golan, "Crisis Theory," in John Turner (ed.), *Social Work Treatment: Interlocking Theoretical Approaches* (New York: Free Press, 1974), pp. 421–56; and Lydia Rapoport, "Crisis Intervention as a Mode of Treatment," in Robert Roberts and Robert Nee (eds.), *Theories of Social Casework* (Chicago: University of Chicago Press, 1970), pp. 267–311. A more

recent and highly comprehensive work is by Naomi Golan, *Treatment in Crisis Situations* (New York: Free Press, 1978).

5. Although the conceptualization of crisis used in the assessment of impact is discussed in Chapter 3, the following tenets provide an introduction to the major underpinnings of crisis theory. (1) All persons seek to maintain equilibrium or a steady pattern of functioning in their lives; (2) when persons are in crisis, their equilibrium or usual style of functioning is disrupted; and (3) crises are, by definition, time-limited in that some state of equilibrium will be achieved within about four to eight weeks. See Gerald Caplan, *Principles of Preventive Psychiatry* (New York: Basic Books, 1964), and Lydia Rapoport, "The State of Crisis: Some Theoretical Considerations," in Howard J. Parad (ed.), *Crisis Intervention: Selected Readings* (New York: Family Service Association of America, 1965), pp. 22–31.

6. To place this matter in perspective, forcible rape after breaking into a house was ranked fourth after (1) planned killing of a policeman, (2) planned killing of a person for a fee, and (3) selling heroin. Forcible rape of a stranger in a park was ranked 13 just after kidnapping for ransom. Forcible rape of a neighbor was ranked 21 after impulsive killing of a stranger, and forcible rape of a former spouse was ranked 62 after neglecting to care for one's own children.

7. For some of the representative works on attribution theory, see Melvin J. Lerner and Carolyn H. Simmons, "Observers Reaction to the Innocent Victim: Compassion or Rejection?", *Journal of Personality and Social Psychology* 4 (1966): 203–10; Kelley G. Shaver, "Defensive Attribution: Effects of Severity and Relevance on the Responsibility Assigned to an Accident," *Journal of Personality and Social Psychology* 14 (1970): 101–13; and Alan L. Chaikin and John M. Darley, "Victim or Perpetrator? Defensive Attribution of Responsibility and the Need for Order and Justice," *Journal of Personality and Social Psychology* 25 (1973): 268–75.

8. The term *cross-cultural* is used to refer to ethnic-racial comparisons across the Anglo, Black, and Mexican American samples studied in this book, the assumption being that each sample represents cultural differences related to history, ethnicity, class, and minority-majority relations. The terms *White* and *Anglo* are used interchangeably to denote the dominant group, the terminology determined (as in daily life in San Antonio) by the minority group being discussed vis-à-vis the dominant group (for example, Black-White, but Anglo-Mexican American). Where all three groups are discussed and compared, the racial-ethnic nomenclature of Anglo, Black, and Mexican American is used consistently. These are the racial-ethnic identity labels most frequently used in the city where Mexican Americans are a numerical majority and where Anglo is a generic term—the literal meaning of which has been lost—denoting the dominant (White) group.

THE WHITE PATRIARCHY AND RAPE

2

There is little doubt that rape laws originated as property laws. This thesis has been documented in a number of sources and was argued most recently, and most convincingly, by Brownmiller (1975) and by Canadian social scientists Clark and Lewis (1977). The property thesis, however, leaves something to be desired as an explanation for the "rape problem." It is rather like explaining the "Black problem" today in terms of slavery. The fact that both women and Blacks have a history as chattel is indisputable; that such a status persists to the present day is, however, questionable. While women are still unequal under the law, few would seriously contend—and be able to support—that women are property in a literal sense. In fact, only the most power-hungry and insecure of men want or need to own a woman, for as Emerson pointed out, "If you put a chain around the neck of a slave, the other end fastens around your own."

While the status of women today is a product of their history vis-à-vis men, a history that includes their being defined as property, that property status does not maintain present sexual inequality. An intricately interwoven system of racial-sexual stratification which systematically differentiates rewards, prestige, and power maintains such inequality. That is to say that there are sets of sex- and race-related statuses and roles that are characteristically accompanied by greater rewards, prestige, or power than others, and movement from one set into another is restricted (Schlegel, 1977, p. 3). Gunnar Myrdal ([1940] 1964) and Helen Hacker (1951) were ahead of their time as social scientists in their treatment of the female in American society. Myrdal's classic study of Blacks in America includes an appendix entitled "A Parallel to the Negro Problem" (1964, pp. 1073–78) in which he conceptualized the role of Blacks as analogous to that of women and children under the power of the *pater-familias*. The problems of both groups, Myrdal concluded, are not accidental: "They were...originally determined in a paternalistic order of society" (p. 1078). Several years after Myrdal's original work, Hacker examined the question of whether women constitute a minority and concluded that women have the objective, but not the subjective, attributes of a minority group: "they lack a sense of group identification and do not harbor feelings of being treated unfairly because of their sex membership" (1951, p. 62). She touched, but never quite focused, on the reason for women's lack of subjective awareness—that is, that they are socialized in a male world. Although the chief socializing agent of a child is the mother, females are socialized to identify themselves in relation to males, to take their "place" in a patriarchal social system, just as minorities are socialized to take their "place" in a White-dominated society.

Power: White and Male

A few years ago, an article by Robert Terry appeared in the *Civil Rights Digest* which described the "White Male Club" in America. Terry presents only a brief description of the already well-documented "power elite," but he goes beyond that to focus on the interlock of racism and sexism as an integral part of the American social system: "Racism and sexism in America are not problems simply to be listed alongside other problems. They are part of the club's foundation." Furthermore, "racism is fundamentally white racism and sexism is fundamentally male sexism" (1974, p. 74). Because this interlocking power elite excludes women and non-Whites, it is safe; the White Male Club perpetuates itself without conscious effort on the part of its members.

In the 1960s, power, more than any other subject and perspective, came to characterize a sociology of inequality and conflict. Power was the paradigm most frequently employed in works dealing with inequality, minorities, and even deviant behavior. There is a well-established knowledge base: the persons who make decisions, who exercise power, and who occupy the elite positions of power are overwhelmingly White, Anglo-Saxon, and male (Hunter, 1959; Mills, 1956; Domhoff, 1967; and Dye, 1976). The last-named characteristic has been so taken for granted that few social scientists have even attended to sexual stratification in power constellations. It remained for feminists to articulate sexual stratification as a part of the system of power. As Clark and Lewis point out:

Our society is characterized by institutions and practices (and the socialization process necessary to support them), which consistently and systematically ensure that only men rise to positions of power and authority in the public world, while women remain at home, in the private sphere, under the legal ownership and control of their husbands (1977, p. 176).

This description of sexist power is very similar to a description of racist power that issued from Black militants more than a decade ago.[1] For example, Carmichael and Hamilton define racism as "the predication of decisions and policies on considerations of race for the purpose of subordinating a racial group and maintaining control over that group" (1967, p. 3). Chicanos have recognized a similar kind of power relationship between Anglos and Mexican Americans as illustrated in the following:

...the barrio is best perceived as an internal colony, and...the problem of Chicano politics is essentially one of powerlessness. Powerlessness, in turn, is a condition produced and maintained by the dominant Anglo society through a number of mechanisms, some of which we have begun to identify (Barrera, Muñoz, and Ornelas, 1974, p. 282).

As Clark and Lewis point out, "All unequal power relationships must, in the end, rely on the threat or reality of violence to maintain themselves" (1977, p. 176). For sexual stratification, this threat of violence lies in the superior physical strength of the male and is manifested in its ultimate form as rape. The violence that has characterized ethnic-racial relations is well known and is recorded in a multitude of sources; such violence is far from being past history. Minority revolt can be suppressed, however, as long as the military and police are controlled by the dominant system. In the late 1960s, a number of U.S. cities exploded as Blacks took their protests and anger into the streets in violence, looting, and burning. The reaction from Whites was inevitably a military one as National Guardsmen, military troops, and riot police turned city after city into armed camps; in the final count of casualties, the lives lost were almost all Black. In similar fashion, Chicanos confronting specific issues of discrimination-inequality have been met in some communities with a military "show of force." The decade of the 1960s altered substantially—but not fundamentally—the American system of racial-ethnic stratification, but at great cost to minorities. The power of the dominant system impacts heavily on all minorities and men and women in very different ways.

Rape, or the threat of rape, is an important tool of social control in a complex system of racial-sexual stratification. Fear of rape keeps not only the female in her "place," but fear of the accusation of raping a White woman keeps minority males in their "place" as well. Reynolds (1974) asserts that rape law, as it is applied in the criminal justice system, is a threat only to those men who "rape inappropriately." More specifically, a number of empirical works suggest what "inappropriate rape" is: rape of a White female by a minority male; rape of an inappropriate victim (one whose reputation and/or activity are not imputable); and rape involving a weapon and/or excessive violence (Clark and Lewis, 1977; and Holmstrom and Burgess, 1978). For minority men, lynching, capital punishment, and inordinately long prison sentences are handed out for their inappropriate rape of White women, while White males are often free to rape minority women. All women, regardless of race-ethnicity, live in a White, male-dominated society where the dynamics of male-female interaction are convoluted by the dynamics of racial power. In a racially and sexually stratified society, a high incidence of rape is predictable. Rape symbolizes not only a key element of social control working to maintain the system, but also the anger and violence engendered by such a system. Females are victimized several times over. Anglo females are potentially appropriate victims for Anglo males and are vulnerable to inappropriate rape by minority males, the latter, no doubt, symbolizing some of the anger and frustration that grow so naturally in a system of unequal power. Minority females appear to be the appropriate victims of both inter- and intragroup rape. If they are raped by White males, it is assumed that they "asked for it" or were simply unpaid prostitutes. If they are raped by minority males, police and other public officials have been known to react as if this is typical in-group behavior for minorities.

Some view rape as an attempt to maintain power on the part of White males and as an imitative power quest by minority males. In her history of rape, Brownmiller documents the place of rape as a ritualistic aspect of war, raids, and revolution. In writing about rape of White females during the revolution in the Belgian Congo, she quotes a Black American minister who had been there for many years as saying, "It [rape] is hard on the children and women but the Belgians deserve it" (1975, p. 145). A Belgian evacuee—a plantation owner—unwittingly described the system of racial-sexual stratification against which the Congolese finally revolted. His response to the reports that the Congolese were raping many White females was: "Why, I've known these people like the back of my hand . . . I've been working with them and sleeping with their women for 35 years and I never expected to see this" (Brownmiller, 1975, p. 146). No doubt, intergroup minority-dominant rapes are frequently just a retaliation in kind for past oppression. As Frantz Fanon points out, "The development of violence among the colonized people will be proportionate to the violence exercised by the threatened colonial regime" (1968, p. 88). There is a further projection of the White male patriarchy in rape. In raping minority women, minority males frequently are doing no more than imitating the White male; as Curtis suggests, Black-on-Black rape is "the symbolic expression of the white male hierarchy" (1976, p. 131).

A theory of racial-sexual stratification posits women and minorities in a White-dominated patriarchal system and minorities in subsystems within the dominant system. What follows is an effort to examine the risks of rape that are endemic to the roles of White females and to the roles of Blacks and Mexican Americans. These risks have their origin in a history of slavery and colonialism but are maintained by the current system of racial-sexual stratification as conceptualized in Figure 1. The diagrammatic representation of a White patriarchal system is predicated on three assumptions which must be kept in mind as the discussion progresses:

1. The system for minorities and females is ultimately supported by force or threat of violence.

2. The system is characterized by economic inequality and limited opportunity for minorities and women, the impact of which defies measurement in terms of frustration, anger, and closure of life choices.

3. The system is characterized by institutionalized political power which works to keep minorities and women in subordinate positions, denying them equal representation in strategic decision-making processes while making laws and public policy that maintain their subordinate status.

Blacks

Black history is replete with victimization and punishment experienced in relation to rape. This discussion deals with three areas that are linked by historical and/or contemporary causation with sex- and race-related attitudes and behavior (Black and White): (1) Black history: sex and survival, (2) sexual racism, and (3) the dynamics of a community of victims.

Black History: Sex and Survival

The institution of slavery effectively turned Black people into property. Property is for use, and Blacks were used for work much as animals were. But Blacks were also used sexually: they were used for breeding purposes to increase the White slaveowner's property, and as sexual favors and as sexual fantasy for Whites (Stampp, 1956, pp. 245–51). Black females were at the disposal of the White slaveowner and any other White male to whom he wished to grant a favor (Rawick, 1972, p. 79). In many cases, sex between White male and Black female was really rape, but the slave woman had no legal protection from the sexual aggression of White males. In fact, several court decisions upheld such behavior (Staples, 1973, pp. 40–41). After emancipation, only the "on paper" legal status changed for Blacks, and because of their economic dependence on Whites, Black women were not much better off in terms of sexual autonomy. A number of social scientists have suggested that the sexual exploitation of Black women insured and supported the "sexual purity" of Southern White women (Staples, 1973, p. 41; Dollard, 1957, pp. 135–38; and Stember, 1976, pp. 39–40). In the double standard of male-female behavior among Whites, men were expected to be sexually experienced, while women were to enter marriage sexually "pure." It was not uncommon then for White males to gain sexual experience and pleasure from their aggression with Black females, while respecting and protecting the virginity of White females (Dollard, 1957, p. 139).

In slavery, Black males were powerless to defend women; such attempts

FIGURE 1. The System of Racial-Sexual Stratification

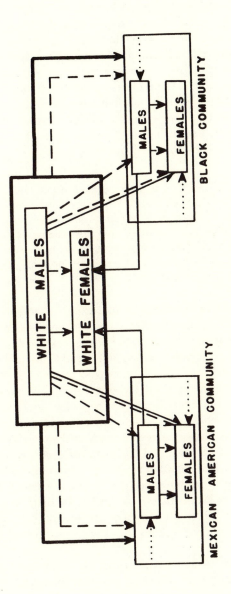

DOMINANT SYSTEM POWER (INSTITUTIONALIZED)
PHYSICAL POWER/STRENGTH
ECONOMIC, POLITICAL POWER
COMMUNITY PRESSURE (FAMILY, PEERS, CHURCH)

would surely result in a severe beating or perhaps even death. Legal marriages for slaves did not exist, nor, of course, were traditional husband-wife relationships recognized. Black women fell into the category of "unprotected," and this lack of male "ownership" made them all the more vulnerable and attractive to White males (Dollard, 1957, p. 145). Because of economic and political oppression, Black males were not substantially more powerful once slavery was ended. Their powerlessness was demasculinizing on two levels: it was destructive in terms of their personal relationships with women, and it was a constant reminder of their subordinate status. White males epitomized masculinity; they possessed (owned), protected, and/or used females; Black males had no such power. The anger of Black males for all generations was expressed by W.E.B. DuBois:

I shall forgive the white South much in its final judgment day: I shall forgive its slavery, for slavery is a world-old habit; I shall forgive its fighting for a well-lost cause, and for remembering that struggle with tender tears; I shall forgive its so-called "pride of race," the passion of its hot blood, and even its dear, old, laughable strutting and posing; but one thing I shall never forgive, neither in this world nor the world to come: its wanton and continued and persistent insulting of the black womanhood which it sought and seeks to prostitute to its lust (1921, p. 172).

Blacks of both sexes had to deal with the sexual exploitation and rape of females, which was initiated legally in slavery and continued as an integral part of the White patriarchy. Their reactions were defensive and very different. In the history of slavery and subsequent second-class citizenship, Black males were forced—by threat of survival—to adapt to a powerless position. Some adapted by determined striving for middle-class status characterized by a steady job, homeownership, a family, and a wife who did not have to work. To be able to support his family, and especially a wife who does not have to work, has long been a mark of middle-class respectability and success for Black males. The importance attached to this achievement, however, may be less that of a status symbol, as has been assumed, than simply that of keeping the wife at home where she is less vulnerable, less accessible to White males.[2] Certainly, the Black male is less powerless today than ever before, but he is not powerful. The system in which he has social and economic well-being is still controlled by White males.

Not all, or even most, Black males could adapt to the middle-class goal since they never achieved the job security by which to begin the uphill climb. Some adapted by perfecting various "hustles" which enabled them to "work the system." Some adapted by escape through drugs and alcohol. Still others adapted by cultivating an exacerbated male sexuality which, in fact, represents a kind of self-fulfilling prophecy for Whites. Whites, perhaps originally to perpetuate breeding, encouraged the identity of Black males in terms of uninhibited sexuality. Later, the myth was perpetuated largely to satisfy the Whites' own vicarious and pragmatic needs. It seems clear that the Black male was given sexual license by the White patriarchy in exchange for his economic and political autonomy. But the threat posed by the image of uncontrollable Black male sexuality became a means of maintaining control over all Blacks as well as over White females. The male sex organ became the identity of the Black male as well as his tenuous link with life itself, for while he might be given approval for uninhibited sexual activity with Black women, the least suggestion of sexual behavior with White women was to invite castration and/or death.

Despite the phallic identity of Black males, they have not been identified vis-à-vis females but by a sex role imposed on them by White males for their own gain or usefulness. Nor have Black women ever been primarily identified vis-à-vis males; unlike their White female counterparts, their identity is not dependent on how males view them. The woman's identity is shaped by her history as a Black woman in a White patriarchy to a greater degree than as a Black woman vis-à-vis Black men. Adaptation for survival is more characteristic of Blacks than is sex-role determinism. White women have traditionally been evaluated, valued, and rewarded in terms of sexual purity and sexual faithfulness, a luxury the Black woman could not afford. If her identity as a young girl was in virginity, it was as likely as not lost early by rape or coercion. Staples poignantly describes the plight of the Black woman: "As the violation of her body became routine, Black women could not value that which was not available to her—virginity. She has been sexually used by men of both races" (1973, pp. 40, 42). Not only have Black women frequently been unable to adhere to traditional moral standards of White society, but Black males have also understood the pragmatics of sexual survival (Liebow, 1966; Rainwater, 1970; and Ladner, 1971). Consequently, the rigid sexual stratification, the male-female double standard of morality, is less evident in the Black community than in the White. There is no reason to believe, however, that Blacks "value" sexual promiscuity, sex for profit, or sex by force. In fact, just the opposite is indicated. Conventional sexual mores identified with middle-class Blacks suggest that monogamy, sexual fidelity, and male-female role divisions are symbols of the security of the White, middle-class world and are elusive but sought-after goals for many Blacks.

Sexual Racism: The Black Male-White Female Enigma

"Rape is to women as lynching was to Blacks: the ultimate physical threat by which all men keep all women in a state of psychological intimidation" (Brownmiller, 1975, p. 281). At the root of all racism is the fear of interracial sex and the ascension of Black power. This fear is epitomized and symbolized in the sex act between Black male and White female—whether voluntary or involuntary. Such fears are not equally evoked by sex between White male-Black female for obvious reasons: in the system of racial-sexual stratification, sexual power and privilege extend downward to all females who are, by definition, below the dominant White male (see Figure 1). The power of minority males is not great enough to secure exclusive rights to minority females; their sexual rights are usurped by White male dominance. Minority sexual stratification extends downward to minority females but not upward to White women who are the exclusive property of White males. White males are the only persons in the system with exclusive and inclusive sexual privilege. Sex between Black males and White females (referred to here as Black-White sex) defies both racial and sexual power systems; it threatens the very essence of the "White Male Club"; it is political.

While it cannot be assumed that most individuals consciously relate to Black-White sex as political in the sense that Eldridge Cleaver (1968) perceived and articulated it, it can be assumed that at some gut-level Black males and White females who engage in sexual relations are aware that theirs is an act of defiance. The Black male has not only taken White property, but he has also defied the system of power above him. The White female has not only denied the White male exclusive sexual privilege, but she has also betrayed her entire race by having sex with a Black man. The real issue now is whether the White man can ever again enter the body of a White woman with security. Has the power he has maintained over women by so fragile a balance been stripped away? Because coition between Black male and White female symbolizes the fragile power of the White male patriarchy, it is little wonder that it has been given exaggerated importance and undue attention. There are two schools of thought which attempt to explain the enigma and fascination of Black-White sex. One approach treats the phenomenon as a myth deliberately perpetrated by White males because of their fear of role reversal; the other treats the phenomenon as compensatory for Blacks. Interestingly, neither approach gives attention to the role of the White female.

THE MYTH OF BLACK MALE SEXUALITY

This view is represented by recent and well-documented works by Mann and Selva (1978, 1979) in which they contend that the White male's affinity for Black women, the sanctity of the White female, and the sexual anxieties of the Southern White male all melded together to produce the myth of Black male sexuality. They allege that

. . .with the southern planter's craving for interracial affairs projected upon the black male, the anxieties were compounded out of the fear that the black would attempt revenge by assaulting the white woman. Since . . .the allegedly chaste white woman represented the South itself, the *potential* black rapists had to be controlled in order to preserve and maintain white civilization (1979, p. 170).

This line of reasoning clearly presents the enigma of Black-White sex as a "White problem"—that is, White males *created* the myth of the Black male, his extraordinary sexual endowment and prowess, his savage lust, as a means of controlling White females. As Day explains, "In slave days, when white slaveowners enjoyed black slave women clandestinely, they needed to set up some barriers between their white women and black men so that white women would not do likewise" (1977, p. 197). She goes on to allege that White men created the fantasy of "black beasts with bull-size genitals," and "white women were as much victims of the system as black men" (pp. 197–98). Whether the myth of Black male sexuality was deliberately contrived as a technique of social control or it simply evolved as a stereotype which happened to be useful, it has most profoundly affected Black males. Calvin Hernton recalls his boyhood growing up in the South: "The taboo of the white woman eats into the psyche, erodes away significant portions of boyhood sexual development, alters the total concept of masculinity, and creates in the Negro male a hidden ambivalence toward all women, black as well as white" (1977, p. 245). The myth of Black male sexuality and concomitant White female fear is basic to maintaining the system of racial-sexual stratification. The myth is easily disproved, however, when Blacks and Whites can socialize and interact at the primary group level, but such interaction is also likely to eventually lead to intermarriage and complete assimilation. Whatever its origin, the Black-White sex barrier is today a finely honed tool of the White patriarchy, working not only to protect the White male's proprietarian control over White females, but to maintain racial segregation as well.

SEX AS COMPENSATORY BEHAVIOR FOR BLACK MALES

This view holds that Whites stripped Black males of all identity and withheld from them access to the usual means of masculine achievement—a stable job and economic success. The result is that Black males competed with the only means available—their sex—and compensated for their lack of job stability and economic success by being hedonistic, sexual beings. As Day observes, "Ironically, the one area in which the black male can compete successfully with the white male is in bed" (1977, p. 197). Carried to its ultimate meaning, sex with a White woman becomes a political act. Whether the Black male seeks voluntary sex or engages in the act of rape may simply reflect the degree of his anger, his need to express personal rebellion versus a need for his own personal "revolution." Stember has written that the desire for the majority female is inherent in the nature of minority male sexuality. Relying very heavily on the assumption that it is the *conquest* and not sex per se which is man's greatest source of pleasure and gratification, he asserts that "the height of sexual pleasure is available only to minority males" (1976, p. 160). By comparison, he believes that majority males experience sexual deprivation which generates hostility and a determined effort to prevent minority males from achieving social equality. This "conquest" of a majority female by a minority male may be nothing more than a rebellious act of sexual gratification, or, on the other hand, it may be viewed as a revolutionary act as revealed in Eldridge Cleaver's oft-quoted rationale: "Rape was an insurrectionary act. It delighted me that I was defying and trampling upon the white man's law, upon his system of values, and that I was defiling his women" (1968, p. 14). Or, in a somewhat milder tone, Hernton has written that "at one time or another, in every Negro who grows up in the South, there is a rapist. . . . And that rapist has been conceived in the Negro by a system of morals based on guilt, hatred and human denial" (1977, pp. 251–52).

THE ROLE OF THE WHITE FEMALE

Whether Black-White sex is voluntary or involuntary, the White female also plays a role. With so very little written about interracial sex from her perspective, her image as a mindless sex object has been reinforced. Other than individual case histories of rape victims, there is no evidence as to the female's fear of, or reaction to, rape by a Black male. The literature on sex and race relations does, however, contain evidence of three phenomena in relation to White females and Black-White sex: the myth of the "rape wish;" fear of being "discovered" and publicly ostracized; and evidence that for women too, sex can be an act of defiance, a "revolution."

The myth of the female rape wish is not confined to Black males but is exacerbated by the dimension of race. Some scholars maintain that the fascination with Black male sexuality (reinforced by White males) manifests itself in a kind of masochistic rape wish (Cash, 1941, pp. 115–17; Fanon, 1967, pp. 156, 179; and Stember, 1976, pp. 180–83). No doubt, this phenomenon, to the extent that it is real, would have to be viewed as a great irony, as an unanticipated consequence of the White male's effort to keep Black males and White females separated. Whether the rape wish has any reality apart from its manifestation in a very few neurotic or psychotic women is doubtful. White women do, however, become involved in interracial sex of a clandestine type and, if found out, in order to avoid public disgrace will sometimes deny or redefine the behavior. As the well-known cases of the Scottsboro Boys and of Willie McGee illustrate, White males and females sometimes engage in a conspiracy to cover up the possibility that the sexual involvement was voluntary or that it ever occurred at all. Black males have frequently paid a high price for interracial sex.[3] Both the "rape wish" and the false rape accusation contribute to a skepticism and ridicule of rape: White females have been impressed with a fear of rape until they fantasize about it, thereby raising questions in the minds of males as to whether *any* rape is "real." White females have entered into complicity with White males to deny voluntary sexual involvement with Black males, again alleging a "rape" both know is false. To a great extent, the lack of credibility given the charge of rape today is attributable to the interwoven history of rape and racism where all involved *know* from their own experience (whether that of White male oppressor, White female, or Black male) that rape has been a technique of social control to maintain the White patriarchy.

Rape wishes and voluntary liaisons which *ex post facto* are defined as rape can easily be denied or dismissed as deviant behavior. What is more difficult and threatening for White males to deal with in the present system of racial-sexual stratification is the open, aggressive interest of some White females in Black males. While it should not be implied or assumed that a genuine affectional relationship cannot exist between Black male and White female, in the social context of today's society, it *is* problematic. Just as interracial sex implies conquest, rebellion, and even revolution for the Black male, such an experience can have the same meaning for the White female. To become involved, in either a casual or serious relationship, with a Black male is an overt denial of the traditional role of the White female and a denunciation of White male dominance. For some White females, a sexual relationship with a Black male is nothing more than sport engaged in out of curiosity or boredom, a fact that has caused one Black writer to comment: "One of the ironies of the myth of black supersexuality is that it drove so many carnally curious white women in hot pursuit of black men" (Day, 1977, p. 198). Another motive that impells White women to seek sex with Black men is simply to demonstrate their freedom from racism and from control by White males. As Stember says, "it becomes an act of affirmation of one's own ideological purity to take a black man as a sex partner" (1976, p. 183).

At the present time, there is no empirical evidence to clarify the role of White females in interracial sex, nor is there any empirical validation for either the myth of Black male sexuality or that of sex as compensatory behavior. Interestingly, however, some research on sex-role conformity and race-ethnicity suggests that Black males and White females are generally more conforming (to traditional sex roles) than are Black females and White males (Iscoe, Williams, and Harvey, 1964). Perhaps the reason, as Brownmiller points out, is that "the black man's fortune was inextricably and historically linked to the white woman's reputation for chastity, a terrifying imbroglio that the black man and the white woman neither created nor controlled but still share" (1975, p. 243).

The Dynamics of a Community of Victims

Most Blacks still live in predominantly Black communities, the strength and viability of which are well documented (Williams, 1973; Stack, 1974; and Valentine, 1978). To a great extent, these communities are comprised of primary group relationships, an extensive network of kinship and friendship. Rape risks are pervasive, and the conflicting vested interests of males and females create strains within the community. Black females, in comparison with Anglos and Mexican Americans, are disproportionately victims of rape and are all too aware of their vulnerability (see Table 27, Appendix C). They are also aware, however, that Black males have been victimized by rape. Brownmiller found Black female victimization to be a neglected topic, statistics nonexistent, and attitudes unidimensional: "To black people, rape has meant the lynching of the black man" (1975, p. 233).

Females in Black communities are potential or actual victims of both intra- and intergroup rape. According to both the FBI crime statistics and victimization data, Black females have the highest rate of known rapes, and rapes reported by Black females (by police and victim reports) are largely intragroup (Curtis, 1975, pp. 69, 83; and McDermott, 1979, pp. 14–15). Despite the rather large number of known rapes among Black females, there may be even more unknown. It is very likely that forces extraneous to the Black community result in the underreporting of White-Black rapes, namely, the tradition of White power-Black powerlessness and the nature of police response (Agopian, et al., 1974, p. 101; Brownmiller, 1975, p. 234; Curtis, 1975, p. 83; and Mann and Selva, 1978, p. 20). For a Black female to prosecute a White male assailant, she must defy or ignore the social distance of both sex and race. Her chances of seeing her case successfully adjudicated are minimal; no doubt this fact accounts for the comparatively small number of White-Black rapes that are reported. It can also be assumed that forces within the Black community work to discourage the reporting of intragroup rape. Given the nature of the Black community, the victim is likely to know her assailant or to know someone who is acquainted with or related to him. Thus, there is a sense of a chain reaction of trouble (for family and friends) if an intragroup rape is reported. An additional consideration is the knowledge or belief that the legal-judicial system will not seriously investigate or prosecute a Black-Black rape (Mann and Selva, 1978, p. 20). The forces that work against the reporting of intragroup rape minimize potential community tensions resulting from conflicting risks and/or vested interests. In this sense, the White system and the Black subsystem support each other, but at the expense of Black rape victims.

The tensions and risks surrounding rape for Black males include those related specifically to the charge of rape, those emanating from the overrepresentation of Blacks in the criminal justice system (as both victims and offenders), and the discriminatory treatment frequently experienced in that system (Brown, 1977). While Blacks comprise only about 11 percent of the total population, they represent 48 percent of all arrests for rape (FBI, 1980). The plight of Black males accused of rape has been documented through each stage of the criminal justice system; arrests, convictions, and use of the death penalty are predictable, depending on whether the accused is charged with intra- or interracial rape (Mann and Selva, 1978, pp. 17–35). The history of rape as a repressive tactic of social control continues to have a great impact on Black males and to carry with it a consequent fear; the death penalty and long prison sentences have simply replaced lynching.

In the Black community, tension and ambivalence surround the topic of rape. The system of racial-sexual stratification has assigned Black females to be victims and Black males to victimize. Black females are victimized in a convergence of racism and sexism by both Black and White males. For Black males, rape has been a tool of oppression, whether couched in the myth of the "Black stud" or of the "Black rapist." This discussion of Blacks and their experience in relation to rape is intended to demonstrate that rape risks are inherent in the Black experience. Hence: (1) rape as experienced intrinsically by victims and as manifested extrinsically in community attitudes may reflect this unique Black experience (when compared with Anglos or Mexican Americans); and (2) the anti-rape movement may be a source of considerable tension in the Black community because of a generalized distrust of the criminal justice system and because of opposing male-female vested interests in relation to rape.

Mexican Americans

Much of what has been written about Blacks as a minority group in a system of racial-sexual stratification applies equally to Mexican Americans, despite the fact that their history in relation to the dominant group is very different. Not only have Blacks lived in intimate, if unequal, association with Whites, caring for their homes and their children, but since slavery they have also told Whites what it felt like to be Black in America. While many Mexican Americans have struggled to assimilate into middle-class America, as a group, they have never taunted Whites about their democratic-Christian hypocrisy, nor have they, until recently, interpreted their ethnic experience for Anglos. In comparing Black optimism and hope for racial justice with that of Mexican Americans, Blauner observes, "It appears that Mexicans in the United States have rarely held such illusions about our vaunted democratic system" (1972, p. 163). Whites have not felt the guilt and paternalism toward Mexican Americans that have always been a part of White-Black relations. Nor have Mexican Americans attempted to awaken the American conscience, to wage a campaign for equality based on the rhetoric and idealism of the system they threatened (as Blacks did in the 1960s). Instead, Mexican writers and intellectuals have frequently used the medium of a "foreign" language and have looked to Mexico for audiences and support. This physical proximity to Mexico and the tenacity of the native tongue are crucial to understanding the Mexican American experience in the United States. Mexicans were conquered, colonized, and given nominal U.S. citizenship, but they have been able, by regular travel, visitation, and communication with friends and family (frequently by means of the Spanish language), to maintain their ties with Mexico, often over several generations. While most Mexican Americans are economically dependent on the United States, they have not been dependent on the Anglo culture for their identity as a people.

The indifference which has characterized Anglo-Mexican American relations is changing. Since the early 1960s, there has been a growing movement of "La Raza"—an awareness of a potentially powerful Hispanic minority (of which Mexican Americans are the largest subgroup). They seek redress of grievances as well as representation in the power structure and in the decision-making processes of government. The Mexican American minority today is in a state of political transition. However, they are still racially and sexually stratified in a melding of old and new inequities. The following discussion focuses on three areas that are linked by history and/or current conditions with some sex and minority-related attitudes and behavior among Mexican Americans: (1) Spanish conquest, the shaping of racial-sexual stratification; (2) male and female in church and family; and (3) the dynamics of a community of suspicion.

Spanish Conquest: The Shaping of Racial-Sexual Stratification

To understand something of the heritage of Mexican Americans, it is necessary to go beyond their American experience to the Spanish colonization or conquest of certain Indian populations (in what is today Mexico and the American Southwest), a period that lasted from 1525 to 1810. A number of writers and historians have addressed themselves to this period of Mexican history. Moquin has written that "Spain came to the new world with the Cross in one hand and the Crown in the other...The church...came to call the Indians to the Kingdom of God. The state came to gather wealth" (1971, p. 2). There is some disagreement as to the degree of racism and sexism manifested by Spanish colonizers toward the indigenous Indians. They apparently did mix freely, however, and the Spanish *conquistadores* were encouraged to "marry" or mate with the Indian women to accelerate assimilation. Yet, many such "marriages" were not legal because the Spaniards had wives in Spain; some were not legal because they were not sanctioned by the church unless the woman had first become a convert to Christianity. Machado states that "The Indian women readily gave themselves to the conquistadores" (1978, p. 13), but others have charged that Indian women were raped, branded, and traded as property, and that the church sanctioned such treatment. Nieto-Gomez reports that in order to satisfy the prohibition that no soldier have sex with a non-Christian woman, Indian women were baptized prior to coition (1976, pp. 226–27). A pragmatic explanation of Spanish-Indian relationships is offered by Cotera who notes that "the desirable ticket to status in the new society was the Spanish male. For this reason, while the first relations between the two groups were by force and violence, eventually parents gave their daughters up willingly and women themselves submitted" (1976, p. 30). There is considerable disagreement among historians as to the status of Indian civilization at the time of the Spanish conquest, the humaneness of the Spanish rule, and the volition with which Indian women engaged in sexual relations with the Spaniards. There is no disagreement, however, on the fact that the two groups did intermingle and interbreed and that in the American Southwest the Mestizo element largely replaced that of the Spanish and Indian.

Nieto-Gomez has attributed much of the present-day sexism and racism experienced by Mexican Americans to the Spanish colonization. She traces the roots of *La Hembra y El Hombre* (the woman and the man) to three forces: the Spanish conquest, the *encomienda* grant system, and the colonial Catholic church. She alleges that the Spanish *conquistadores* obtained Indian women both by force and through peaceful means such as trade agreements, alliances, and "gifts" from fathers and brothers (Nieto-Gomez, 1976, pp. 226–27). Elmendorf (1977) supports this view. The *encomienda* system further solidified racial and sexual stratification. In this system, the Spanish Crown granted the recipient a temporary right to demand any service desired from the Indian inhabitants of the land. Frequently, men were used as slave labor and females as concubines and domestic slaves. Elmendorf concludes that the result of the colonial period was "devastating for the native population, and above all for the women, who were not only slaves like everybody else, but also the objects of sexual exploitation" (1977, p. 132). Nieto-Gomez further charges that the colonial church supported and legitimized the *encomienda* system by teaching Indian women to be subservient and long-suffering, and to yield to the wishes of others, especially men. Nevertheless, after a period of initial exploitation, the church did intervene to persuade the Crown to issue protective legislation (Cotera, 1976, p. 27). Yet, the Crown also sought to discourage formal marriage between Spaniards and Indians by refusing to legitimize their offspring and, from time to time, by exporting Spanish women to Mexico to marry Spanish men and produce legitimate heirs, thus reinforcing racism.

In the Mexican culture, there seems to be a dichotomous concept of the "good woman" versus the "bad woman," a dichotomy traceable to the

Spanish conquest. *La Mujer Buena en La Casa Grande* was the upper class Spanish (White) woman, segregated and protected in her fine home. She fulfilled only three socially acceptable roles: those of virgin, wife, and mother, in that order. On the other hand, *La Mujer Mala de La Casa Chica* had a race and class connotation. The *casa chica*, or little house, was frequently a convenience which an Indian mistress maintained for a Spanish man who had a legal wife in *La Casa Grande* (Nieto-Gomez, 1976, pp. 231–33; and Machado, 1978, p. 13). Indian women were not sheltered or protected. Prior to the conquest, some were apparently politically active and shared responsibilities with men outside the home. Under colonial rule, frequently their children were not legitimized by the formality of marriage, and the women themselves were no more than slaves. The Indian woman became the "bad woman" and was contrasted with the White woman. One was seen as a saint, and the other as a whore; there was little in between (Elmendorf, 1977, pp. 131–35; and Stevens, 1973, pp. 94–98).

Little has been said thus far about the Indian male during the colonial period, except that he was in many ways a slave under the *encomienda* system. Until the Spanish Crown issued some stipulations protective of Indians, it was not uncommon to break up a family to coerce the members into labor, a situation denigrating to the male as head of the household (Cotera, 1976, p. 26). In relation to the Spanish invaders, Mexican males were in a powerless position not unlike that of the Black male during slavery. Even the Indian *Caciques* who were allowed nominal rule in some villages were weakened, and some served the Spaniards in menial roles such as artisans, storekeepers, and farmers. Some Mexican writers suggest that males, observing females serving the Spaniards, sleeping with them, and giving birth to the children of the conquerors, felt angry and "in their powerlessness to change things blamed the women" (Nieto-Gomez, 1974, p. 19). Although an *ex post facto* explanation, it has been suggested that the powerlessness of Indian males under Spanish colonialism was the beginning of sharply differentiated and stratified male-female sex roles, and even of the cult of *machismo* (Mirandé and Enríquez, 1979, p. 241). Indian males hated the Spanish conquerors, but they envied and identified with their power. As the Spanish males were waited on and attended by Indian females, so the Indian male wanted to be served, to be treated as master. He, too, wanted to feel powerful, and the female could to some degree restore the dignity the Spanish conqueror had taken from him. "The woman became the symbol of the conquered, subdued Indian, and the man the symbol of the conquering, demanding Spaniard" (Elmendorf, 1977, p. 141). The conquest ended with Mexico's independence from Spain in 1821; the Mestizo people were the product of almost 300 years of sexual racism. They subsequently became a part of a color-class stratified, independent Mexico. Some of their descendants were conquered and annexed to the United States by the Treaty of Guadalupe Hildalgo in 1848; still others have emigrated more recently for political or economic reasons. Racism and sexism are an integral part of the Mestizo history. This heritage, their initial involuntary American "citizenship," and their language and identity with Mexico made it easy for the dominant Anglo group to impose its own system of racial-sexual stratification.

Male and Female in Church and Family

Much has been written about the *machismo* or virility cult of Latino males. Inevitably, its feminine counterpart evolved—*marianismo*. *Machismo* is a term commonly used to refer to exaggerated aggressiveness, intransigence in male-to-male interpersonal relationships, and arrogance and sexual aggression in male-to-female relationships. *Marianismo*, on the other hand, embodies the concept of the spiritual and moral superiority of women compared to men (Stevens, 1973, pp. 90–91). Both concepts are exacerbated versions of masculinity and femininity. Most students of contemporary Mexican culture acknowledge the existence of sharply dichotomized male-female sex roles, but they are inclined to view *machismo* and *marianismo* as externally imposed stereotypes. Sex-role stratification, however, began in the era of Spanish colonialism, and subsequently it was fortified and elevated in importance by two strategic institutions—the Catholic church and the Mexican family.

THE CATHOLIC CHURCH

In several specific ways, the church has contributed to sexual and racial stratification: by idealizing womanhood in the image of the Virgin Mary; by defining the woman's "place" as in the home, subservient to her husband; and by its official stance on birth control. The Spanish conquerors brought the Roman Catholic church with them to the New World, and within ten years it was ingeniously interwoven into the fabric of Mexican Indian culture by means of an apparition of the "Most Holy Mother of God" on the site of a traditional Indian sacred ground. Significantly, the apparition—given the name of Our Lady of Guadalupe—was seen by an illiterate young Indian male. The religious symbol was accepted by the Spaniards and venerated by the Indians, and in 1756 the Lady of Guadalupe was declared patroness of New Spain (Mexico) by Pope Benedict XIV (Stevens, 1973, p. 94). Nieto-Gomez charges that the Spaniards deliberately used the vision as a means of social control "to maintain the subjugation of Indian women" and to "reinforce the Spanish role" because the Virgin Mary was in reality the prototype of the Spanish woman—virgin, wife, and mother (1976, pp. 228, 232). Nieto-Gomez thus charges the church with both racism and sexism: "Eventually church ideology integrated these class and cultural differences into the concept of the ideal woman" (pp. 232–33).

By literal adherence to Pauline Christianity, the Catholic church consigned women to a subservient role vis-à-vis husbands. For example, the Apostle Paul wrote to the Ephesians: "Wives, submit yourselves unto your own husbands, as unto the Lord. For the husband is the head of the wife, even as Christ is the head of the church" (Ephesians 5:22–24). By use of the symbolism of the Virgin Mary as well as Pauline theology, the church teaches that an "ideal" woman is male-identified because she is venerated for her roles as wife and mother. Along with the church's sanctioning of women as male-identified and subservient is the implicit assumption that women are property; they exist for male comfort, service, and enhancement. "Mary draws her worth and nobility from her relationship to her son, Jesus Christ. She is extolled as mother, as nurturer" (Nieto, 1974, p. 39). Finally, perhaps an unintended, but nevertheless very real, consequence of the Catholic doctrine prohibiting the use of contraceptives is the fact that, unless women defy this teaching, they will spend most of their lives in childbearing and childrearing. These are restrictive roles and serve effectively to reinforce sexual stratification.

FAMILISM

Although both Anglo and Mexican writers have expressed critical views with regard to the Mexican American family, few have failed to acknowledge its strength or to point out that more Mexican Americans than Anglos or Blacks live in family units. Criticisms with regard to the family have been focused largely on male-female sex roles and the assumption that the family works to retard or prevent assimilation. These two issues are also crucial to any consideration of racial-sexual stratification. There is some evidence to support the view that the family is the basic social unit for Mexican Americans (Murillo, 1976, pp. 19–20). Research in San Antonio, in fact, provides some empirical support for the belief that Mexican Americans internalize a higher degree of familism than Anglos (Farris and Glenn, 1976). The strength of the Mexican American family lies in its ability to provide for its members—to provide the security, identity, and well-being which the dominant Anglo culture does not. Although the individual is to a degree subsumed by the family unit, this does not diminish his/her individual responsibility. Quite the contrary, it increases it.

In the traditional Mexican American family, individuals do not have to go outside the family unit for help, and the family itself is sustained by the continual role fulfillment of its individual members. "Only in unusual circumstances, dire need, or when there is no alternative will a chicano or his family attempt to seek help from others" (Murillo, 1976, p. 20). This dependence on family can be explained pragmatically and historically. Mexicans and, subsequently, Mexican Americans have lived under conditions of colonized people for much of their history. They were forced to develop their own support systems; the dominant group (Spaniards, French, and Americans at varying times) was not always trustworthy. In order for the family unit to fulfill its role as a "total institution," it was necessary for individual family members to play certain roles. The simple, most logical division of responsibility—and one already provided by the church—was that based on sex. The result was what Elmendorf describes as a family system of "patriarchy interwoven with matriarchy." "Men it appears have the 'outward and visible' signs of power, while women rule through the acknowledged superiority of their 'inward spiritual grace'" (1977, p. 143). In substance, the female represents the nurturing aspects of family life and the male the authoritarian, economic aspects (Peñalosa, 1968; and Murillo, 1976). Together, the interwoven sex roles are sufficient to meet the needs of individual and collective family members. Because of the importance of the family as a social unit, if either male or female fails in his/her respective role obligations, the family as a whole suffers. If the male is unable to support, protect, and control his family, he brings dishonor not only on himself, but also on his entire patriarchal line. If the female fails in her role obligations, she dishonors herself, her husband, and the extended families of both. Mirandé and Enríquez state that the "Chicano family has proved remarkably impervious to external forces," and they point to the domestic role of the woman as the "primary source of preservation of cultural values." They further charge that the submissive Mexican woman is "a creation of social scientists and journalists" (1979, pp. 242–43). In the reality of everyday life, sex roles are more differentiated than hierarchical. There is a sharply defined male "place" (or role) and an equally well-defined female "place." As long as each sex functions within that socially acceptable role, each has respective power.

CHURCH, FAMILY, AND RAPE

Both Catholicism and familism are related to the issue of rape. For a woman to be raped is to dishonor or disgrace not only her, but her family and husband as well. It is to dishonor self because she did not resist enough, she did not fight off her attacker; it is to dishonor her family because individual and family are inseparable; and it is to dishonor her husband because she is his responsibility. Commenting on the case of Inez Garcia who killed one of the two men involved in her rape, Maria Del Drago said, "Inez's failure to resist the rape while it was going on, even if it had been at the cost of her own life, remains shameful to her" (1975, p. 84). Del Drago also characterized the Latin culture in terms of "twin macho assumptions": that a woman belongs to a man, and that a woman dishonored by belonging to more than one man (as in rape) is herself at fault. A Catholic priest testified at the Garcia trial about the church's attitude (the Spanish church in particular) toward rape and the responsibility of a devout Catholic who is confronted with rape or threat of rape. He explained that she "would have to try to resist. . .even to the point of death," and he noted that there is a saint in the church so honored because she died resisting the attack of a rapist. Although Saint Maria Goretti was defending her virginity, the priest said that a married woman would be expected to "resist strenuously any attack upon that particular right of her husband" (Wood, 1976, p. 156). In the context of the traditional Mexican American community, a male might be expected to avenge the rape of his wife, girl friend, daughter, or sister. Del Drago explains that sex roles prescribe certain responses to rape in stating that "we are taught to be gentle, quiet, and shy and yet men do great violence in defense of our 'honor'—our virginity as girls, our fidelity as wives—and we ourselves are taught to resist such 'dishonor' to the death" (1975, p. 54). Yet, while a male will fight, even die, to defend the honor of "his woman," he may find it difficult to forgive her victimization which represents shame for both of them.

The relationship of sex roles, family, and church in a sexually and racially stratified society is obviously mutually supportive and functional. Male-female sex-role differentiation and stratification are functional in the family's fulfillment of its all-important role for minority group members in the midst of a racially stratified society. The vast majority of outside agencies to which Mexican Americans might go for help are controlled by the dominant group. The family is the only minority-controlled, minority-defined institution for Mexican Americans. With its Anglo hierarchy and its sanctioning of the submissive wife and its anti-birth control doctrine, the church supports, even bolsters, racial and sexual stratification.

The Dynamics of a Community of Suspicion

Probably the most influential factor in desegregating Mexican Americans and thereby disseminating the subcommunity is social class. According to Machado, "there is. . .a breakdown of traditional values as a Mexican American moves upward. Familial ties weaken; language. . .yields to bilingualism. On occasion, Spanish is replaced by English. With the replacement comes a greater emphasis on Anglo values" (1978, p. 160). But most Mexican Americans are poor, and while the degree of residential segregation is not as great as for Blacks, in most cities and towns in the Southwest they generally live together in distinctive neighborhoods called *barrios* (Moore, 1976, p. 56). A report by the U.S. Commission on Civil Rights (1970) provides narrative and statistical details on the discriminatory and unjust treatment which these Mexican American communities have suffered at the hands of various agents of the criminal justice system. Police brutality, resulting in several unwarranted murders of Mexican Americans, is a volatile and ongoing issue. Mexican American communities have had a generally negative experience over the years with law enforcement personnel and with the criminal justice system as a whole, resulting in what Moore characterizes as a "culture of suspicion" (1976, p. 91). It is doubtful whether law enforcement personnel have treated Mexican Americans any worse than Blacks. However, the Mexican American experience is compounded by two variables not present in the Black experience. First, they have been subjected to control by more agencies than have Blacks: the Immigration and Naturalization Service, the Border Patrol, and (in Texas) the Texas Rangers, founded in 1835 specifically to handle "the Mexican problem" (Moore, 1976, p. 93). Second, the Mexican American experience is complicated by the language barrier. No small number of Mexican Americans grow up with Spanish as their first and only functional language. The distrust of the criminal justice system, the language barrier, and the existence of the family as a kind of total institution suggest that, in the Mexican American community, one's family, relatives, and friends are inclined to "take care of business" as much as possible without seeking help from outside sources.

A substantial literature (historical, sociological, and psychological) exists on race and rape; there is, however, very little on Mexican Americans and rape. It is difficult, if not impossible, to assess the degree to which the problem of rape impinges on the *barrio* and its residents. Since most crime statistics are recorded in racial categories only, there are very limited data on Mexican American rape victims and offenders. Where statistics are recorded by ethnic group as well as by race, Mexican American victims are frequently underrepresented when compared with their representation in the general population (see Table 27, Appendix C). There is no proof as to whether the statistics reflect low reporting or low victimization. Some facts, however, do point to low reporting. While language, cultural, and spatial barriers may shield Mexican American females somewhat from intergroup sexual contact, most live in poor neighborhoods where crime and victim rates are high. Furthermore, the fact that sex roles are culturally differentiated suggests that when traditional female sex-role expectations are violated, Mexican American women may be particularly vulnerable to intragroup rape. In light of what is known about Mexican American communities, there are strong forces working against the reporting of rape. Specifically, the woman and her family are shamed and dishonored; there is distrust of the Anglo-dominated criminal justice system; husband, brother, father, or another family male may insist that the rape is his to avenge.

If the political-economic powerlessness of Mexican American males (depicted in Figure 1) leads to imitative and/or retaliatory behavior manifested in intra- and intergroup rape, this is not clearly supported by the available data. Mexican American males are frequently underreported as offenders. However, where victim-offender statistics are available, the proportion of Mexican American offenders generally exceeds the proportion of

Mexican American victims (Table 27, Appendix C). For all minority males, the charge of rape (particularly of a White female) can be used as a form of social control or oppression, although the actual use of this tactic has most frequently been against Blacks. The difference in the Black and Mexican American experience with the charge of intergroup rape reflects the different histories of these minorities vis-à-vis Whites. As a whole, as mentioned earlier, Mexican Americans have never lived in prolonged, intimate association with Whites in the same way that Blacks have. The Mexicans already had a well-established culture and social system when the White settlers came to the Southwest. Through the years, they have maintained a separate cultural existence supported by language differences and suspicion of Anglo-dominated institutions.

What these facts suggest is that Mexican American males may be relatively free of outside constraints to engage in intragroup rape. However, the community exercises its own internal control via a system of family honor which may serve to minimize such behavior. Some intergroup rape can be expected, based on the political reality of minority-dominant relations, but probably less than is the case with Blacks and Whites because Mexican Americans and Anglos historically have not been sexual rivals as much as strangers. Intergroup rape of a Mexican American female is less likely to be avenged by the family than intragroup rape, but forces within the community are still likely to work against reporting, namely, distrust of the Anglo system and a need to protect family honor. The limited facts available suggest that rapes in the *barrio* may be more underreported than among either Blacks or Anglos. Even if Mexican Americans placed their trust in the institutions of the dominant society (and clearly they tend not to), the family and the Catholic church seem to hold the victim responsible for her rape. Thus, the development of viable support systems may be blocked on several fronts.

Variations on the Sex-Role Script

The preceding analyses of Blacks and Mexican Americans in relation to the dominant group suggest that these unique group experiences (past and present) have produced sex roles differing in content, degree of inequality, and impact on daily life. The feminist explanation of rape as emanating from sexual stratification assumes a uniformity in differentiation, stratification, and socialization that does not exist across different class, race, and ethnic groups. Male and female are universal differentiations, but in America *masculine* and *feminine* are concepts rooted in the White core-culture, perfected and propagated by the middle and working classes. They have become scripts for the masses to follow. These different masculine and feminine script themes are summarized by Chodorow (1972) as "doing" (for males) and "being" (for females).

The masculine role is an active one, and the female role, passive. Masculine is strong, assertive, rational, able to "get things done"—dominant. On the negative side, being masculine means not crying, being a leader, in control, seldom showing emotion, and having a tolerance (if not a propensity) for violence. Feminine is nurturing, sensitive, moral, submissive, empathetic—giving. The negative side of feminine is enigmatic, unpredictable, coy, seductive. Women use sex as a promise and as a reward and punishment. Men, motivated by the promise, are pursuers—sometimes rewarded, sometimes punished, frequently "outwitted" in the pursuit. Females can reduce the strong, powerful male to a mass of bruised ego, but they can "put him back together" by being seductive, by playing the "clinging vine." All of this is strangely contradictious of the sweet, giving female and the strong, dominant male; the "battle of the sexes" is all part of the well-written and well-learned script. However, the role strains to male "doing" and female "being" are strong and anger-producing. This is the stuff of which rape is made, and one has to look beyond it to see that the "battle" between male and female is really over power. The male has it, the female subverts it; the male flounders, and ultimately his only means of maintaining power is his superior physical strength.

The White middle class in America wrote the script which calls for male and female to give up the "battle of the sexes" to become the "happy couple." They become professional male and female; role-conflicts become role-complements. The male role is "doing" in the competitive world outside the home where he must become an economic and occupational success, providing for and protecting his home and family. The female "being" is perfected at home, by being a "homemaker," wife, and mother. The home is a retreat and offers respite for the husband and a place of growth for the children, but it may become a trap for the woman. She is constantly required to give: social and emotional support to her husband, and *everything* to her children. Her own being is expressed only in relation to others. She is expected to nurture, to support; she may often feel drained and too rarely replenished or rewarded. Women can tolerate this gross inequity in the male-female roles only if they have neither the time nor the awareness to question the ascribed female role. As women have become better educated, borne fewer children, and been freed from the continual demands of housework, they have expressed the discontent Betty Friedan wrote about in *The Feminine Mystique* (1964).

The complementary-role family of middle America has evolved into a system of sexual bargaining where males and females of more equal status bargain for rewards in marriage. Today's marriage has become a system of social exchange where each role includes both rights and duties, but the roles are basically unchanged. The wife "nurtures" the family; the husband performs his economic role obligations. As Scanzoni explains, "The economic rewards he [husband] provides motivate the wife to respond positively to him, and her response to him in turn gives rise to a continuing cycle of rectitude and gratitude" (1972, p. 65). The White middle class has refined and promulgated the male-female script, shaping up a system of social exchange with conflict built in, simmering just beneath a thin veneer. But some White middle-class women, many of them housewives, finally did rebel. The feminist movement evolved from what Friedan termed "the problem that has no name...that voice within women that says: 'I want something more than my husband my children and my home'" (1964, p. 27). This was the same awareness that produced early feminist treatises such as *Sexual Politics* (Millett, 1969), *Born Female* (Bird, 1969), and *The Female Eunuch* (Greer, 1970).

To the degree that females are successfully socialized to their role, to the feminine script, they have learned to fear rape and to be controlled and limited by their fear. In some ways, females have also been taught to expect rape, perhaps unconsciously, because they know that by their feminine role they participate in it—not by "asking for it" or by any active "rape wish," but by just "being" feminine. It is very likely that a majority of White-White rapes go unreported because of this participatory guilt, particularly those where some voluntary victim-assailant interaction preceded the attack. What White females are more likely to report are stranger-to-stranger attacks over which they had no control and in which their activity or behavior was unimpeachable. They are also more likely to report intergroup rapes because minority males lack socially acceptable access to White females, if only because they (White females) are the property of White males.

The feminist movement originated with White, middle-class females; the anti-rape movement is an attack on their own sex-role conformity as well as that of men. Where this kind of awareness has permeated public attitudes, it can be expected that an empirical link can be found between traditional sex-role attitudes and attitudes about rape—or, specifically, that anti-rape attitudes will be associated with nontraditional sex roles and attitudes supportive of women's liberation. Where sex-role consciousness does exist, it is likely to mitigate ethnic-racial and class-sex differences in attitudes about rape. However, racism and poverty may have shaped the experience of Blacks and/or Mexican Americans (and perhaps poor Whites) to the extent that sex roles do not have the centrality of importance that they do for most Whites. Minority women have had to cope with racial-ethnic stratification and its dehumanizing impact on both males and females. Because most minorities are also poor, they have had to cope with survival first. Racism and poverty have been overpowering, obscuring, and at times subsuming of sexism. In general, minority women have yet to confront sexual inequality from the same social location as that of White middle-class women; they cannot afford it. They have yet to reach the stage of comfort and leisure that allows them to become introspective, to say "I want more."

Summary

Sex and race-ethnic related roles are shaped by history and are maintained by a system of racial-sexual stratification. Sex roles among Blacks and Mexican Americans (in comparison with Anglos) can be expected to differ perceptibly because each group has experienced a unique history and presently exists in a position of powerlessness compared to the dominant group. The separate social realities of Anglos, Blacks, and Mexican Americans suggest that there are clearly identifiable sex-role patterns, which are the product of sexual and racial stratification. The preceding analysis would suggest, for example, that for Anglos (perhaps excluding the very poor) the pattern of sex-role interaction can be described as *sexual bargaining*—competitive, reward-seeking behavior between males and females. For Blacks, the pattern is aptly described as *sexual survival*—male-female roles are largely adaptive and secondary in importance to survival in a White, racist society. For Mexican Americans, the pattern of male-female interaction is that of *sexual differentiation*—sharply dichotomized male-female role complements which together form the nucleus of the family as a total institution.

To be Black, Mexican American, or Anglo in America is a compendium of historical experience and contemporary racial and sexual inequality. This thesis is fundamental and essential to the empirical study of rape, for rape is a manifestation of power, of inequality. Consequently, rape risks are unequally distributed in terms of power-powerlessness, sex and/or racial-ethnicity. Therefore, it is reasonable to assume that how one deals with the experience of rape, that the kinds of attitudes about rape manifested by racial-ethnic communities, are largely determined by the differential statuses (power), roles, and related attitudes that are now a part of being Black, Mexican American, or Anglo, and male or female. This work attempts to document and illuminate these differences and associations.

Notes

1. Sexism is defined as "cultural beliefs and social practices premised upon the superiority of one sex, usually the male, and accompanying masculine values." See Clarice Stasz Stoll, *Female and Male: Socialization, Social Roles, and Social Structure* (Dubuque, Iowa: William C. Brown Co., 1974), p. 220. For a discussion of the

interrelatedness of institutionalized racism and sexism, see Joe R. Feagin and Clairece B. Feagin, *Discrimination American Style: Institutionalized Racism and Sexism* (Englewood Cliffs, N.J.: Prentice-Hall, 1978), pp. 1–40.

2. Ironically, most economists have noted in recent years that almost without exception the common characteristic of Black middle-class families today is that both husband and wife work; it is their joint income which pushes them into the middle class.

3. For a detailed summary of both the Scottsboro and McGee cases, and similar cases, see Susan Brownmiller, *Against Our Will: Men, Women and Rape* (New York: Bantam Books, 1975), pp. 250–82. For an autobiographical account of the Scottsboro case, see Clarence Norris and Sybil D. Washington, *The Last of the Scottsboro Boys* (New York: G. P. Putnam's Sons, 1979).

THE SAN ANTONIO RESEARCH: A DUAL APPROACH TO RAPE

3

Setting

The research setting is San Antonio, Texas, a city with a population in excess of 800,000. Broken down by race-ethnicity, the city is approximately 52 percent Mexican American, 39 percent Anglo, 8 percent Black, and 1 percent other. Although Mexican Americans are a majority in the city proper, there are a number of incorporated areas within the San Antonio city limits that are predominantly White, as reflected in the racial-ethnic breakdown for the county: 48 percent Mexican American, 44 percent Anglo, and 8 percent Black and/or other. The city purports to be bicultural. However, it is residentially segregated and economically and politically dominated by Whites, interspersed with a small number of "successful" Mexican Americans and a few charismatic-type leaders who have cultivated some popular constituency among Mexican American voters. While there is a sizable population of middle- and upper middle-class Mexican Americans in the city, those who are poor are far more representative. For this reason, Mexican Americans are defined here as a minority, even though they are in the numerical majority. It should be acknowledged, however, that there are a number of characteristics of San Antonio's Mexican American population which, combined, may significantly differentiate them from Hispanics in other parts of the United States—for example, their size, economic diversity, and cultural impact on the region.

Ties between San Antonio's Mexican American population and Mexico are strong, even for those who have been there for several generations. The city and Mexico are welded together, not just by history and tradition, but by family ties, communications media, and frequent travel. Mexico, whose border is only 150 miles from San Antonio, is easily accessible by automobile, bus, train, or air. Spanish is the first language in a majority of

Westside households, and it is the only language spoken in some. In talking with Mexican Americans in the city, it is not unusual to find that they have been to Mexico at least once during the past year and that they have either family or friends there. Sizable numbers of resident Mexican nationals and illegal Mexican aliens live in the city, although no accurate statistics are available on either. To give some grasp of the strength of the Mexican American culture in the city, of 340 public attitude interviews completed among Mexican Americans for this research, 131 (38.5 percent) were conducted in Spanish at the request of the participant.

With respect to San Antonio as the research setting, some of the city's specific characteristics made it especially suitable for a cross-cultural study with a dual focus on victim responses and public attitudes about rape. (1) The Anglo, Black, and Mexican American populations are residentially segregated and differ enough socioeconomically and in terms of group consciousness to be treated as separate racial-ethnic communities. (2) While rape in San Antonio has received some increased attention in recent years, this is probably no more than in most cities of comparable size. (3) A population of victims was potentially accessible through a community volunteer program that provided support services to rape victims.

Racial-Ethnic Nomenclature

We recognize that the racial-ethnic identity terms—Anglo, Black, and Mexican American—used throughout this research differ from those used in other parts of the country. For this reason, we should explain our rationale for selecting these terms while rejecting others. We did not use the term *Chicano* because in San Antonio, Chicano tends to be identified with political militancy or "lower class" Mexicans and is eschewed by most older Mexican Americans and by many of the middle classes, or those with middle-class aspirations. We did not use the term *Hispanic* because, while it does not have a negative connotation locally, neither does it convey a sense of personal identity or national origin. The identification as *Mexican American* seems to be preferred in San Antonio in that it emphasizes the mixture of the two cultures *and* American citizenship.

Use of the label Mexican American in referring to one's own group and Anglo in reference to the dominant group apparently had its origin in racism, back to the time when Mexican Americans were overtly treated as a separate race. At least with respect to official records and the Bureau of the Census, Mexican Americans have been classified racially as Caucasian since 1940. More recently, of course, Mexican Americans have won the right to be recognized as a separate ethnic-identity group, as reflected in the 1980 census. Historically, the term Anglo came into use in the Southwest to distinguish the dominant from minority groups since both groups are theoretically Caucasians (and White). The label persists to the present.

Within their own group, Anglos call themselves "Whites," but in referring to their group (in the third person) versus Mexican Americans in the city, they generally use the term *Anglo*. Likewise, they will use the term *White* when the "other" group under discussion is Black.

In short, the ethnic-racial nomenclature used is that which we hear in daily conversations, and our selection was supported by some data from the public attitude portion of this research.[1] Finally, to put to rest one other possible question, we did not give serious consideration to the suggestion that, for the sake of consistency and egalitarianism, we should use the terms *Anglo/White Americans, Black/Afro Americans,* and *Brown/Mexican Americans.* Aside from being cumbersome, these terms do not capture the identity of the three racial-ethnic groups as they relate to each other in San Antonio, and that was our purpose.

Rape in the City

Rape in San Antonio seems to be no greater a problem than in most cities of comparable size. In fact, statistics on known rapes are slightly lower than might be expected. There were 304 cases of reported forcible rape or attempted rape in the city in 1978 and 364 in 1979. If rape rates (the number of rapes per 100,000 population) from the FBI crime statistics for metropolitan areas are compared, the San Antonio metropolitan area has a rape rate of 40.5, while the average for the metropolitan areas of the United States as a whole is 41.1 (1980).

A very low-key anti-rape movement began in the city in 1974, when three unlikely forces converged in support of rape victims and against rapists: (1) the news media coverage of several brutal, violent rapes over a relatively short period of time; (2) a female candidate for mayor who used the rape issue for political purposes; and (3) a feminist group attempting to garner support for a rape crisis center and to recruit community volunteers to work with and for rape victims in an advocacy-support role. The "front-page" kind of rape cases come and go; the female mayor was elected; federal money was secured for a rape crisis center which interested the city politicos only until the funds were depleted. The only enduring anti-rape force in the city is the volunteer group begun in 1975 which, although still functioning, is weakened and floundering with no paid staff, only limited funds, and a continual attrition of volunteers. The group has succeeded admirably, however, in effecting some positive institutional changes in the treatment of rape victims in the county medical facilities and by police personnel, but the processing of rape cases in the criminal justice system still leaves much to be desired. For example, in the 1978 San Antonio Police Department Annual Report, of the 262 reported cases of forcible rape (excluding attempted rape), 63 percent were shown to be "cleared by arrest," while this same report showed only 76 arrests. Similarly, in 1979, of 331 forcible rape cases, 62 percent were cleared by arrest, while 101 actual arrests were made.

Statistics from the district clerk's office on the prosecution of rape cases show a *total* of 49 and 65 defendants convicted (by plea or trial) of rape—both forcible and attempted—1978 and 1979, respectively. These statistics are offered here to give some indication of how the crime of rape is presented and processed by the agencies of criminal justice; we think that rape in San Antonio is not unique. Our work is a case study using victim and public attitude data from one city to test some of the propositions of a theory of racial-sexual stratification and to examine empirically the rape-as-crisis assumption.

Research Procedure and Rationale

The system of racial-sexual stratification, with its roots in slavery and colonialism, has produced and still maintains minority-dominant group differences in sex roles and in how males and females view themselves as sexual beings in relation to one another. Rape is one result of compounded sexual and racial inequality. Rape is the ultimate proof of male power over females, and it is the final breach of a social barrier erected by society between the dominant group and some racial and/or ethnic minorities. In a social system characterized by sexual and racial-ethnic inequality, *rape risks* become a predictable manifestation of power and powerlessness. Rape risks impact on males because rape (by legal definition in most states) is a male crime; it represents the loss of exclusive sexual privilege and/or proprietarian control over a woman; and it "costs" males when significant females fall victim to rape. Minority males experience an added risk—as suspected assailants—in relation to rape (or alleged rape) of majority females. For women, to know a rape victim or offender personally, no doubt, extracts a certain emotional price, but it also increases one's sense of vulnerability; hence, rape risk is experienced primarily as victimization or potential victimization.

By using racial-sexual stratification as a theoretical perspective, several propositions can be extracted relevant to the present research. (1) The impact of the rape experience for victims is expected to differ consistent with community (racial-ethnic) attitudes about rape, about sex roles and male-female sexuality. (2) Attitudes about rape (conceptualized in terms of feminist-nonfeminist) can be expected to vary among racial-ethnic groups because of historically different experiences and because of the present system of stratification which results in different minority-majority rape risks for both males and females. (3) Attitudes about male-female sex roles and/or sexuality (conceptualized as feminist-nonfeminist) can be expected to vary among racial-ethnic groups for the same historical and contemporaneous reasons.

The research setting allows for examination of these propositions as well as pursuit of other, more specific questions. The description of the research moves from an analysis of the rape experience from the victim's perspective to a community view of rape with samples of Anglos, Blacks, and Mexican Americans. These samples are treated as representative of separate communities, providing different social statuses and roles and a vastly different history and experience with regard to male-female relationships, sex roles, and rape. While there is much to be learned from both the victim and the community perspectives, only when they are intermeshed can we begin to fathom rape as both an experienced and a perceived phenomenon.

The Intrinsic Meaning of Rape: The Victim Research

Recognition of the intrinsic meaning of any life experience provides at least an initial foundation for understanding that experience. Despite the fact that the rape-related literature demonstrates both increasing awareness and concern over the problem, that literature also indicates that, as yet, there has been no empirical assessment of the rape experience. Utilizing the victim's perception of her experience as our data source, we attempted to explore the intrinsic meaning of rape and to assess its impact from the perspective of those who have experienced it. While that part of the work based on victims' perceptions is largely exploratory and descriptive, the impact of the rape experience is objectively and systematically assessed through quantitative measurement.

Assessing the Impact of Rape[2]

As defined here, "impact" is a generic term that refers to the effects of the rape experience on victims. However, we were concerned not only with obtaining a general description of the effects of this experience, but also with seeing whether the impact of rape varies significantly in relation to victim characteristics, assault characteristics, and/or victim support systems. Accordingly, seven independent and four dependent variables were used to assess the impact of rape. The independent variables (age-at-assault, time-since-assault, victim race-ethnicity, inter- versus intragroup rape, stereotypic versus nonstereotypic rape, institutional support systems; and personal support systems—see Appendix A.1) were developed either in response to the literature which suggests that rape is a crisis (or that it precipitates a crisis for the victim) or from the theory of racial-sexual stratification. Four dependent variables—crisis response, feelings about men, general functioning, and health concerns—were developed as impact measures.

CRISIS RESPONSE

The extent to which the prevalent rape-as-crisis conceptualization might be valid—for which victims, under what set(s) of circumstances—is an important research question because it has direct implications in relation to the use of the crisis intervention strategy in counseling rape victims. As noted previously, earlier victim research has neglected to conceptualize crisis adequately. Although this failure may simply be a reflection of the degree to which the term has been incorporated into everyday language, the result is that a multidimensional concept has been grossly oversimplified. From both a clinical and a theoretical perspective, this lack of conceptual clarity is problematic. To avoid this same error, we used the following conceptualization of crisis, which includes three interrelated factors: (1) a hazardous event that poses some threat to the individual; (2) an inability to respond with adequate coping mechanisms; and (3) a resultant temporary disruption of the individual's usual pattern of functioning.[3] In order to measure the relative degree of crisis response, a sixty-item, paper and pencil Crisis Scale (Halpern, 1973) was administered. This instrument produced a Crisis Score for each victim, and these scores represent one measure of Crisis Response.[4]

FEELINGS ABOUT MEN

A series of questions (resulting in a Feelings About Men/FAM Score) was developed to examine the degree to which the rape experience might have affected victims' feelings toward men in five interpersonal dimensions: communication, trust, nonsexual affection, general comfort, and sexual attraction-interest.[5]

GENERAL FUNCTIONING

Several questions related to routine activities were used to assess the degree to which victims' "normal" or typical pattern of functioning might have been disrupted following the assault. General Functioning Scores could indicate a change toward a comparatively passive, withdrawn style of functioning characterized by decreased concern or interest, or a change in the direction of increased activity.[6]

HEALTH CONCERNS

A measure (Health Concerns Score) was developed to determine the extent to which victims might have experienced health problems or concerns as a result of the rape. Victims were given a list of eleven health concerns and were asked to check each one they had experienced since the rape. For each concern checked, they subsequently were asked if that problem was directly related to the assault.[7]

Sampling, Interviewing, and Data Analysis

Data were obtained from sixty-one female rape victims (age fourteen or older) who were seen by, or had contact with, a volunteer or staff person from either the Alamo Area Volunteer Advocate Program, Inc. (AAVAP) in San Antonio or the Austin Rape Crisis Center (ARCC) in Austin, Texas (see Appendix B.1 for details). Both programs operate on an "on-call," around-the-clock basis providing information and support to rape victims. Express permission to conduct this study was obtained from administrators of both programs, and a staff member or volunteer from the program was used to make the initial contact with victims. If a victim was receptive to the idea of participating in the research, she was then contacted by a member of the research team who arranged the interview.[8] Of the sixty-one interviews completed, thirty-nine (64 percent) were from the AAVAP population and twenty-two were secured through the ARCC and by victims who referred us to other victims.[9] While it is clear that these victims do not constitute a random sample in the "pure" research sense, it is equally obvious that a random sample of rape victims is a pragmatic impossibility since many women never report the incident to police; and many undoubtedly do not seek medical attention, the services of rape crisis centers, or advocacy programs. To compound this sampling limitation, it can always be argued that there is something inherently "different" about the person who agrees to be interviewed versus the one who refuses. Suffice it to say that obtaining a random sample of rape victims was, and surely remains, problematic; in all likelihood, the victims who participated in this study are no more and no less representative than victims who have been included in other research. It is to be hoped that in time, rape victims will no longer feel intimidated and stigmatized, so that future research will include the hidden, as well as the more visible, victims.

Data were collected during personal interviews using a semistructured interview schedule designed for this study; the average time per interview was just under an hour and a half. All materials (schedules, consent forms, and response cards) were available in Spanish for respondents who did not speak or read English, or for those who preferred that the interview be conducted in Spanish. The interview schedule was designed to elicit data in the following areas: (1) demographic-background information; (2) circumstances of the assaults; (3) opinions about rape (definition, cause, and prevention); (4) impact of the rape experience; and (5) perceptions of service-delivery efforts. The actual process of locating, contacting, and interviewing victims spanned nearly six months during 1977; the time lapse between the rape and the research interview ranged from one to thirty-six months. The victim data were computer analyzed using selected procedures from the Statistical Package for the Social Sciences (SPSS) (Nie, et al., 1975). Basic descriptive statistics as well as analysis of variance and bivariate regression analysis were used in the analyses of the victim data. The .05 level of significance was set for all tests of association.

The Victims

Some of the more relevant descriptive characteristics of the sample are presented in Table 1, and, as can be seen, there is considerable diversity

TABLE 1. Selected Demographic Characterisitics of the Victim Sample

CHARACTERISTICS	NUMBER	PERCENT
Age at Interview		
Range 15-67 years	61	100
Mean 26.6 years		
Median 23.4 years		
Race-Ethnicity		
Anglo	32	52
Black	11	18
Mexican American	18	30
Religious Preference		
Catholic	22	36
Protestant	29	47
Other	4	7
None	6	10
Marital Status		
Single (Never married)	26	43
Divorced/Separated	22	36
Married[a]	11	18
Widowed	2	3
Education		
Range 4-19 years	61	100
Mean 11.9 years		
Median 12.1 years		
Currently Employed	28	46
Family Income[b]		
Range $1,188-22,000	55[c]	90
Mean $6,567		
Median $6,004		

[a]Two respondents indicated common law relationships; in Texas, these are viewed as legally binding, in which case they are included here as married.

[b]Family income denotes total income from the respondent and, where applicable, support from husband, parents, or other family members.

[c]N = 55 because 3 persons did not know income; 3 said they had "no" income.

within this group of sixty-one victims. While the average age at the time of the interview was just under twenty-seven years, a broad range of fifteen to sixty-seven years is apparent. Anglos represented just over half the respondents, while almost 20 percent were Black and nearly 30 percent were Mexican American. Protestants outnumbered Catholics; nearly 10 percent of the respondents reported having no religious preference, and the remaining 7 percent were categorized as "other." Although one-third of the respondents had not completed high school, nearly a third had some college and a few were college graduates (7 percent). Since some were still in school at the time of the interview, it seems likely that the average educational level may be skewed downward somewhat. In addition, nearly a third reported having had some other educational or vocational training such as business school, medical technology, or cosmetology courses. As shown in the table, almost half the respondents were employed at the time of the interview: 8 percent (of the total sample) were in professional or managerial positions; 26 percent were in clerical or sales positions; and just over 11 percent were service workers. Among the respondents not categorized as formally employed were homemakers-housewives (20 percent) and students (13 percent). The remaining respondents (21 percent) were unemployed, and most indicated that they were actively job-hunting. For the forty-six respondents who reported an individual income, the mean was nearly $5,500 a year with a median of $4,800, the range from $768 to $13,200 annually. These figures are substantially lower than those reported in the table, which reflect total family income. For the eleven respondents who were married and living with their husbands at the time of the interview, data on husband's education, occupation, and income indicate that, with one exception, all appeared to be in relatively marginal working-class positions.

The Extrinsic Meaning of Rape: The Public Attitude Research

In view of the theoretical and conceptual linkages established in the previous chapter, it seems clear that a macro-level approach to rape must take into account not only sexual inequality, but racial-ethnic inequality as well. A lesser approach precludes a holistic grasp of the extrinsic meaning of rape. On a conceptual level, this component of the research was designed to deal definitively with the concept of rape and with the concepts of sex roles-women's liberation, sexuality, and minority rape risks. On the operational level, data were collected by means of a structured interview schedule in five areas: (1) attitudes about rape; (2) attitudes about sex roles; (3) beliefs about male-female sexuality vis-à-vis rape; (4) minority-related rape risks; and (5) demographic characteristics. Since this is the first cross-cultural study of public attitudes about rape, it must be considered exploratory, and it is unlikely that complete congruence has been achieved between concepts, definitions, and measurement. (See Appendix A.5 for a discussion of reliability and validity in relation to ethnic-racial differences.) While the research is directed toward investigation and comparison of cross-cultural attitudes, it is also intended to go beyond the descriptive level to suggest some linkages between sex- and race-related attitudes and attitudes about rape among Anglo, Black, and Mexican American communities. Theoretical hypotheses which evolved from the theory of racial-sexual stratification are stated explicitly in Chapter 8 where all supporting data can be considered and evaluated.

Assessing Attitudes About Rape

Given that one of our objectives was to determine how each of the three samples perceives rape, no operational definition of rape was provided the respondents. Instead, as with the victim sample, three items (two of them open-ended) were used to tap the public's definition of rape and their opinions as to its cause and prevention. In contrast with these abstract opinion questions, a series of scenarios was used to quantify Attitudes About Rape which were conceptualized as three-dimensional—relating to definement of the situation, attribution of fault to the victim, and willingness to prosecute the alleged assailant. The scenarios are presented here as they were seen by the respondents except that numbers have been added (and the order rearranged) to simplify subsequent discussion.

S1: A young woman in her mid-twenties was required to work late at night in a dark and deserted part of town. As she left her office to go to the bus stop, she was attacked by a stranger with a gun. She was dragged into an alley where she was beaten and forced to have sex with him. Later, a night watchman found her unconscious.

S2: A secretary in her late twenties had to work late at night in a deserted part of town. As she walked from the office to her car after work, she was stopped by a stranger who demanded that she follow him into an alley. There, he forced her to have sex with him. He then told her to stay where she was, and he ran away. A night watchman found the woman, frightened and dazed, but otherwise unhurt.

S3: A teenage female had an argument with her parents and left home. She wanted to go to another city to stay with a friend. Because she had no money, she decided to hitchhike. She accepted a ride with an older man who pulled a gun on her, took her to a wooded area, and forced her to have sexual intercourse with him. He then told her to get back in the car and that he would take her where she wanted to go.

S4: A teenage female had an argument with her parents and left home. She wanted to go to another city to stay with a girl friend, but she had no money. She accepted a ride from a young man she knew slightly through some friends. After driving about twenty miles, he pulled off the road in a deserted area and told her that she would have to have sex with him. After some resistance on her part, he forced her to have sexual intercourse with him.

S5: A working woman in her mid-thirties stopped by her favorite bar for a drink after work. She talked briefly with some people there, but talked with one man more than anyone else. As she started to leave, he offered to drive her home. At her apartment, she asked him in for some coffee. Once inside, he immediately pulled a gun and forced her to have sex with him.

S6: A woman in her mid-thirties went to a singles bar after work to have a drink with some friends. She got into a conversation with some people she had not met before. A man in the group started to leave when she did and he offered her a ride home. When they got to her apartment, he asked if he could come in for a cup of coffee. Once inside, he attempted to seduce her; when she said no, he forced himself on her and had sexual intercourse.

S7: A known prostitute was assaulted and forced to have sexual intercourse with a young man in his late teens. The youth beat the woman and threatened her with a knife before escaping. The victim was able to identify her assailant as a member of a gang which frequently hangs out in the downtown park.

S8: A young college student was forced at knife point to have sex with a man she had been dating for several weeks. They supposedly had an understanding that there would be no sexual involvement. The attack came after she refused to spend the weekend with him.

S9: A husband and wife had an argument. The husband was very angry so he went to a bar to have a few drinks. After several hours he returned home to find his wife in bed asleep. He woke her up and demanded that she have sex with him. She refused, but he slapped her across the face and, although she resisted, forced her to have sexual relations with him.

With the exception of the husband-wife assault (S9), all scenarios met the legal definition of rape in Texas. Each was designed to vary certain components which the literature suggests are integral to the concept of rape (for example, victim's activity and/or reputation, use of a weapon, injury, victim-assailant relationship). After having read each scenario, respondents were asked to give their judgment or opinion in terms of (1) whether the situation was a rape; (2) whether the female was at fault; and (3) whether they would be willing to prosecute the alleged assailant.[10] Responses to each of these three dimensions were then combined across all nine scenarios to form composite Rape (definition), Fault (assessment of female responsibility), and Court (willingness to prosecute) Scores.[11] These three composite scores were used as measures of presumably independent dimensions of Attitudes About Rape where low scores are viewed as suggesting feminist attitudes (definement of the situation as rape, low assessment of fault, and willingness to prosecute), while high scores are seen as indicative of conservative, nonfeminist attitudes about rape.[12] In addition to the three composite measures, a Credibility Measure was developed to examine responses to a particular "kind" of rape. By adding the three responses on any one scenario (for example, the "date rape" depicted in S8), its overall perceived credibility can be compared with the credibility given to any other scenario.

Sex Roles and Women's Liberation

TRADITIONAL SEX ROLES

The concept of sex roles seems to contain the commonality of two gross constructs: (1) the assumption or belief that men and women are basically different in terms of psychology (some would tie this to biological differences, some to socialization); hence, there are certain personality, temperament, and emotional differences associated with "male" and "female"; and (2) the assumption or belief that males and females behave differently as a result of the above.[13] Thus, sex-role attitudes were dichotomized conceptually in terms of stereotypic, traditional *beliefs* about differences between males and females, and attitudes about stereotypic, traditional male and female *behavior*. An earlier work by Kammeyer (1966) offered a two-index standardized measure of stereotypic sex-role attitudes (see Appendix A.2). The Kammeyer items were used with some minor modifications in wording to make them more amenable to all three samples. The two indices seem to deal with gross sex-role stereotypes in terms of (1) beliefs (SR Beliefs) about how males and females differ in relation to attributes, characteristics, and emotions; and (2) attitudes about traditional male-female sex-role behavior (SR Behavior), particularly with regard to stereotypic male authority and the woman in her "place"—that is, home and/or some limited jobs.

WOMEN'S LIBERATION

The concept of women's liberation was more difficult to operationalize and measure because it is theoretically unspecified and behaviorally idiosyncratic. Definitive concepts of women's liberation run the gamut from radical feminist ideology to a version of Marxist feminism, to male-female egalitarianism, and finally to the vulgarized version of "doing your own thing." Since no single standardized or pretested measure of women's liberation was found (amenable to the constraints of the research design), women's liberation—like traditional sex roles—was dichotomized conceptually in terms of *beliefs* about women's liberation and attitudes about *behavior* thought to signify women's liberation. Two composite measures—Women's Liberation Beliefs (WL Beliefs) and Women's Liberation Behavior (WL Behavior)—were constructed, comprised of items from Yankelovich (1974) and Mason (1975), and some developed by the authors (see Appendix A.2).[14] Essentially, there are three major themes in the Belief Index: (1) equality—males and females are not basically unequal, nor are they inherently "masculine" or "feminine"; (2) self-appreciation—women are worthwhile and interesting apart from their traditional relationships to men; and (3) awareness of male dominance at an institutional level. Items in the Behavior Index suggest two dominant themes: (1) rejection of the traditional "place" of women as exclusively homemakers, wives, and mothers, with the assertion of women's right to work for equal pay and to pursue their own fulfillment and interests; and (2) rejection of the double standard of behavior for males and females, affirming women's right to equality in such areas as sexual freedom, mobility, and social activity. At best—from a theoretical level—the Women's Liberation indices measure a tendency toward male-female equality; at worst, they may be a vulgarized measure of women's liberation. The two indices, in fact, may not be congruent. For example, while some women may approve of acting "liberated," at the same time they may reject, or give little thought to, any feminist beliefs or ideology.

To the degree that these four indices (SR Beliefs, SR Behavior, WL Beliefs, and WL Behavior) are capable of measuring attitudes about traditionality or liberation in sex roles across the three ethnic-racial samples (see Appendix A.5 for discussion), it is theoretically hypothesized that nontraditionality in sex-role beliefs and behavior and high support for women's liberation will be associated with feminist attitudes about rape.[15]

Male-Female Sexuality and Rape

Sexuality means, literally, the quality or state of being sexual. However, it has been generalized to describe the entire area of personality related to sexual behavior. Sexuality has traditionally been assumed to be very different for males and females. Female sexuality in America is believed to be characterized by conflicting forces of good and evil. The good and virtuous woman is coupled with the seductive enchantress who causes men to lose control and become weak and malleable. The result of these conflicting strains is that females are typically viewed as having a dual sexuality; the good, virtuous female side is seen as the result of socialization, but beneath this lurks a repressed sexuality. Properly socialized women cannot consciously "give in" to their sexual self; men must overpower or outwit them. Consequently, men are ambivalent as to which side of women they prefer, and women (because of their repressed sexuality) are frequently assumed to harbor a "rape wish." Myths and ambivalence about female sexuality build in a certain skepticism about rape. People in general, and men in particular, must always be wary of the charge of rape, for a woman may have simply given lead to her natural sexuality only to have her social self deny her role in what happened and label it as rape. Or she may have failed to restrict (as prescribed by her role) the sexually aggressive male, hence, precipitating her own rape. Male sexuality is perceived as less complex than female sexuality. Sexual behavior is man's "nature." It is kept under control for social reasons, but the pressure to keep it under control is less than for women, presumably because women are biologically tied to childbearing and childrearing and are therefore ascribed a higher purpose, a moral responsibility. The end result is that women have seemingly inherited the responsibility of keeping not only their own sexuality under control, but that of men as well.

To the degree that persons hold the view that sexuality (or the sex drive) is a controlling (albeit subconscious) drive rather than a controlled drive, they may also hold the view that rape is simply an extension, or a natural result, of male-female interaction. A series of items was developed in an effort to get some measure of public beliefs (perhaps myths) about the dynamics of male-female sexuality and to test how these beliefs were associated with attitudes about rape. The underlying assumption is that persons who think of female sexuality as containing a rape wish or who doubt that a woman can "really" be raped (short of overt violence and/or a weapon) would tend toward conservative, nonfeminist attitudes about rape, as would those who see rape as a mere extension of the dynamics of "normal" male-female interaction. Although male sexuality is ostensibly more simplistic or unidimensional than that of females, the fact that males are seen as sexual beings may also lead to the perception that they are potential rapists. Consequently, additional belief items were included which relate directly to male sexuality. Questions were asked to determine whether rape is viewed as pathological behavior—that is, the product of mental illness or exaggerated anger-hatred toward women; presumably if this is true, it (rape) is not "natural sexuality." We also wanted to explore whether rape is generally viewed as a "bum rap"—the false accusation of a guilty, repentant, or vindictive female. Seven items were used to assess beliefs about female sexuality and six to assess beliefs about male sexuality and rape (see Appendix A.3). These thirteen items were subsequently factor analyzed to produce three underlying dimensions of beliefs about male-female sexuality for each sample.[16]

Minority-Related Rape Risks

As argued earlier, the majority-minority experience with regard to rape is very different because of (1) fear of interracial rape on the part of Whites, (2) higher minority rates of victimization, (3) a history of prejudicial and discriminatory treatment of minority victims and suspects by public officials, particularly in the criminal justice system, and (4) higher arrest rates for minority males. Several questions were designed to probe attitudes about minorities in relation to rape as both victims and suspects, and about attitudinal and experiential differences vis-à-vis rape among the three racial-ethnic groups.

INTERGROUP

This item was specifically designed as a rough measure of each group's perception of rape as an intergroup phenomenon (as opposed to intragroup or both inter- and intragroup). Since statistics on known rapes indicate that rape is a predominantly intragroup phenomenon, Intergroup can be taken as a crude indicator of racial-ethnic bias (or perhaps as general sexual distrust of one group for another).

DISCRIMINATION

In an effort to elicit perceptions of how minority persons are treated—as victims or as suspects—by law enforcement and other institutional representatives, a series of four questions was developed, related separately and specifically to Blacks and Mexican Americans. Responses to all four items were summed to form a composite measure of perceived (or experienced) minority Discrimination in relation to the crime of rape.

VICTIMIZATION

Official statistics indicate that minority groups have had more direct experience with crime as victims and as suspects than have majority group members. Three items dealing with victimization experience (rape/sexual assault and other violent crime) were developed, and affirmative responses on the items were summed to form a Victimization Score. Since it is clear that some respondents would be unlikely to admit their victimization experience to an interviewer, these scores should be viewed as conservative estimates of respondent victimization.

Demographic-Background Characteristics

The data documenting the relationship between attitudes (conceptualized along liberal-conservative continua) and certain demographic, socioeconomic characteristics are substantial.[17] The very limited data that exist with regard to public attitudes about rape suggest that these same associations hold—that is, that feminist (anti-rape) attitudes are associated with higher, as compared with lower, socioeconomic characteristics (Klemmack and Klemmack, 1976; and Feild, 1978). In the present work, the direction selected demographic characteristics were expected to take in relation to attitudes about rape was based on these limited data, but with sex and race-ethnicity treated as control categories because of differing vested interests and rape risks. While the primary focus of this part of the research is the relationship between sex and race-related attitudes and rape, it must be acknowledged that any measure of attitudes about rape might just as easily result from demographic-background characteristics. Therefore, for the purpose of statistical analysis, sex, age, education, income, and religion were selected (based on zero-order correlation coefficients) to represent background characteristics of respondents. Operational definitions of these background variables are found in Appendix A.4.

Data Collection and Analysis

A stratified random sample design was used in securing personal interviews with 335 Anglos, 336 Blacks, and 340 Mexican Americans, with each sample almost equally divided between males and females. Only persons age eighteen or older were allowed to participate.[18] (Specific details of the sampling procedure are noted in Appendix B.2.) The research design dictated that interviews be conducted by a person of the same racial-ethnic identity and the same sex as the respondent, and a local research firm was contracted to provide experienced interviewers.[19] With eighteen interviewers (six Anglos, six Blacks, and six Mexican Americans, three males and females per group) in the field, it took nearly six months (in 1976–1977) to complete the 1,011 interviews. All of the Mexican American interviewers were bilingual and were prepared to interview either in Spanish or English depending on the respondent's preference.[20] The public attitude data were coded, computer processed, and analyzed using selected procedures from the SPSS program (primarily one-way analysis of variance with a priori contrasts and multiple regression analysis). The .05 level of significance was used in tests of association, except for the contrasts where the more stringent .01 level was set.[21]

The Respondents: Three Samples

Table 2 provides some descriptive and comparative data on each of the three samples. There is considerable disparity on socioeconomic characteristics among the samples, with the Mexican Americans having the lowest and Anglos the highest socioeconomic indicators. In comparison with 1970 census data for the city as a whole, the Black and Mexican American samples appear to be representative, while the Anglo sample is somewhat more middle class than Anglos throughout the city. This prob-

TABLE 2.   Descriptive Characteristics of Respondents in Three Samples

CHARACTERISTICS[a]	ANGLO	BLACK	MEXICAN AMERICAN
Sample Size	335	336	340
Male	169	167	167
Female	166	169	173
Age (years)			
Mean	38	41	43
Median	34	40	43
Education (years)			
Mean	14	11	7
Median	14	12	8
Religion (percent)			
Protestant	60	85	6
Catholic	28	5	86
Other	12	10	8
Currently Married (percent)	74	44	65
Number of Children			
Mean	2	3	4
Median	2	2	3
Family Income (dollars)[b]			
Mean	16,578	8,232	6,231
Median	14,400	7,250	5,460

[a]Characteristics are those of the respondent except for family income (combined respondent and working spouse).

[b]These data represent actual or estimated family income. Income was estimated for either the respondent of spouse or both in approximately 19 percent of the cases (varied by ethnic group) where the respondent refused to provide information on family income but did provide information on occupation and education. The procedure for estimating income is that described by the U.S. Bureau of the Census, "Methodology and Scores of Socioeconomic Status," Working Paper No. 15 (Washington, D.C., 1963).

ably stems from the fact that the census tracts with the greatest concentration of Whites formed the population from which the sample was drawn (see Appendix B.2); hence, some poor Whites who live in mixed neighborhoods were excluded. It is probably safe to assume that the Anglo sample has restrictive generalizability to middle-class Whites, while the Black and Mexican American samples are more representative of the whole of these two populations. Whether these three samples are representative of Anglo, Black, and Mexican American populations outside of San Antonio (or perhaps the Southwest) is open to question. Generalizations from the present research (beyond San Antonio as a case study) should, therefore, be withheld pending replication in other geographic settings. It is clear from Table 2, however, that the minority samples differ markedly from the Anglo sample and, in some respects, from each other. Whether each of the three represents a different social reality in relation to the phenomenon of rape is the focus of subsequent chapters.

Concluding Note

No research is without methodological flaws or shortcomings, the present work included. Many readers, no doubt, prefer not to be bothered (or bored) with methodological details and procedures; others feel that a work stands or falls on its methodology. We have attempted to steer a middle-of-the-road course in this chapter. Because the work involves two complementary, yet distinct, research endeavors, and because one of those involves three autonomous samples, it is, at best, complex. Both portions of the work involved large numbers of variables which we attempted to assess by some objective, systematic means. Unless these measures and their operational definitions are understood, the research findings cannot be evaluated in proper perspective. And because this work is ground-breaking in attempting to quantify victim impact and racial-sexual attitudes, we are acutely aware of the importance of stating what we did (and why). Considerable time and effort were invested in developing interview schedules that would minimize interviewer bias and subjectivity. For example, there were no interviewer ratings *of* victim responses, only ratings given *by* victims. Response categories were developed to be exhaustive and mutually exclusive, and the resultant findings are therefore unambiguous. In subsequent chapters, we interpret and give meaning to findings, but our theoretical perspective is made explicit from the beginning. We also present major findings in tabular form so that they can stand alone, independent of whatever meaning we may give them. In sum, the findings from this research can be examined, scrutinized, and accepted or rejected as they are. By describing the variables, data collection, and analysis in some detail (here and in the Appendices), we have tried to avoid the confusing and often ambiguous presentation of findings that has characterized previous research, particularly that involving victims. In so doing, we feel that we have made it possible for others to replicate this work and thereby build a sound knowledge base vis-à-vis the intrinsic and extrinsic experience of rape.

Notes

1. In relation to the use of these minority-majority identity labels, an open-ended question in the public attitude survey asked respondents what term they used to identify themselves as members of a particular racial or nationality group. Over 72 percent of the Mexican American sample said Mexican American; 68 percent of the Black sample said Black. The dominant group showed no such consensus in identity; 38 percent said White; 25 percent said Anglo; 16 percent said American; 12 percent said Caucasian, and so forth.

2. In this part of the study, rape was defined as sexual intercourse forced on a female by one or more males—not her husband—without the female's consent. This definition closely approximated the legal definition of rape in most states at the time the research was conducted. Attempted rape, husband-wife rape, rape of a child, and cases involving incest were excluded, not only because they differ in terms of legal status, but also because we made a conscious decision to focus on rape. In particular, we felt that including data from victims of incest and child rape might obscure or confuse the findings on the impact of rape since the behavioral and social-psychological dynamics of these phenomena may well differ.

3. This conceptualization is a synthesis derived primarily from the theoretical works of Gerald Caplan and Lydia Rapoport. See Caplan, *Principles of Preventive Psychiatry* (New York: Basic Books, 1964), and Rapoport, "Crisis Intervention as a Mode of Treatment," in Robert Roberts and Robert Nee (eds.), *Theories of Social Casework* (Chicago: University of Chicago Press, 1970), pp. 267–311.

4. The Crisis Scores could range from 0 to 240; presumably the higher the score, the greater the degree of crisis. However, it should be acknowledged that the Crisis Scale elicits continuous data with no definitive point (or score) at which an individual can be viewed as "in crisis." Realistically, scores can only be viewed as suggesting a comparatively greater or lesser degree of crisis. The scale is comprised of ten groups of statements, each reflecting one aspect of a crisis reaction. Victims were asked to rate each of the sixty statements as being more or less valid descriptions of their present feelings/behavior compared with their feelings/behavior before the rape. Response categories (0–4) were: *much less true, less true, same as before or not applicable, more true,* and *much more true.* Sample items include: I find it hard to keep my mind on a task or job; I feel I've got more trouble than I can handle; and My life is worthwhile.

5. Feelings About Men Scores could range from 5 to 15, with high scores indicating that victims feel better now and low scores indicating that their feelings are not as good now as before the assault. Victims were asked to select a response by comparing their present feelings about men with their feelings before the assault. Response categories (1–3) were *not as good, about the same,* and *better.*

6. General Functioning Scores could range from −4 to +4, with high scores reflecting increased activity/concern and low scores reflecting decreased activity/concern. Items included in this measure related to functioning in terms of cooking, housekeeping, spending time with friends, and running errands. Response categories (1 to 3) were *more, about the same,* and *less* (now as compared with before the rape).

7. Health Concerns Scores could range from 0 to 15, with the score indicating the actual number of concerns experienced by victims as a result of the assault. In addi-

tion to the eleven items on the list, victims could add up to three other concerns, and an earlier item related to alcohol use was included in scoring. Examples of items on the checklist included fatigue, stomach trouble, headaches, and nightmares.

8. Unlike the procedure used in some studies, we did not interview victims immediately after the rape when they were initially seen by someone from a service-delivery program. Our rationale was twofold: (1) we wanted to maintain a separate identity with a research, rather than service-delivery, role; and (2) in order to assess impact from a crisis perspective, there had to be a time lapse between the rape and the interview.

9. In all cases, caution was exercised with regard to the protection of respondents' privacy. Specific guidelines were followed in making initial contacts, all respondents read and signed an informed consent agreement prior to being interviewed, and a procedure was established to provide counseling referrals for victims, if necessary. In cases involving minors, signed consent was also obtained from the parent(s).

10. Each scenario was presented on a separate card, the order having been determined by a random-numbers selection. After reading each scenario, respondents were asked to select the statement that best reflected their views in relation to the following:

WHICH ANSWER BEST DESCRIBES YOUR OPINION ABOUT THIS?

I *strongly agree* that this is rape.
I *agree* that this is rape.
I *disagree* that this is rape.
I *strongly disagree* that this is rape.

DO YOU THINK THAT THE FEMALE WAS AT FAULT?

She was *not at all* at fault.
She was *somewhat* at fault.
She was *very much* at fault.

WHICH ANSWER BEST DESCRIBES YOUR OPINION ABOUT WHAT SHOULD BE DONE?

I *strongly agree* that the man involved should be arrested and taken to court.
I *agree* that the man involved should be arrested and taken to court.
I *disagree* that the man involved should be arrested and taken to court.
I *strongly disagree* that the man involved should be arrested and taken to court.

11. Following the collection of all data, Fault Scores were standardized to be comparable with Rape and Court Scores. Therefore, each of the three composite scores had a possible range of 9 to 36. The lower the R Score, the stronger the agreement that the nine scenarios did depict rape; the lower the F Score, the less inclined the respondent was to blame the victims for the rape; the lower the C Score, the more willing the respondent was to prosecute the assailants.

12. The terms *feminist* and *conservative* are used here in a general descriptive sense to refer to different ideologies about rape. *Feminist* is used to mean anti-rape attitudes emanating from the women's movement and defining rape simply as sex

without the woman's consent. *Conservative* is used to refer to a more limited definition of rape—for example, qualified acceptance of the validity of rape according to
the female's activities, reputation, assailant's use of force, victim-assailant relationship, and so on.

13. A number of works present arguments and empirical findings with regard to
sex differences and sex-role socialization. See, for example, Janet Saltzman Chafetz,
Masculine/Feminine or Human? (Itasca, Ill.: F. E. Peacock, 1974); Sue Cox (ed.),
Female Psychology (Chicago: Science Research Associates, 1976); Carol Tavris and
Carole Offir, *The Longest War* (New York: Harcourt Brace Jovanovich, 1977); and
Barbara L. Forisha, *Sex Roles and Personal Awareness* (Morristown, N.J.: General
Learning Press, 1978).

14. In attempting to operationalize and measure women's liberation, a conscious
effort was made to avoid the more controversial theoretical and ideological aspects
of the concept (for example, conceptualizing women as an oppressed minority or as
an exploited underclass in the capitalist system). Knowledge of San Antonio as a
relatively conservative, provincial city suggested that the randomly selected
respondents would not likely be familiar with these views. Realistically, they would
be more likely to relate to women's liberation in behavioral terms such as the Equal
Rights Amendment, abortion, equal opportunity, and equal pay. In effect, some
items in the Belief Index reflect a merging of feminist ideology with a more popular-
ized version of women's liberation. See, for example, Cox, *Female Psychology*, pp.
1–20; Annette M. Brodsky, in *Female Psychology*, pp. 372–77; and Barbara S.
Deckard, *The Women's Movement* (New York: Harper and Row, 1975), pp.
376–413.

15. It should be pointed out that, although both sex roles and women's liberation
were conceptualized in terms of dichotomous beliefs and behavior, all four indices
are, in reality, attitudinal measures. Attitudinal measures were selected over
behavioral measures because of the inherent problems in attempting to determine
(with any degree of accuracy) what people really do. This approach also had the advantage of allowing males as well as females to respond to the same items.

16. These measures of beliefs about Male-Female Sexuality may be tautological
when treated as causal (independent) variables in relation to attitudes about rape.
There are conceptual distinctions, however, which justify their inclusion. The male-
female sexuality items were aimed at measuring the degree to which male-female
role-bound sexual behavior is believed to be an integral part of the phenomenon
labeled as rape. On the other hand, the rape scenarios measure specific judgments
about rape which may be influenced by these male-female beliefs. Zero-order correlation coefficients, in fact, reveal only low to moderate correlations for the male-
female factors (extracted from the thirteen items) and R, F, and C Scores.

17. For some representative works that deal with attitudes (prejudice, politics,
race, or sex) in some liberal-conservative context while taking into account
socioeconomic characteristics, see Gordon Allport, *The Nature of Prejudice* (New
York: Anchor Books, 1954); Gary T. Marx, *Protest and Prejudice* (New York:
Harper and Row, 1969); Harriet Holster, *Sex Roles and Social Structure* (Norway:
Universitetsforlaget, 1970); Angus Campbell, *White Attitudes Toward Black People*
(Ann Arbor, Mich.: Institute for Social Research, 1971).

18. As in the victim study, participants were not interviewed until the purpose of the research had been explained to them and they had read and signed an informed consent agreement.

19. Specialized training regarding the subject matter and design of the study was provided by the researchers before any interviewer was allowed in the field. Debriefings were held with interviewers throughout the course of their work to review the quality of their interviews and to handle any problems that might arise.

20. The interview schedule was available in Spanish as were all related materials (such as consent form and response cards). Interviewers were thus prevented from making impromptu translations that might have altered the meaning of items.

21. *A priori* contrasts are a kind of specific comparison test used to explore the data beyond the overall F test. The rationale for having used this additional data analysis technique was twofold: (1) sex and race-related differences had been predicted in advance (that is, given the theoretical framework of Chapter 2); and (2) as an exploratory study, we felt it was important that possible differences between groups not be overlooked. Therefore, *t*-tests were used to protect against Type II errors, but a more stringent level of significance (.01) was also used to offset the probability of capitalizing on chance differences (Type I errors).

THROUGH VICTIMS' EYES

4

In striving to understand rape, to achieve some grasp of what rape victimization means, it becomes necessary to identify and examine some of the components of the total experience. While it is widely assumed that rape is a traumatic event in the life of a woman, we can best understand its intrinsic meaning by sharing her victimization as she remembers (however selectively) and continues to feel its impact. From the women who agreed to talk about their experiences, we hoped to learn the circumstances and consequences of rape, their needs immediately following the rape, and how well they felt these needs were actually met. The following sections provide a description of the rape experience and its impact as given by the sixty-one victims we interviewed. Where meaningful comparisons can be made, data from other sources are presented to place our findings in a broader context.

Characteristics of the Assaults

Age

As shown in Table 3, the average age of victims at the time of the assault was almost twenty-six years, although the modal age was twenty-three. Just over one-third of the victims were twenty-one or younger, about 44 percent were between the ages of twenty-two and twenty-nine, and nearly 20 percent were thirty years of age or older. In comparison, findings reported by Schram indicate that more than half of the victims represented in their police data (N=1,261) were under the age of twenty-one and approximately 15 percent were over the age of thirty (1978, p. 17).[1] This difference suggests that victims in the present study tended to be somewhat older than those represented in police records in that there were higher percentages of victims in the twenty-two to twenty-nine and "over thirty" groups. However, this difference may be attributed to the fact that victims under the age of fourteen at the time of the assault were excluded from our research. Data related to the assailants' ages are based on estimates provided by victims, and some must be viewed as educated guesses since there were cases in which victims stated they could not be sure. Based on their estimates, more

TABLE 3. Selected Characteristics of the Assaults

CHARACTERISTICS	NUMBER	PERCENT
Age of Victim		
Range 14-67 years	61	100
Mean 25.7 years		
Median 22.9 years		
Mode 23 years		
Assailant Age (in Years)[a]		
Under 25	21	34
25-30	21	34
Over 30	15	26
Number of Assailants		
1	45	74
2	11	18
3-5	5	8
Assailant Race-Ethnicity		
Anglo	20	33
Black	16	26
Mexican American	22	36
Other/Unknown	3	5
Victim-Assailant Race-Ethnicity[b]		
Intragroup	38	62
Intergroup	22	36
First Contact with Assailant		
Broke into home	22	36
Accosted without warning	20	33
Social situation	13	21
Accepted a ride	6	10

[a] Age of assailant is grouped since respondents rarely knew exact ages; these are actually estimates. Also, N=57 because four respondents were unable to provide any data.

[b] N=60; one respondent never saw the assailant and therefore could not specify his race-ethnicity.

TABLE 3 *(continued)*

CHARACTERISTICS	NUMBER	PERCENT
Location of Assault		
Victim's home	22	36
Alley/Park/Street/Vacant Building	20	33
Vehicle	10	16
Assailant's home	6	10
Other	3	5
Threats by Assailant		
Explicit threats	29	47
Verbal intimidation	17	28
Physical force	7	12
None	8	13
Use of Weapon		
Knife	17	28
Gun	10	16
Other	3	5
None	31	51
Victim Injuries		
Nonspecific/minor	24	39
Specific head/neck	14	23
Serious/moderate	3	5
None	20	33

than two-thirds of the assailants were thought to be thirty years of age or younger. In comparison, Schram reported that the majority of offenders represented in their police data were between the ages of eighteen and twenty-five. Findings from the present study reflect equal numbers of assailants in the eighteen to twenty-five and twenty-five to thirty age brackets (just over one-third each), about 26 percent believed to be "over thirty," and 5 percent unknown.

Inter- Versus Intragroup Rape

In keeping with the theoretical framework of Chapter 2, one of the more critical assault-related variables was that of victim's and assailant's race-ethnicity, or the phenomenon of inter- versus intragroup rape. As shown in Table 3, just under two-thirds of the assaults occurred between persons of the same racial or ethnic group. Specifically, 85 percent of the Anglo assailants chose Anglo women as victims, and nearly two-thirds of the Mexican American assailants chose Mexican American women as victims. The exception to this pattern is in relation to Black assailants. By a margin of 56 to 44 percent, Black assailants chose Anglo, then Black women as victims; there were no Black-Mexican American assaults reported by our sample. These findings indicate that intragroup rape was more typical, but when intergroup rape did occur, the pattern was one of minority assailant-majority victim.

Victim-Assailant Relationship

The question of victim-assailant relationship has been a crucial one in attempting to understand both the situational dynamics of rape and subsequent responses—institutional and personal—to rape victims. For example, it is evident that the victim's credibility is less in question if she can say that the assailant was a total stranger since this fits the stereotyped perception of rape as a randomly committed, unpremeditated offense. Clark and Lewis have reported data clearly suggesting that the nature of the victim-assailant relationship influences the classification of rape complaints (as founded or unfounded) by police. Based on 104 rape complaints filed with the Toronto police, 52 percent of those involving assailants who were strangers were classified as founded; yet, when the victim and assailant were "acquaintances," 24 percent were founded, and when the victim and assailant "knew each other well," only one of five complaints was classified as founded (1977, p. 71). All other things being equal, something of a "credibility continuum" seems to exist on the variable of victim-assailant relationship. It is of considerable interest to note that in the present study the majority of victims (72 percent) said they did not know, nor had they ever seen, their assailant prior to the rape. Of the seventeen victims (28 percent) who did know their assailant, five said they knew him "by sight," that is, they had "seen him around" the neighborhood; five others said they knew him casually or had met him earlier that day or evening; and the remaining seven victims indicated that the assailant was someone known by, or related to, their husband, family, or friends. While our findings suggest that most of these rapes involved victims and assailants who were total strangers, it is of no real comfort to find that in one of every four cases, men known to these women (albeit rather tenuously in some instances) were to become their assailants.

Setting and Circumstances

As shown in Table 3 regarding the first victim-assailant contact, twenty-two victims (36 percent) described situations in which the assailant forcibly broke into their homes or gained entry through fraudulent or deceptive means. For example, in one case the assailant had attended a party given by the victim's husband; some time later, he returned to the victim's home saying he was there to meet with her husband. After allowing him in to wait (the husband was not there at the time), the assailant overpowered and raped her. In another case, a man knocked on the victim's door and asked her to call the police because there had been an accident outside. As she was dialing the phone, he came into the room brandishing a knife and raped her.

While these kinds of cases were atypical of the sample as a whole, they do serve as a reminder that some rapes involved a degree of premeditation and planning on the part of the assailant. Apparently, the same may be said for the twenty victims (33 percent) who described being somewhere outside their homes when they were suddenly accosted. This category included situations where the assailant produced a weapon or physically attacked and threatened the victim, seemingly without warning. To illustrate, one victim reported that she was walking home from a local grocery store early one evening when a man stopped to ask if she knew "Susan." As she walked past him, he grabbed her from behind and, with a knife in hand, took her to a vacant house nearby and raped her.

Not surprisingly, the location of the assault was often dictated by the initial contact between victims and assailants. While women raped in their own homes were most likely assaulted by a stranger who forcibly broke in or, in a few cases, by a man who "conned" his way in, women who were accosted elsewhere without warning were usually in a public place. In these cases, the actual rape most often occurred in an alley, a deserted street, a park, or a vacant building. The findings also indicate that only one of five assaults occurred following some voluntary social interaction between victims and assailants (for example, having attended the same party), and only one in ten was related to the victim's having been hitchhiking or riding with someone she had just met. If these findings approach being representative, it is time for the perennial question of victim-precipitation to be laid to rest. It is somewhat puzzling that victim-blaming continues to be such a prevalent response to rape. However, the larger irony may be the proverbial "Catch 22" situation in which many victims find themselves. On the one hand, women are socialized to stay at home where they are ostensibly safe from so-called street crime; on the other hand, women are also taught to be kind, polite, and helpful. But these findings seem to suggest that the woman who remains at home, *and* the woman who tries to be a "good samaritan," *and* the woman who goes about minding her own business, are *all* at risk in relation to rape.

Threats, Weapons, and Injuries

Although we recognize that the act of rape is, by definition, a threat to a woman (physically, emotionally, and sexually), we nevertheless attempted to get beyond the obvious to learn how threats are used and perceived in rape incidents. Not surprisingly, nearly all victims (87 percent) reported having been threatened in some way by their assailants. As shown in Table 3, threats ranged from an initial use of physical force (where the assailant threw the victim to the ground, hit, slapped, or otherwise overpowered her), to explicit threats where the rapist wielded a weapon while saying he was going to injure or kill her, to verbal intimidation without a visible weapon. Specifically, the category labeled verbal intimidation included vague verbal threats that the victim would not be hurt "if she cooperated," or threats to the effect that he (the assailant) would "find her" if she "caused him any trouble." To illustrate the difference between an explicit threat and verbal intimidation, a response such as "He told me if I didn't do what he said, he'd kill me, and he held a knife to my neck," was considered an explicit threat. In contrast, a frequent form of verbal intimidation was "Be quiet...I don't want to hurt you." It was also clear in some cases that assailants knew the victim had a child in the house or nearby, and this provided a further dimension to their threats. These victims tended, rather matter of factly, to indicate that they chose not to scream or resist very strenuously because they were afraid for their children.

There is considerable difference in terms of the threat variable in our data compared with findings from the Toronto police data. While threats were reported by the vast majority of victims in our study, Clark and Lewis indicate threats recorded by police in only 37 percent of their 104 cases (1977, p. 68). For some reason, few of the victim studies in the United States have reported findings regarding assailant threats. Comparisons are further complicated by the use of different response categories where data are available. For example, Bart reported that 44 percent of the 1,071 victims responding to the *Viva* questionnaire were threatened, but these are undifferentiated as to form or degree (1975, p. 7). McCombie reported that approximately half of the seventy victims seen through the Rape Crisis Intervention Program at Beth Israel Hospital were threatened with death, and 22 percent were threatened with injury or disfigurement (1976, p. 148), but it is not clear whether these categories are mutually exclusive. And while the interview guide used by Holmstrom and Burgess (1978) included questions related to threats, findings were not reported.

Suffice it to say that victims in the present study experienced a high number and degree of threats—verbal and physical—in their rape experiences. What accounts for this pattern is not known, although it could be part of a larger pattern of violent crime characteristic of the region. For example, national crime statistics compiled by the FBI indicate that, among the four geographical regions in the nation, the South holds the dubious distinction of having the highest murder rate and is second only to the Western region in both aggravated assault and forcible rape rates.[2] Therefore, it could be argued that the Southern region, including Texas, tends to be violence prone. In that case, threats by assailants, use of weapons, and injuries sustained by victims during rapes might be expected to be more prevalent in this study compared with those by McCombie or Holmstrom and Burgess who carried out their research in the Northeast.

As reflected by the figures in Table 3, this alleged pattern of violence does seem to hold true in relation to use of a weapon and victim injury. In almost half the cases, victims reported that the assailant had a weapon; that is, a gun, knife, or some other object (for example, a metal belt-buckle, a rock, a kitchen utensil) was wielded as a weapon. McCombie reported weapons were used in 41 percent of her seventy cases (1976, p. 148), while no findings are available from other studies. As to injuries sustained by victims, in this study a continuum was developed to differentiate between serious and relatively minor injuries. As shown in Table 3, nearly a third of the victims reported no injury at all. Almost 40 percent reported minor, nonspecific injuries, which included bruises, superficial cuts/scratches, wrist and/or ankle sprains, and general soreness from having been beaten and/or kicked on various parts of the body. Another 23 percent received specific injuries to the face, head, and neck, including black eyes, cuts to the mouth or lips, swollen jaw, and welts and/or bruises around the throat from having been choked. In the remaining cases (5 percent), moderate to severe injuries were sustained, including concussions, wounds requiring surgical repair, and broken bones. Comparisons are again difficult to make in relation to other studies because different coding categories were used. However, as a broad point of reference, McCombie reported injuries among 41 percent of her seventy cases (1976, p. 148), while Holmstrom and Burgess reported (based on ninety-two cases) that "63 percent of the adult...victims had at least one sign of *general* physical trauma" (1978, p. 88). In comparison, 67 percent of those in the present study reported some degree of injury as a result of the assault.

Feelings About Assailants

As a sort of closure question related to circumstances of the assaults, respondents were asked: "Can you tell me how you feel about the man (men) who assaulted you?" Although responses were grouped into five categories, just over two-thirds fell into a single category of angry and/or punitive feelings. Proportionately more Mexican American victims (78 percent) expressed angry/punitive feelings, compared with approximately two-thirds of the Anglo and about one-half of the Black victims. It is evident that only in response to an open-ended question could the intensity of feeling come through so clearly. Statements such as "I hate him" or "I'd like to kill him" were common among the forty-one responses placed in this one category. However, some responses were much more emphatic and explicit. As an illustration, the following is a quote from a single woman in her early twenties who was interviewed three months after she had been raped by three men: "I hate them, and for me, hate is a big word. It wouldn't bother me to shoot them. I wouldn't care at all if they died." Nor does it appear that the intensity diminishes over time, as illustrated by the response of a young housewife and mother who was interviewed more than two years after the assault. "I *hate* him because he made my baby watch it." Some victims seem to have given thought to what they would like to do if they were to encounter their assailants under different circumstances. A young secretary raped a year before the interview said, "I think I'd kill him and I don't think I'd feel guilty. In fact, I think I'd enjoy it."

Finally, there were those who had thought far enough along to have considered the "ultimate" revenge for rape. As described by a housewife and mother raped fifteen months before the interview, "I'd like to kill him if I could get away with it, or let him experience something like what he put me through." Or, as another woman, the mother of four, coolly said one year after she was raped, "I'd like to see him dead—or better yet, castrated." To find that victims of rape feel angry and punitive toward their assailants is not startling. However, from the interviewer's perspective, to have heard and seen these feelings expressed repeatedly, to recognize their compounded depth and intensity, is to sense and feel a reservoir of unresolved anger and rage.

With regard to the other response categories, six victims (10 percent) described their primary feeling toward the rapist in terms of fear and/or apprehension. Specifically, they felt afraid of him, and they experienced strong feelings of apprehension at the thought of ever seeing him again. Five others (8 percent) gave responses that were categorized as generally negative statements about the assailants—for example, "He's low and filthy"; "He's a coward"; or "He's repulsive." Interestingly, another five victims (8 percent) described feeling somewhat sympathetic toward their assailants, perhaps in an effort to understand and/or rationalize what had happened. Statements such as "I feel sorry for him"; "He has a problem"; or "He needs help" were typical of responses in this category. Finally, four victims (7 percent) basically said they had no identifiable feelings toward their assailants. It is, of course, impossible to say whether these are true reflections, or whether they might be interpreted as indicative of some degree of denial, perhaps as a means of self-protection. In any case, responses in this category included "I don't have any feelings one way or the other"; "I just blocked it out"; or "It never happened."

The Assaults: A Summary

The findings presented thus far provide an overview of the assaults as described by this victim sample, and they help to provide some tentative answers to the following questions: who are the rapists, and under what range of circumstances do assaults occur? Data gathered from these victims indicate that most assailants were thought to be thirty years of age or younger. Nearly two-thirds of the assailants raped women of the same race or ethnic group as themselves, and nearly three-fourths of the rapes were committed by a lone assailant. The majority of assailants were strangers to their victims, and in all likelihood, the assailant either broke into the victim's home or otherwise attacked her without warning. Most rapes occurred either in the victim's home or somewhere in the open such as a street, an alley, a park, or a vacant building. About half the assailants had a weapon, most often a knife. Nearly all assailants threatened their victims, and most (victims) sustained some degree of physical injury as a result of the assault.

Since these data were provided by a group of victims from a nonrandom sample, we cannot assume that this description reflects the reality of all rapes. In fact, what these data seem to suggest is that most victims who participated in this study were involved in rather stereotypic assaults. That is, most described the kinds of rape incidents commonly perceived as "good" or "real" in that the following criteria were met: (1) the victim and assailant were total strangers; (2) the victim was accosted without warning; (3) the victim was explicitly threatened ("preferably" with a weapon); and (4) the victim suffered some degree of observable injury. So, while it might be said that a reasonably accurate description of stereotypic rape has been presented, it should be acknowledged that these assaults represent only one circumstantial or contextual "kind" of rape. Other "kinds" of rape situations, especially those that fail to meet the criteria of a "good" or "real" rape, were most likely selected out by the victims who elected not to report to the police, not to seek medical treatment, and not to contact a rape crisis program. The most obvious examples of so-called questionable assaults are those that occur within the context of what is generally consensual social interaction ("date rapes"), those in which the assailant is a former husband or lover, and those in which the victim herself feels somehow responsible for what happened, perhaps because of poor judgment or carelessness. From a research and knowledge-building perspective, it is unfortunate that the data gathered here do n' t include these kinds of rape experiences.

The Impact of Rape: Victim Assessments

In thinking about the ramifications of rape, a number of very basic, pragmatic questions come to mind. We asked some of these questions in an effort to determine whether the victim's feelings about men had changed and whether their typical pattern of acting and relating to others had been altered. We tried to get a sense of what being a "rape victim" was like, how victims coped, and how they felt about their lives. The findings presented in this section provide some qualitative description of the impact of the rape experience.

Feelings Toward Men

It is rather obvious to expect that victims of rape might feel less than positive toward men, that there may well be some generalized "fallout" as a result of the experience. But it seems equally clear that such feelings are not likely to be unidimensional. Furthermore, the critical factor in trying to examine the impact of rape has to do with change, in this case, how do victims feel toward men *now* compared with before the assault? To tap this aspect of impact, victims were asked to think about their feelings toward men in general (rather than toward any specific man) and then to indicate whether they felt *better, about the same,* or *not as good* now (compared with before the assault) in terms of the following interpersonal dimensions: (1) communication or talking with men; (2) trust; (3) showing affection (nonsexual); (4) general level of comfort around men; and (5) sexual attraction or interest. Responses to these items are summarized in Table 4, and as shown, few victims indicated that they felt better with regard to these interpersonal dimensions. Responses in the better category ranged from none on communication to four (7 percent) on general feeling of comfort. At the opposite end of the spectrum, 77 percent reported feeling not as good in relation to trusting men, 66 percent indicated their level of sexual interest was not as good, and nearly 60 percent said their feelings of affection toward men were not as good as before. Across all five dimensions, the majority of responses fell into the category of "not as good."

When each dimension of feelings toward men was examined separately by victims' race-ethnicity, the following findings emerged: (1) Mexican American victims were apparently the most adversely affected in terms of communication, Anglos the least; (2) in relation to trust, 94 percent of the Mexican American victims, 73 percent of the Blacks, and 68 percent of the Anglos reported feeling not as good; (3) there was considerable diversity of responses in relation to nonsexual affection in that 94 percent of the Mexican American victims stated they did not feel as good, compared with 64 percent of the Black and 37 percent of the Anglo victims; (4) in relation to comfort around men, negative feelings were less in evidence for all groups, although Anglos were the only group with as many responses in the *same* category as in the *not as good* category; and (5) Mexican American victims were the most adversely affected (81 percent), Anglos the least (56 percent), and Blacks in between (73 percent) on the sexual attraction dimension. Overall, the two most adversely affected dimensions were trust and sexual attraction, while communication and general level of comfort were, relative to the other dimensions, the least affected.

General State of Mind

We were also concerned with giving victims a chance to describe, in their own words, their feelings and general state of mind during the month or two after the assault. Their responses were grouped into five categories, each reflecting a different theme. Although one victim said she could not remember anything about that time and another indicated that the rape did

TABLE 4.   Victims' Feelings Toward Men in Five Interpersonal Dimensions (N=61)

DIMENSION		COMPARATIVE FEELINGS		
		BETTER	*SAME*	*NOT AS GOOD*
Communication-Talking	N	0	29	32
	%	—	47	52
Trust	N	1	13	47
	%	2	21	77
Affection-Nonsexual	N	3	22	36
	%	5	36	59
Comfort	N	4	25	32
	%	7	41	52
Sexual Interest-Attraction[a]	N	1	19	39
	%	2	32	66

Note: Not all percentages add to 100 because of rounding errors.
[a]N = 59 because two respondents were undecided.

not really affect her, responses from the remaining fifty-nine victims evolved into the following: (1) 41 percent described feeling apprehensive and afraid; (2) 27 percent felt confused and unable to maintain control; (3) 15 percent said they became depressed and tended to withdraw from social interaction; (4) 12 percent described feeling guilty, embarrassed, and/or ashamed; and (5) 5 percent expressed anger and/or hostility. It is clear that the process of analyzing responses and placing them into content categories for a more organized presentation of findings loses a great deal in terms of affective tone. For this reason, selected responses are presented to illustrate more realistically the nature of victims' descriptions.

That rape victims experience fear both during and after the assault is hardly a surprise. The depth of this feeling, the existence of variables that serve to compound it, and the lengths to which some victims go in an attempt to cope are illustrated in the following responses from three victims: (1) "Fear, I was more careful. Every time I went somewhere, I thought I saw the men who assaulted me." (2) "I was frightened. I felt okay for the week he was in jail, but after they let him out I felt frightened again." (3) "Terribly frightened, paranoid—I walked around with a knife in my hand around the apartment." The second most frequent response was a feeling of general confusion, sometimes evidenced by an inability to make decisions. While one victim simply said, "I was confused. I didn't know what I wanted," another was more explicit in stating, "My life was in limbo. I wasn't getting things together; I felt I couldn't take control of things. I was real scared; I thought of death . . . and felt vulnerable, like I was physically falling apart."

The frequency of responses in the next three categories is smaller, but the feelings expressed are not less intense. For example, some victims who experienced a sense of depression said they became preoccupied with the assault: "I couldn't get it off my mind and just thought about it constantly." Another victim who talked about feeling depressed and sleeping more than usual explained, "My dreams were so much better than my real life that I didn't want to wake up." Those who felt embarrassed or ashamed often expressed the feeling that somehow others "knew" about the rape: "I felt like people were looking at me for what had happened"; or, more explicitly stated, "I felt dirty, unclean . . . I couldn't let anyone touch me or get physically close." Some victims who described feeling angry evidently generalized their anger beyond the predictable target of the assailant. In some cases, it was directed toward family members who had not been supportive of the victim, while for others it was directed toward men in general: "I hated men, didn't want them near me. I wanted to smash them in the face whenever they got close to me."

Mobility, Coping, and Change

One of the ways in which individuals sometimes attempt to cope with residual feelings about an unpleasant experience is to try a "change of scene." As noted previously, one of the major difficulties in the victim research was our inability to locate victims seen through AAVAP, in many cases because they had moved since the assault (see Appendix B.1). In an effort to explore the "change of scene" thesis, victims were asked if they had moved since the assault, how often, and whether the move was related to the assault. As a caution, however, it is obvious that victims who were never located by the research team may have been the most highly mobile, in which case these findings probably represent a conservative picture of victim mobility. Fifteen victims, or one out of every four in this sample, changed residences as a result of the assault. While most of those who moved did so only once, the range was from one to four times. In response to whether the move was related to the assault, victims who said yes tended to do so rather emphatically. For example, one victim stated, "Definitely. I loved where I was living. That's one thing that made me really angry, to have to move because of this. I moved in with a relative; I think it would be very difficult to live alone now." For many of those who moved because of the assault, it was not uncommon to find that they felt afraid to live alone; consequently, several said they had moved back home with their family or had moved in with a roommate. Others explained that they moved because the rape had occurred in their home and they simply could not stay there. One victim poignantly said, "I moved away from where it happened because living there made it all come back."

In exploring impact further, victims were asked to provide a self-assessment as to whether they felt they were generally getting along *better*, *about the same,* or *not as well* as before the assault occurred. Interestingly, responses were almost equally distributed: twenty-two (36 percent) said better, eighteen (30 percent) said about the same, and twenty-one (34 percent) said not as well. When these responses were examined according to victims' race-ethnicity, Anglo victims had the most evenly distributed assessments, with about one-third in each rating level. Mexican American victims generally approximated this distribution, with one-third indicating they were getting along better, 28 percent about the same, and nearly 39 percent not doing as well as before. In comparison, Black victims showed the most definitive pattern in that a majority (55 percent) said they felt they were getting along better, 27 percent about the same, and only 18 percent felt they were not getting along as well. It should be noted that victims who indicated they were getting along better were not suggesting that this experience was "good" or "positive" in the usual sense. Rather, their assessments seem to reflect that they had managed to come through the experience feeling somewhat stronger than before.

This distinction came across more clearly on the next question which, because it was open-ended, allowed for more detailed responses. Victims were asked: "In relation to this experience, do you feel that it has caused you to think or act or feel any different than before?" Only four victims (one Black and three Mexican Americans) said that they had experienced no discernible changes. Responses from the remaining fifty-seven victims were grouped into four categories: (1) 35 percent described an increased sense of fear; (2) 33 percent reported a heightened sense of distrust; (3) 21 percent indicated they felt stronger or more in control; and (4) 10 percent described a lowered sense of self-esteem.

For Anglo victims, increased fear was the most frequent response (41 percent) to the question of how they are different now, while lower self-esteem was cited least often (6 percent). For Blacks, heightened distrust was cited most frequently (40 percent), and lower self-esteem the least (10 percent). In comparison, Mexican American victims reported increased fear and heightened distrust with equal frequency (33 percent), while their least frequently cited response was feeling stronger or more in control (13 percent). Interestingly, despite the open-ended form of this question, responses were easily grouped. For example, responses reflecting increased fear included those where victims stated they were "afraid to go out much anymore," or afraid they might meet or see their assailant. Heightened distrust or a general lack of trust is evident in the following responses from three victims:

(1) "I don't trust people as easily as I did before. I'm not as friendly to just anybody." (2) "You have to watch people; you can't trust anybody." (3) "I act different toward men...no trust. I'm not as ready to start new relationships."

Victims whose responses were categorized as feeling stronger or more in control demonstrated considerable thought as seen in the following: "Yes—it has caused me to take a firmer grip on things, but not to worry disproportionately...Now I believe there's a reason for everything and you have to, and can learn to, accept things as they come in life—you can come away from a crisis a better person." Toward the other end of the spectrum, however, were responses indicating that some victims suffered a loss of self-esteem as a result of this experience. One victim said, "I feel dirty now—I don't like men." Another described her feelings in more detail: "Yes, I keep lowering myself. I don't feel I'm worth anyone's time so I don't have people around like I used to...I feel unclean, unworthy." Six victims described changes that reflected a decreased sense of worth or self-esteem; in line with the pattern emerging from other impact findings, half of these respondents were Mexican American, two were Anglo, and one was Black.

"The Worst Thing..."

If, as has been argued here, the rape experience is the culmination of numerous effects rather than a singular incident of violent sex, then what do victims themselves identify as "the worst thing about this experience"? Other studies suggested that the sex act(s) would *not* be cited as the worst thing, and this was borne out by these findings. Responses to this question fell into five categories: (1) intense fear (26 percent); (2) feelings of helplessness or powerlessness (25 percent); (3) the sex act(s) (20 percent); (4) negative personal effects or consequences (16 percent); and (5) judgmental attitudes of others (13 percent).

Clearly, there can be little doubt as to the pervasiveness of fear as a response to and as an after-effect of the rape experience. Victims who described fear tended to fall into two groups: those who related their fear to the rape itself, and those who indicated that they still felt afraid in general, that their lives were still disrupted because of fear. An example of fear specific to the rape incident was, "I was scared—I thought I was going to be killed." In contrast is the following response which reflects a persistent and disruptive sense of fear: "The fear that I had afterwards—the generalized feeling of fear that has not gone away completely. Also, being afraid to be alone, which I'd always enjoyed before. The idea that in a 20 minute period of time, my life could be affected the way it has been." Feelings of helplessness or powerlessness were described almost as often as fear. One victim stated, "The feeling of being helpless. I've never felt that way—ever." Another explained, "It's really a feeling of being victimized, feeling helpless. There's no retribution for the victim, even if they catch the guy."

About one of five victims indicated that the sex act(s) was the worst thing about this experience. Some simply said, "the rape itself" or "being raped," while others were more explicit in describing the pain of forced sex and/or their feelings of disgust and revulsion in relation to a particular sex act. The category of negative personal effects or consequences included responses like the following: "The effect it had on my marriage, not being able to cope with my husband's reaction"; "How it's affected my attitude, my ability to cope, my decision-making ability"; "I'm not able to communicate with people like I used to—I don't trust anyone; I especially don't trust or like men and I worry about how this is affecting my feelings toward my son."

The last category in response to this question includes situations where victims encountered negative and/or judgmental attitudes from others. One victim said, "People were judging me, even after I told them the truth." Another responded, "I guess that I went to the hospital and went to the police and all that, and he never got caught. They never did anything about it." With respect to racial-ethnic group variations, no two groups described the same thing as the worst part of this experience. For Anglos the worst thing was the feeling of helplessness (34 percent) followed by intense fear (22 percent), whereas Black victims reported the sex act(s) and judgmental attitudes with equal frequency (27 percent), and Mexican Americans most often described intense fear (39 percent). Once again, these findings raise the question of whether it is a valid premise to treat all rape victims alike. While it is clear that variations exist with regard to the circumstances of assaults in general, it is also important to keep in mind that women from different racial-ethnic groups are likely to perceive and experience rape in different ways as well.

Victims' Needs, Support Systems, and Services

Related to the impact of rape is the question of victims' needs. What do victims perceive as their immediate needs following the rape, and to what extent do they feel these needs were actually met? With respect to potential sources of support, how do victims see their families and/or friends? What about victims' perceptions of institutional support systems such as police officers, medical staff, and rape crisis counselors? Given the view of rape as comprised of both intrinsic and extrinsic meaning, it seems clear that the act itself is but one aspect of the larger experience with which victims must cope. The way in which significant others and representatives of service-delivery systems relate to and treat rape victims comprises no small part of the total rape experience. The following findings address these issues in an attempt to identify some of the factors that may either mitigate or retard the victim's efforts to cope successfully with her rape experience.

Victims' Needs — Met and Unmet

Toward the end of the interview, we asked victims to describe what they most needed or wanted immediately after the assault. Responses evolved into five categories: (1) twenty-six victims (44 percent) indicated they needed or wanted a generalized "someone" to provide support and understanding, or simply someone to talk to; (2) thirteen (22 percent) specified certain persons—for example, a family member, friend, or husband—they wanted to be with them; (3) eleven victims (19 percent) said they wanted various forms of physical comforts, such as a bath, sleep, or a cigarette; (4) five others (8 percent) indicated a need for medical attention, police intervention and/or protection; and (5) four victims (7 percent) said they wanted to be alone, to cry, or to "run away from it all." Two others (excluded from these percentages) could not recall what they needed or wanted. The most definitive pattern is the apparent need or desire for "someone" to be there with the victim to provide support, understanding, and emotional comfort. If the first two categories are combined, clearly two-thirds of the responses would be directed toward needing or wanting someone supportive and understanding.

The same pattern of needs holds true when responses are examined by victims' race-ethnicity as well. The most frequent response among Anglo and Black victims was for a generalized "someone" to be there (47 and 70 percent, respectively), and among Mexican American victims, the most frequent response (35 percent) was for a specific person to be there. However, the actual degree to which victims felt these needs were met varied considerably: thirty victims (51 percent) indicated that their needs were met as much as was possible at the time; thirteen (22 percent) said their needs were partially met or were met only after some delay; and sixteen (27 percent) indicated that their needs were not met at all. Looking at variations among the racial-ethnic groups, it seems that Anglos and Blacks fared considerably better than Mexican Americans in terms of feeling that their needs had been met. Nearly 63 percent of the Anglo and 50 percent of the Black victims reported their needs were met as much as possible. In comparison, some 70 percent of the Mexican American victims indicated that their needs were met only partially or not at all. However, it is possible that Mexican American victims built in a higher probability of nonfulfillment of their needs because (unlike Anglo and Black victims) they wanted a specific person to be there.

Support Systems—Personal and Institutional

The importance of a concerned, supportive, and understanding response to rape victims has been noted before, and the findings related to victims' needs seem to reinforce this. In an attempt to identify which persons were perceived to be the most helpful, a forced-choice format was developed wherein victims were asked to indicate whether given persons were *very helpful, somewhat helpful,* or *not at all helpful* to them. Victims' assessments of persons from two groups were obtained: those referred to as significant others and those who represent various institutions which victims encountered subsequent to the assault. More specifically, significant others included parents, other family members, husbands, boyfriends, and close friends; institutional representatives included clergy, professional counselors (for example, psychiatrists, psychologists, and social workers), medical staff, police, and rape crisis workers. Table 5 shows the median ratings for both groups as well as the number of victims who provided an assessment of each.

The median ratings for significant others ranged from a high of 2.7 for boyfriend or fiancé to a low of 1.9 for father. With respect to institutional representatives, rape crisis workers had the highest rating (2.9), while clergy (minister, priest, or rabbi) had the lowest rating (2.0). In a general sense, it is of some concern that both father and mother were perceived as less helpful in comparison with the remaining significant others. Among the institutional representatives, rape crisis workers were clearly perceived as the most helpful. The comparatively low ratings for professional counselors and clergy may suggest a need for them to reexamine their approach to working with victims of rape.

An Evaluation of Services

An attempt was made to move beyond the personalized question of helpfulness into the area of service evaluation. A forced-choice format was developed where victims were asked to rate specific services as *excellent, good, fair,* or *poor.* Only those working under the auspices of an institutional service-delivery system were evaluated (that is, rape crisis program, medical, law enforcement, and legal-judicial). Median ratings are shown in Table 6 as well as the number of victims who provided an evaluation of each service within each system.

As shown in Table 6, median ratings for the services provided by the rape crisis programs were quite positive, although as a whole—with the exception of the district attorney—all the ratings indicate fairly positive evaluations. While some of these findings must be treated cautiously because so few victims were able to provide a rating, the general indication is that the rape crisis programs are doing a comparatively good job, while the services of prosecutors leave something to be desired. There is, of course, no question that the evaluation of the rape crisis programs might be inflated because of the connection between the researchers and the programs themselves. However, in only a very few cases was the research interviewer the same person who had been the service deliverer for the rape crisis program.

TABLE 5. Median Ratings of Helpfulness of Personal and
Institutional Support Systems

SOURCE OF SUPPORT	MEDIAN RATING	NUMBER[a]
Personal		
Boyfriend-Fiancé	2.7	29
Husband	2.5	12
Other family[b]	2.5	39
Close Friends	2.4	53
Mother	2.2	37
Father	1.9	22
Institutional		
Rape Crisis Worker	2.9	48
Medical Staff	2.3	54
Police	2.2	54
Professional Counselor	2.1	20
Clergy	2.0	9

Note: Responses were coded so that 3 = Very Helpful, 2 = Somewhat Helpful, 1 = Not at all Helpful; the higher the rating, the more helpful the person.

[a]Each number indicates how many respondents provided a rating in each category. If a victim had no contact with a particular person or institution or if the rape had not been discussed, the item was coded not applicable.

[b]This item was open-ended, allowing victims to specify which family member; other responses included brothers, sisters, aunts, grandparents, sons, and daughters.

Overall, these ratings suggest that there is room for improvement among all four service-delivery systems. In particular, the comparatively low ratings for the law enforcement and legal systems are cause for concern, especially in relation to the district attorney's office. In general, these findings suggest that there may be some basis in reality for the perception that victims sometimes receive less than adequate services from police and prosecutors, and this may account for the fact that some victims fail to pursue prosecution actively. The importance of rape crisis programs is documented in two dramatic ways in this research. Since the most frequently verbalized need of victims was for a generalized "someone," obviously rape crisis center personnel can meet this need by simply being available. However, these findings also indicate that when rape crisis personnel are available, they are perceived as doing a good job.

TABLE 6. Median Ratings of Service-Delivery Systems

SERVICE-DELIVERY SYSTEM	MEDIAN RATING	NUMBER[a]
Rape Crisis Program		
In-person	3.8	48
By telephone	3.9	27
Medical		
Physician[b]	3.6	30
Medical Examiner[b]	3.1	39
Nursing Staff	3.0	50
Law Enforcement		
Reporting officer	3.0	52
Detective	2.9	52
Legal-Judicial		
District Attorney	1.5	10
Judge	3.8	4

Note: Responses were coded so that 4=Excellent, 3=Good, 2=Fair, 1=Poor; high ratings indicate a positive evaluation related to the quality of the service.

[a]Each number indicates how many respondents provided an evaluation of a given service. Obviously, there is considerable variation in terms of the number of victims who evaluated specific services; some of this variation is explained by the fact that not all victims could recall exactly who they had seen or in what capacity each person was acting.

[b]In Bexar County, a rape victim who wishes to file charges must be seen by the medical examiner who is responsible for the collection of medical evidence. The category of "physician" may include a doctor called in for consultation, a specialist called in to treat specific injuries, or (in Austin) the initial examining physician.

When victims were asked if there was anyone from the four service-delivery systems who they felt had treated them badly or disrespectfully, twenty-three (38 percent) said yes. Specifically, more than half the Blacks (54 percent), nearly 39 percent of the Mexican Americans, and approximately 31 percent of the Anglos felt they had been treated badly or disrespectfully by someone. Among those who felt this way, thirteen (56 percent) identified the reporting police officer and/or the detective as having been involved, another five (22 percent) described situations involving medical personnel, and three victims (13 percent) specified the district attorney. Of the other two victims, one identified a detective and a nurse jointly, and one identified the defendant's attorney. The exact nature of what had happened centered around one of the following areas: 39 percent said their needs were ignored, 35 percent felt they were confronted with judgmental attitudes, and 26 percent felt that services were inadequate. When we look at the responses according to victims' race-ethnicity, the findings suggest that Anglos were critical of the services they received, whereas minorities were critical either because they felt their needs were ignored or their reports of rape were met with skepticism. Half of the Anglos cited inadequate services, nearly three-fourths of the Mexican Americans cited having needs ignored, and among Blacks, judgmental attitudes were described most often (83 percent).

A few quotes from among the responses will serve to illustrate these concerns or criticisms more effectively. For example, an Anglo victim in her twenties described the following situation categorized as inadequate services: "The nurse—she was abrupt and tacky. She started to give me a penicillin shot before asking if I'm allergic, and I am." Another response in this category came from an Anglo victim who felt that the medical staff had not done its job adequately: "They expected me to check [myself] over for bruises...the doctor did not seem to do his job, the nurse didn't respect me." Other Anglo victims felt that the detectives made little effort to apprehend the suspect; one said, "They listened to me, but they never did anything. They never called, never tried to get the guy." In a similar vein, but more indicative of having needs ignored, were the following responses from two Mexican American victims. One woman in her early twenties said that because the police did not believe her, they refused to take her to the hospital for medical attention, despite the fact that she needed to see a doctor. Another victim, in her thirties, described the detectives as "very impatient...They asked a lot of questions when they knew I was in no shape to answer them."

In comparison, proportionately more Black victims encountered situations in which they felt that the reporting officer(s) and/or detective(s) were being judgmental. An older Black woman raped more than two years before the interview said that the police officer "seemed to have the attitude that it was my own fault even though I was asleep in my own home and he [the assailant] broke in the back door." In another instance, a Black woman in her late twenties talked with two detectives; she described one as "fine," but said the other kept referring to her as "gal" which she compared to calling a Black man "boy." She felt that this detective never took the rape seriously, and "he acted as if this was the kind of thing I should be used to." An even more blatant example of judgmental attitudes was described by a Black victim in her twenties who heard the patrol officer say to his partner: "This girl claims she was raped. I don't know how true that is."

The fact that nearly two out of every five victims in this study reported an encounter similar to those just described gives cause to wonder about how this experience might affect victims' willingness to actively pursue prosecution. Although this question was not explored here, we did ask the following: "If you filed charges against the man who attacked you, what happened to the case?" Eight of the sixty-one victims (13 percent) said they did not report the assault, and, therefore, charges were never filed. Of the fifty-three victims who reported the offense, forty-four (83 percent) pursued prosecution and made a statement to detectives. The nine who did not continue with efforts to prosecute cited one or more of the following reasons: they knew they could not identify the assailant; they did not want to go through a trial with its consequent publicity; they did not think it would do any good. Of the forty-four who gave their statements to detectives, twenty-eight did not know the status of their case at the time of the interview, on the average, nine months after the assault.

Among the sixteen victims who made the initial report, gave a statement to detectives, and could indicate the current case status, five had seen their cases rejected or dismissed by the district attorney's office. The remaining eleven said their cases had been accepted: seven were pending indictment or trial, and four had been adjudicated. In these last cases, final disposition included one felony conviction and subsequent imprisonment of the assailant; one misdemeanor conviction and subsequent fine (the result of plea bargaining in which the rape charge was reduced to simple assault in exchange for the guilty plea); one minor released to his parents as ordered by the juvenile court; and one man committed to the state mental hospital in lieu of prosecution.

These figures, coupled with the earlier findings related to inadequate services and judgmental attitudes, do not evoke optimism with respect to the law enforcement and legal-judicial systems. Victims repeatedly described a similar process of reporting the offense, filing charges, and then hearing nothing further. From a young Black woman raped more than two years before the interview: "I filed charges, but nothing ever happened." From an Anglo in her her twenties, raped some three months before the interview: "I filed charges, but nothing has happened. The police know his identity and where he is, but they haven't apprehended him for some reason." From a young Mexican American assaulted approximately eight months before the interview: "I reported, gave a statement, but never heard anything about it from the police or the D.A."

A similar kind of "information gap" was also apparent among some victims whose cases had been accepted by the district attorney's office. In fact, three victims said they had already been to court; yet, they were still unclear as to the status of their respective cases. Two of these victims had each been called to court three times, but neither could say what was being done in terms of prosecution. The district attorney's office seemed to feel little obligation to inform the chief witness (the victim) of the status of the case, especially if she was a minority. Such a lack of accountability is nowhere more evident than in the case of one victim who said that on three separate occasions she took time off from work, rode the bus to the courthouse, and sat in the courtroom until everyone left, at which time she also left. Because she neither spoke nor understood English, she did not know that her case had been postponed each time.[3] There were, however, other (perhaps more sophisticated and/or assertive) women who knew as much as could be known about their cases. For example, one victim assaulted three months before the interview knew that an arrest had been made, that the defendant was in jail unable to post $10,000 bond, and that no trial date had been set. Two others (each assaulted about two months before) indicated that they were awaiting a decision from the grand jury regarding an indictment. As a general conclusion with respect to these findings, it is probably quite sufficient to say that a rather definitive "information gap" exists between victims and those whose role it is to enforce and carry out the law.

Profile of the Rape Experience: A Composite

The limitations of rape victim research are well known, particularly those associated with sample size and representativeness. Hence, the profile of the rape experience developed here should be viewed cautiously. While this study represents the first in-depth look at the rape experience with a focus on racial-ethnic group variations, more research will be needed before we can say, with a high degree of certainty, whether these findings generalize to other rape victims. The following profile is descriptive of the composite or "typical" rape experience as drawn from the sixty-one victims who participated in this research.[4]

The typical victim is single and in her mid-twenties. She is a high school graduate and is just as likely to be employed as not; if she is working outside the home, it is probably in a clerical or sales position. Her income averages nearly $5,500 a year, although her family income is somewhat higher. This woman is most likely to have been raped by one man, who is the same race-ethnicity as she, and who is in his early to mid-twenties. The assailant is someone she does not know; most likely, he has broken into her home or has otherwise accosted her without warning. The victim is raped in her own home or somewhere on the street, in an alley, a park, a vacant house, or a building. There is a fifty-fifty chance that the assailant has a weapon, and, if he does, it is probably a knife. It is almost certain that the victim is threatened by her assailant, often having been told that she is going to be killed. Finally, the victim is likely to suffer at least minor injury as a result of the assault.

Following the assault, the victim is likely to call the police, a female friend, or simply the nearest person for assistance. Immediately after the rape, the victim wants an understanding and supportive person to be there with her. Shortly after the rape and for many months thereafter, the victim experiences a combination of angry and punitive feelings toward her assailant, often taking the form of hatred and/or a verbalized desire to kill him. Her feelings toward men are likely to have changed in a negative direction. In relation to her feelings and general state of mind for a month or two after the assault, the victim seems to feel either apprehensive and afraid, or confused and unable to maintain a sense of control over things. Chances are about one in four that the victim changes her residence as a result of the assault, and there is about a one-in-five chance that she obtains a new, unlisted phone number as a result of her experience. Among those victims who discuss the rape with significant others, parents are perceived as less helpful than boyfriends or fiancés.

Based on her own assessment that she feels stronger, more in control, the victim is slightly more inclined to say that she is doing better now than before the assault. However, the probability of this response is slightly higher if the victim is Black; if the victim is Mexican American, there is a higher probability that she says she is not doing as well now as before the assault. It is nearly certain that the victim has noted some changes in the way she thinks, acts, or feels, and these changes are likely to be an increased sense of fear or a heightened feeling of distrust toward people in general and men in particular. The worst thing about the entire experience may be intense fear, a feeling of helplessness, the sex act itself, or judgmental attitudes from others following the rape. The exact nature of this response is apparently related to the victim's race-ethnicity.

While it is not known to what extent this profile is generalizable, it does provide a systematic, qualitative sense of the rape experience as discussed by these sixty-one women. Given the kind of rape experience encountered by most of them, the fact of their survival is a credit to them; that some have been able to find something positive and growth-producing in the experience is a testament to their strength and coping skills. Findings reported thus far suggest an impact continuum ranging from almost negligible to severely debilitating. Rather than belabor the point, however, quotes from three victims are used as illustrations and as closing reflections on this chapter. At the end of the interview, victims were asked if there was anything they wanted to add. In response, one victim said, "I don't think it messed me up all that much; I filed charges is all." Another offered the following comment: "I think the most important point in rape is your attitude toward it. People should be better informed, then maybe they'd feel less guilty, less ashamed. It really shouldn't ruin a person's life." And finally, among the most poignant responses:

I've had lots of traumatic experiences. The way I was brought up was to "give 'em hell" in relation to problems. This was the biggest challenge—can I whip this one too? And if it happens again, I don't think I could live through it. This has been the hardest thing I have ever had to cope with—I just don't think I could do it again.

Notes

1. These data are based on rape complaints made to police in Seattle, Detroit, Kansas City, New Orleans, and Phoenix during 1974–1975.

2. For the year 1979, the murder rate in the Southern region was 13 per 100,000 inhabitants compared with 10, 8, and 8 for the West, North Central, and Northeast, respectively. With regard to aggravated assault, the South was second to the West with a rate of 306 versus 356 per 100,000; the same pattern held for forcible rape where the rate for the South was 71, exceeded only by the West with 96 per 100,000 population. See U.S. Department of Justice, *FBI Uniform Crime Reports: Crime in the United States, 1979* (Washington, D.C.: U.S. Government Printing Office, 1980), pp. 7, 14, 20.

3. This is just one example of a situation where followup services were initiated by the researchers. A Spanish-speaking volunteer from AAVAP was contacted so that each time this victim was subsequently called to court, she had someone to accompany her and to translate.

4. Some findings included in the profile were omitted from the earlier presentation of data.

RAPE: THE PROLONGED CRISIS

5

The qualitative findings of the preceding chapter depict rape victimization as a complex montage of people, events, and responses, the essence of which we have hopefully captured through the victims' own perceptions and reflections. While this approach yields data rich in detail and provides insight into the intrinsic meaning of rape, we sought to move beyond the descriptive level into a more objective, systematic analysis. Our approach in this chapter might aptly be described as empirical exploration in that a concerted effort has been made to measure the impact of the rape experience and test the rape-as-crisis assumption.

Measuring the Impact of Rape

As discussed in Chapter 3, a dual conceptual framework derived from crisis theory and the theory of racial-sexual stratification guided this quantitative analysis. Each of the seven independent variables (see Appendix A.1 for operational definitions) was statistically analyzed with each of the four impact measures in an attempt to uncover significant relationships. Our statistical procedures included one-way analysis of variance (with group contrasts as appropriate) and bivariate regression analysis.[1] As a result of the quantitative analyses, tentative answers to the following questions are discussed: (1) Are there identifiable variations in victim responses to rape, and, if so, what specific variables account for these variations? (2) How does the conceptualization of rape-as-crisis fare under empirical examination?

Crisis Response

The *a priori* assumption that rape precipitates a crisis is consistently interwoven throughout the victim literature, but, as yet, no empirical data have been offered to support it. Not only is this problematic in the sense of our need to know about or to understand victim responses to rape, but it also raises questions about the widespread use of the crisis intervention model with rape victims. While this may ultimately prove to be the most viable and effective model for helping victims, at this time, its use seems to be based on a combination of good intentions and folk wisdom. In all fairness, however, the complexity of crisis theory itself has, no doubt, retarded efforts to systematically examine the rape-as-crisis conceptualization. In this study, for example, we were confronted with an inherent constraint in measuring the impact of rape in terms of crisis responses; that is, an absolute determination as to the presence or absence of crisis cannot be made. Crisis responses are both fluid and relative. Therefore, although they are measurable, the resulting conclusion can only suggest that a comparatively greater or lesser degree of crisis exists at a given point in time. In addition, it would be an error in logic to suggest a simplistic, cause-and-effect relationship between rape and crisis response. Obviously, the rape experience cannot be isolated as the single, causal factor since the survey methodology does not allow for control of all extraneous variables. Having acknowledged this, the design of the quantitative analysis nonetheless enables us to measure relative degrees of impact (that is, variations in victim responses) as well as to examine the "fit" between the rape experience and crisis theory.

As noted in Chapter 3, crisis responses were measured as victims' scores on the Crisis Scale. The possible range of scores is from zero to 240; presumably, the higher the numerical score, the greater the degree of crisis. For the victim sample as a whole, the actual range of scores was from 40 to 153, with a mean of 114.3 and a standard deviation of 22.5. A one-way analysis of variance was run on Crisis Scores by age-at-assault, time-since-assault, victim race-ethnicity, inter- versus intragroup rape, and stereotypic versus nonstereotypic rape. The personal and institutional support system variables (treated as interval level data) were each entered into a bivariate regression with Crisis Scores. Results indicate that only victim race-ethnicity is significantly associated with crisis ($F=5.87$; $df=2,58$; $p \leq .01$). Since the association was significant, group contrasts were analyzed to examine the variations more carefully. Table 7 summarizes the means, standard deviations, and significance of t-values obtained on Crisis Scores by victim race-ethnicity.

As shown in the table, the mean score for Anglos fell in the middle of the three groups and is very close to the grand mean for all respondents. In comparison, Black victims had the lowest mean score, while Mexican Americans had the highest. In addition, two of the group contrasts are statistically significant—those between Anglo-Black and Black-Mexican American victims. Keeping in mind the word of caution about absolute conclusions, we do not know, based on these data, to what extent a given group was or was not "in crisis." What we do know, however, is that the data suggest that Mexican American and Anglo victims, as separate groups,

TABLE 7.   Means, Standard Deviations, and Group Contrasts on
Crisis Scores by Victim Race-Ethnicity

VARIABLE	ANGLO		BLACK		MEXICAN AMERICAN	
	MEAN	*SD*	*MEAN*	*SD*	*MEAN*	*SD*
Crisis Score[a]	113.41	21.21	98.45	18.91	125.72	21.46

GROUP CONTRASTS: SIGNIFICANCE OF *t*-VALUES[b]	
Anglo with Black	.05
Anglo with Mexican American	ns
Black with Mexican American	.01

Note: ns = not significant.
[a]Theoretically, cumulative Crisis Scores could range from 0 to 240; the higher the score, the greater the degree of crisis.
[b]Significance is based on the two-tailed probability of *t*.

were each experiencing a significantly higher degree of crisis than were Black victims. Relative to one another as groups, Mexican Americans evidenced the greatest degree of crisis, Blacks the least, with Anglos in between.

Feelings About Men

In the preceding chapter, findings were presented descriptive of victims' feelings toward men in five interpersonal dimensions (see Table 4). For the quantitative analysis, an impact measure was developed giving each victim a FAM (Feelings About Men) Score. Since the literature suggests that male-female interaction is often problematic for rape victims, we considered the FAM measure one of strategic theoretical and pragmatic importance. We were particularly concerned with exploring this dimension of impact because it is clear that victims must continue to interact with men on some level, despite the fact that the rape experience may produce some generalized negative feelings. The possible range of scores of the FAM measure is from 5 to 15; low scores indicate that victims' feelings about men (across the five interpersonal dimensions) are not as good now as they were before the assault, while high scores indicate that their feelings are better now than before. The actual range for this sample was from 5 to 12, and it is of interest that Anglo victims were the only group to have scores as high as 12;

the maximum score among both Blacks and Mexican Americans was 9. The grand mean for all respondents was 7.1, with a standard deviation of 1.9. Results of the statistical analyses indicate that only one variable is significantly associated with this impact measure, and again this variable is victim race-ethnicity (F=5.27; $df=2,58$; $p \le .01$).

Data from subsequent group contrasts on FAM Scores by victim race-ethnicity are summarized in Table 8, and, as shown, the mean score for Black victims fell between the other groups and was identical to the grand mean. In comparison, Anglos had the highest and Mexican Americans had the lowest mean FAM Scores; the group contrasts indicate that their scores differed significantly. While these statistics suggest that Anglo victims had significantly higher mean scores than Mexican American victims, they should not be interpreted as an indication that Anglos feel "good" or especially positive about men as measured here. In fact, none of the racial-ethnic groups had a mean score that could substantively be interpreted as suggesting that their feelings about men were better (or even the same) at the time of the interview compared with before the rape. Thus, while the statistical analysis enables us to identify which groups differ significantly from one another (Mexican Americans and Anglos), it is equally important to recognize that all three groups experienced negative changes in their feelings about men—Mexican Americans the most, Anglos the least, with Blacks in between.

General Functioning

Since disruption of one's "normal" or usual pattern of functioning is viewed as an integral component of a crisis response, a General Functioning measure was developed as another way to examine the rape-as-crisis conceptualization as well as to assess, in a generalized way, the impact of rape. Although questions were asked in relation to several areas of functioning (for example, parental, student, and employee role functioning), only the items that were applicable to nearly all respondents were used in developing the General Functioning measure. These items included routine activities such as household cleaning, cooking, shopping or running errands, and visiting with neighbors or friends. The range of possible scores is from -4 to $+4$; low scores indicate a change toward a passive style of functioning, characterized by decreased interest or concern with taking care of routine activities, while high scores indicate a change toward a more active pattern of functioning. The actual range for this sample was from -4 to $+2$, although only Anglos had scores as high as $+2$; the highest score among Blacks was $+1$, and for Mexican Americans, the highest score was 0. The grand mean was -1.3, with a standard deviation of 1.6. Once again, the statistical analyses indicated that the only variable found to be significantly associated with the impact measure was victim race-ethnicity (F=3.32; $df=2,53$; $p \le .05$.[2]

TABLE 8. Means, Standard Deviations, and Group Contrasts on Feelings About Men Scores by Victim Race-Ethnicity

VARIABLE	ANGLO		BLACK		MEXICAN AMERICAN	
	MEAN	*SD*	*MEAN*	*SD*	*MEAN*	*SD*
FAM Score[a]	7.69	2.13	7.10	1.64	5.94	1.21

GROUP CONTRASTS: SIGNIFICANCE OF *t*-VALUES[b]	
Anglo with Black	ns
Anglo with Mexican American	.001
Black with Mexican American	ns

Note: ns = not significant.
[a]Feelings about men scores could ranges from 5 to 15; the higher the score, the more positive the feelings.
[b]Significance is based on the two-tailed probability of *t*.

Group contrasts involving additional statistical tests indicate that Anglo and Mexican American victims differed significantly, as did Black and Mexican American victims. Table 9 summarizes the means, standard deviations, and significance of *t*-values for all three groups. As shown in the table, the mean score for Anglos was the closest to the grand mean; the mean for Blacks was somewhat higher; and the group mean for Mexican Americans was substantially lower. Negative mean scores for all three groups suggest that their overall functioning tended to change toward becoming more passive or withdrawn, that the respondents were less concerned with routine activities than they had been prior to the rape. Mexican American victims, with a group mean of −2.06, evidenced the strongest movement in this direction. Although Blacks also tended to move toward a more passive style of functioning, their group mean of −0.60 indicates that they were less inclined in this direction than either Mexican American or Anglo victims.

Without placing either a positive or negative value on one's style of functioning, these data do seem to suggest that victims' "normal" or usual functioning was altered or disrupted following the assault. This is clearly reflected in the victims' own descriptions of how their routine activities were affected.[3] For example, with respect to household cleaning, it was very common to have victims explain that they "just didn't care how things looked," "just didn't want to do anything," or simply said, "the hell with it." In general, a theme of lethargy, apathy, and/or desire to withdraw from

TABLE 9.   Means, Standard Deviations, and Group Contrasts on General
Functioning Scores by Victim Race-Ethnicity

VARIABLE	ANGLO		BLACK		MEXICAN AMERICAN	
	MEAN	SD	MEAN	SD	MEAN	SD
Functioning Score[a]	-1.10	1.68	-.60	1.58	-2.06	1.25

GROUP CONTRASTS: SIGNIFICANCE OF *t*-VALUES[b]	
Anglo with Black	ns
Anglo with Mexican American	.05
Black with Mexican American	.05

Note: ns = not significant

[a]General functioning scores could range from −4 to +4; negative scores indicate passive functioning or withdrawal from usual routine, while positive scores indicate increased activity. A score of zero indicates no change.

[b]Significance is based on the two-tailed probability of *t*.

everything and everyone seemed to characterize victims' responses to taking care of routine activities. The only exception was in relation to the activity of going out shopping or running errands. On this item, the direction of change was still toward a more passive style characterized by withdrawal, but the reasons given by victims were clearly different. While some described themselves as disinterested, others explained that they were afraid to go out, or they felt too tense or anxious at the thought of seeing—or being seen by—the rapist. Regardless of the reasons, however, changes in functioning were found to have occurred among all groups as evidenced by a tendency to withdraw from routine activities. Mexican American victims showed the strongest movement toward a more withdrawn style of functioning. Black victims showed the least movement in this direction, and Anglos were in between.

Health Concerns

One area that has yet to be discussed vis-à-vis the impact of rape is that of health concerns. Findings from some of the earlier studies have suggested that it is not unusual for rape victims to experience a variety of health problems subsequent to the assault. In an effort to explore this matter as another dimension of impact, a series of questions was included in the interview schedule in order to collect descriptive data on victims' health concerns.

Following the collection of data, a new variable was created as an impact measure for use in the statistical analysis. Essentially, the Health Concern Score is the actual number of problems or concerns experienced by victims following the assault. However, it should be made clear that the concerns included in this measure were, by victims' own assessments, related to the rape. These scores do not include every health concern or problem reported, only those perceived by victims as having been caused or precipitated by the rape. Since these data are not presented elsewhere, this discussion includes both statistical and qualitative-descriptive findings.

The possible range of scores on the Health Concerns measure is from 0 to 15; the actual range was from 0 to 10, with a mean of 4.5 and a standard deviation of 3.0. Unlike the results of the earlier statistical analyses, no significant associations were found between the independent variables and this impact measure. Nonetheless, the data related to victims' health concerns are revealing. For example, only six victims (10 percent) reported no health concerns related to the assault, while fifteen victims (25 percent) reported from seven to ten concerns each. As a result, when the victims reporting no concerns are excluded, the average number of concerns is five per victim; in fact, these fifty-five victims reported a total of 277 health concerns related to the rape. Although the relationship was not statistically significant, the same pattern of racial-ethnic group variations found in earlier analyses again emerged: Mexican American victims reported the highest average number of health concerns (5.2), Black victims the lowest (3.4), with Anglos in between (4.6). Table 10 provides a summary of findings where victims' concerns are ranked-ordered according to the frequency with which each was cited.

As shown in the table, more than half of the victims who experienced health concerns reported difficulty in relation to sleep disturbances and nightmares. Although in some cases these two problems overlapped, many times they did not. Some victims, for example, indicated that they had a great deal of difficulty going to sleep because noises frightened them or they generally felt too uneasy and fearful to close their eyes; a few said they had to leave a light on at night to ease their anxiety. Most victims reporting problems with nightmares said that they were specifically about the rape and that it was like "reliving the whole thing." Among the thirty-three victims (60 percent) who reported "panicky feelings," most said that any reminder of the circumstances of the assault or the assailant triggered that feeling. Specific examples included seeing a man who resembled the assailant, being alone (especially at night), and/or hearing noises (again, this was said to be especially problematic at night). The most frequently reported concern was tension (82 percent), and for most victims, this term subsumed a wide range of responses—for example, feeling "uptight" in general, and particularly around men, feeling afraid, apprehensive, or "paranoid."

TABLE 10. Rank-Ordered Frequencies of Victims' Health Concerns

HEALTH CONCERN	NUMBER	PERCENT
Tension	45	82
Panicky Feelings	33	60
Sleep Disturbances	32	58
Nightmares	32	58
Inability to Relax	23	42
Headaches	22	40
Alcohol Consumption	18	33
Poor Appetite	18	33
Fatigue	15	27
Suicidal Thoughts	15	27
Stomach Trouble	13	24
Dizziness	5	9
Other[a]	6	11

Note: Percentages are based on an N of 55, the number of victims who reported health concerns related to the assault.

[a]Victims could add as many as three concerns of their own. Six victims each added one concern: epileptic seizures exacerbated by the assault; manic behavior; chain-smoking; back problems; seizures from concussion; frigidity.

For the most part, the remaining concerns do not require elaboration, but because of their relative seriousness, changes in drinking habits and thoughts of suicide are discussed briefly. With respect to alcohol consumption, seven of the eighteen victims who said their drinking habits had changed as a result of the assault indicated they now drink less, whereas the other eleven said they drink more now. For those who reported drinking less, the change was described as related to specific circumstances of the assault. For example, victims who were raped after having left a club or party (where there had been drinking) tended to report they quit drinking altogether, or now they only have a drink at home, nowhere else. For most victims, however, the change was in a somewhat more predictable direction of more frequent or heavier drinking, mainly in an effort to keep from remembering or thinking about the assault. While a few said they needed a drink to relax or to sleep, several victims candidly admitted they were drinking in an effort to "forget" or to handle their feelings; for one or two victims, drinking had become a very serious concern.[4] Among the fifteen victims (27 percent) who reported thoughts of suicide, three volunteered the information that they had attempted to kill themselves at some time following the assault. Two of these women indicated that the rape was like the proverbial "straw that broke the camel's back" in that other, preexisting problems played a part, but the rape was just "one thing too many to handle." Although several victims said that the assault, "on top of" marital, financial, or medical problems, had prompted them to consider suicide, most were clear in stating that the rape became the most influential precipitating factor. The depth and intensity of their feelings are reflected all too clearly in their own words: "There wasn't anything left for me, the future didn't look too bright"; "I just wanted to give up"; "I felt guilty and dirty, like something out of the gutter...completely and totally ruined." We should add, however, that the victims who made these and similar statements were eager to let us know that they had managed to overcome these feelings, that while they might still feel "down" once in awhile, they were going to "make it."[5]

Summary—Discussion

The findings derived from the preceding quantitative analyses allow us to suggest tentative answers to the questions posed in the beginning of this chapter. With respect to the question of whether there are identifiable variations in victim responses to the impact of rape, one variable—victim race-ethnicity—was found to be significantly associated with three of the four impact measures. However, in stating this finding, we are simultaneously acknowledging that our empirical examination of the rape-as-crisis assumption produced some mixed results. Specifically, our conceptualization of crisis included three interrelated factors: (1) a hazardous event that poses some threat to the individual; (2) an inability to respond with adequate coping mechanisms; and (3) a resultant temporary upset in one's usual pattern of functioning. We accepted as given that the rape incident represents a hazardous event to the individual and that such an incident poses a threat, either in the sense of literally being threatened by the assailant (as 87 percent of these victims were) or in the sense of a perceived threat to one's sexual autonomy, personal identity, and/or one's very survival. However, it is the other elements of this conceptualization that evolve as somewhat contradictory vis-à-vis crisis theory.

The descriptive findings *suggest* that victims experienced difficulty in coping with the rape. More objective empirical evidence (such as the Crisis Scores, FAM Scores, and Functioning Scores) *documents* this idea by revealing the relative degree to which victims' lives were, in fact, disrupted. But the conceptual dilemma, or perhaps paradox, is that not one of the independent variables derived from crisis theory was found to be significantly associated with any measure of impact. In other words, we have the rape incident as a hazardous event which poses some threat; we have qualitative-descriptive data from victims which reflect their own perceived difficulties in coping; and we have objective, quantitative evidence to support these victim perceptions, all of which lend support for the rape-as-crisis conceptualization. Yet, the independent variables derived from crisis theory, those variables which—if found to be significantly associated with the impact measures—would solidify the evidence in support of the rape-as-crisis conceptualization, consistently failed to do so. Theoretically, victim age-at-assault (viewed as stages representing periods of developmental crisis) should have been associated with crisis response. Time-since-assault should have indicated that recent victims were experiencing a significantly greater degree of crisis than other, further removed time groups. The number of personal-institutional support systems should have had some significant effect on crisis response. Clearly, these variables were not associated with relative degrees of crisis response, nor were they significantly related to any measure of impact.

In effect, we found degrees of crisis response, degrees of change in feelings about men, and degrees of change in victims' usual style of functioning, all significantly related to the race-ethnicity of the victim. In contrast, we also found that the severity of the impact of rape is neither significantly greater nor lesser for adolescent compared with adult victims; for victims recently assaulted compared with those raped many months earlier; and for victims with many versus few (or no) personal and/or institutional support systems. In addition, specific assault variables such as inter- versus intra-group rape and stereotypic versus nonstereotypic rape were found to have no significant effect on the degree of impact experienced by these victims. In other words, to the extent that the impact of rape has been tapped by our measures, victims experienced comparatively more or less impact depending only on their race-ethnicity.

Rape-As-Crisis: A Reconceptualization

A Continuum of Impact

Realistically, the data suggesting that most of the victims in this study suffered adverse effects from (or related to) the rape experience are neither surprising nor startling. The end result of our systematic exploration into possible variations in victim responses is yet another matter, particularly in light of the fact that *only* victim race-ethnicity was identified as a significant variable with respect to the impact of rape. What ultimately emerged from our analysis is a definite pattern of variations in response to the rape experience, a pattern that appears to be consistent in both source and substance. This pattern can best be conceptualized as a continuum (see Figure 2) on which the mean scores (substance) are plotted for the racial-ethnic groups (source) on each impact measure. However, to dispel the notion that we are using *source* as synonymous with *cause*, we refer back to the theoretical framework. In this context, race-ethnicity is a *conduit* of experiences, roles, and statuses. While being Black or Mexican American is the source to which these data take us, a macro-level understanding of racial-sexual stratification takes us beyond—to fundamental cause.

Keeping in mind that higher scores on crisis and health concerns, and lower scores on feelings about men and general functioning, suggest adverse or negative impact, *all victims are shown as having been affected to some degree across all dimensions,* but especially in terms of changes in their feelings about men and general style of functioning. The impact continuum also clearly depicts the pattern of racial-ethnic variations in which Mexican American victims were found to be the most adversely affected in all four dimensions, Blacks the least (with one exception on feelings about men), with Anglo victims at some point in between. Specifically, as a group, Mexican American victims evidenced the greatest degree of crisis, the most negative changes in their feelings about men, the most withdrawn pattern of functioning, and the highest average number of health concerns. In contrast, the opposite pattern held for Black victims on three of the four measures (they evidenced the lowest degree of crisis, the least withdrawn style of functioning, and the fewest average health concerns). On the other hand, Anglos were between Black and Mexican American victims on all measures except for changes in feelings about men where they reversed their position with Blacks and were the least negatively affected.

FIGURE 2. The Impact of Continuum: Variations in Victim
Responses to Rape

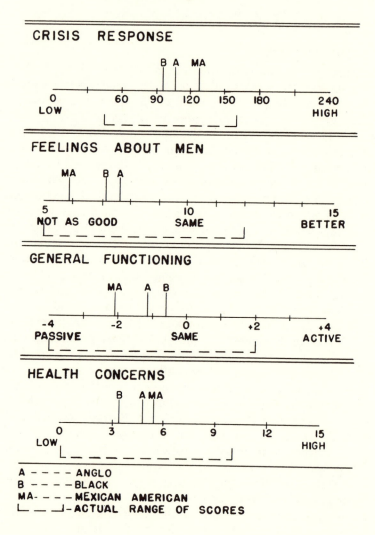

CRISIS RESPONSE

FEELINGS ABOUT MEN

GENERAL FUNCTIONING

HEALTH CONCERNS

A ─ ─ ─ ─ ANGLO
B ─ ─ ─ ─ BLACK
MA ─ ─ ─ ─ MEXICAN AMERICAN
L ─ ─ ⌐ ─ ACTUAL RANGE OF SCORES

Residual Crisis Effects

Although the rape-as-crisis conceptualization neither can nor should be rejected based solely on these findings, several pertinent questions should be raised with respect to crisis theory. For example, one of the basic tenets holds that crises are, by definition, time-limited, that while "the total length of time between the initial blow and the final resolution of the crisis may vary,...disequilibrium is time-limited, usually lasting up to four to six weeks" (Golan, 1978, p. 9). For this group of victims, assaulted from one to thirty-six months prior to the interview, the degree of affective and behavioral upset they experienced was not found to differ according to time. Instead, some degree of disequilibrium (that is, changes between pre- and post-rape) was found to exist among all groups. This may suggest that the experience of rape precipitates some degree of crisis, yet, rather than achieving a quick resolution (that is, a return to a pre-crisis level of functioning), rape victims may be left with a variety of disruptive residual effects. In essence, it appears that we have not only tapped some measure of active crisis, but we also seem to have documented some degree of longer term, residual impact, perhaps suggesting that rape is more accurately viewed as a *prolonged crisis*. However, since some crisis theorists have noted that resolution of active crisis may leave the person functioning at one of three levels (better, not as well, or about the same as before), it is impossible to determine exactly what we tapped: it may be a prolonged crisis response, or it may be a crisis resolution which has left victims functioning at a "lower" than pre-crisis level.

Given all the data presented here, qualitative and quantitative, victims' own perceptions as well as statistically analyzed scores, we are inclined to believe that rape is more appropriately conceptualized as a prolonged crisis. Although victims do manage to cope and function, the impact of the rape experience persists in the form of residual crisis effects. By and large, victims do not simply reestablish their pre-crisis state of equilibrium. Rather, they experience fundamental changes, affectively and behaviorally. In general, they seem to experience both fear and anxiety to the extent that they become more defensive and self-protective. As a result, their behavior is changed in substantial and specific ways: they restrict their mobility, their interaction with men is hampered by distrust and generalized discomfort; they are comparatively apathetic and withdrawn from a variety of routine activities; and they suffer from some assault-related health concerns. One victim may have unknowingly articulated the essence of residual impact for us when she said, very matter of factly: "I will never be the same because the worst thing about rape is that you learn how vulnerable you are." While there may be class-related and cultural differences, most females in America are taught at an early age that they can control (and they are responsible for) their own sexual experience. How frequently do we (still) teach little girls to "act like a lady" so they will be "treated like a lady"? Once this defensive and protective veneer is shattered, what remains? Are rape victims ever again the same? Do they, at some unknown point in time, lose or overcome the residual effects of the rape experience, or are victims irreparably changed? Only a carefully designed longitudinal study of impact can adequately address these questions, and given the inherent problems in any victim research, such an undertaking would be an extremely arduous task.

Micro- and Macro-Level Implications

These findings raise complex but fundamental questions: Are the residual effects of rape solely a product of the sexual assault, or is the victim's initial crisis actually prolonged or sustained as a result of how others perceive and react to the reality of rape? Is the crisis model the most viable for understanding the dynamics of rape victimization, and, consequently, is crisis intervention the most appropriate treatment strategy for meeting the needs of rape victims? Essentially, we are suggesting that, while the victim's initial response may well "fit" the theoretical concept of crisis, we cannot overlook the fact that she is a person-in-context. That is, she must not only contend with her own response to the rape, but she must also deal with the reactions of significant and generalized others, reactions that are incorporated into, and ultimately become a part of, her rape experience.

Our concern with the crisis model is not just academic. To the degree that service-delivery personnel are actually knowledgeable about and trained to use the crisis intervention model, certain class and culture-bound expectations may be established with regard to how rape victims *should act* and for *how long*. For example, in discussing the crisis intervention model in relation to rape victims, Golan has stated:

After several weeks of extensive work, most women tend to integrate the experience and place it appropriately in their past. Should the client be unable to master the trauma within a reasonable time, the worker may evaluate the need for continued therapeutic treatment in the light of the ego's inability to handle stress of this magnitude (1978, pp. 218–19).

In this case, Golan is simply following the practice principles suggested by the time-limited tenet of crisis theory. In fact, a basic six-session format for crisis intervention is widely accepted, even though data supporting the efficacy of this practice are very limited. Given our findings, the obvious question is, what happens to the victim who fails to integrate and resolve this experience in this predetermined time frame? Unfortunately, we know relatively little about the specific assumptions that are made and acted on under the rubric of *rape crisis* services. Our guess is that such services run the gamut from attempts to implement a relatively pure crisis intervention model to just doing what seems "right" at the time. What we do know is that rape crisis services (which evolved as one pragmatic response to the feminist anti-rape movement) are largely staffed by White, middle-class counselors and that they have been comparatively more successful in reaching White, middle-class victims than minority victims.[6]

The findings from our victim study suggest a reconceptualization of crisis that would include not only what appears to be a prolonged crisis response (residual crisis effects), but also racial-ethnic variations in the impact of rape. This means we must eliminate or at least modify several expectations: that rape precipitates some kind of unidimensional crisis for all victims; that the rape itself is the singular source of stress; that six to eight weeks is sufficient time for the crisis to be resolved; and that a pre-crisis state of equilibrium or level of functioning will be reestablished. We offer several reasons for suggesting this reconceptualization. If a tentative hierarchy of impact were developed based on our findings, Mexican American victims would be at the top having experienced the greatest degree of negative impact, followed by Anglo and then by Black victims. If rape crisis personnel and clinicians who work with victims do not temper their expectations of how victims "should" respond, how soon they should "get over it," then both Black and Mexican American victims are likely to encounter problems as they seek help in relation to resolving the effects of the rape experience. While Black victims may be met with skepticism because they do not appear to be sufficiently upset, Mexican American victims may risk being labeled as seriously disturbed because they "overreact" or fail to recover quickly enough. Both examples represent risks that are a part of the crisis model when that model is oversimplified and implemented on the basis of class and culture-bound expectations.

The second question we have raised deals with the macro-level sources of the rape problem. Is a crisis response to rape, in fact, kept alive or sustained by the social reality of racial-sexual stratification? In a system of minority-dominant relationships (sexual and racial-ethnic), rape risks and the impact of rape are compounded by sex, color, national origin, and class. Are women held responsible for rape simply because they are female and socialized to be responsible for sexual control (theirs and that of men)? Are women more or less vulnerable to the prolonged crisis depending on their social world or racial-ethnic community? While we cannot promise answers to all of these questions, we hope to find some explanations in the public attitude data.

Notes

1. Group contrasts (also known as specific comparison tests) were used when the F ratio from the analysis of variance was significant and the independent variable had

more than two levels. This additional procedure enabled us to identify which specific groups differed significantly from one another.

2. In this analysis of variance, degrees of freedom were smaller because data were missing for five respondents who said these functioning items were not applicable to them.

3. Unlike the Crisis and Feelings About Men measures, the original general functioning items allowed for further open-ended response after the initial rating had been obtained. This enables us to provide some elaboration through victim quotes.

4. It is very important to acknowledge that, despite the clearly defined task of the interviewers to collect data, specific problems being experienced by victims were not ignored for the sake of the research. In cases where victims expressed concern about their ability to handle or control their drinking, interviewers explicitly discussed counseling referrals with them. Whenever a situation arose where there seemed to be a need for further service, the interviewer (or a member of the research team) checked back with the victim to be sure she understood that additional help was available to her.

5. The same comments as noted previously apply with regard to victims experiencing severe depression and/or suicidal thoughts. In some cases, as we talked with victims about counseling referrals, we found that they were already seeing someone for therapy, in which case they were encouraged to continue. The important point is that the research team gave priority to the well-being of respondents; no victim who seemed to be in need of followup services (whether the need was for counseling in relation to the rape or for something else) was left without information regarding a variety of alternative resources; and someone from the research team made a point to check back with victims at a later time.

6. During the course of this research project, the authors received correspondence from rape crisis centers throughout the country, requesting *any* information we had on minority victims. The bulk of these inquiries acknowledged that (1) rape crisis services were being underutilized by minority victims; or (2) service-delivery personnel felt unprepared in relation to working with minority victims.

VICTIMS AND NONVICTIMS: ON RAPE, ITS CAUSE AND PREVENTION

6

Central to the design of this research was the objective of collecting data that would describe and systematically explore the rape victim's experience as well as describe and explain public attitudes about rape at the level of the racial-ethnic community. In the preceding two chapters, we have attempted to examine the intrinsic meaning of rape from the victim's perspective and to assess the impact of that experience. Before proceeding to the other aspect of rape—its extrinsic meaning, the meaning given it by ordinary people in the realm of everyday reality—we will examine one small piece of the research where the two faces of rape reality intersect, where we have an opportunity to compare victim and public perceptions of rape. Specifically, three questions were asked of both the victims and the three public samples. Responses are presented here as descriptive and definitive of the phenomenon of rape as perceived by victims and their communities. It is especially interesting to compare the opinions of the victims (who have experienced rape) with those of the public samples (the majority of whom have not experienced rape). The items on which common data were collected are as follows: (1) selection of a definition of rape; (2) opinion as to the primary cause of rape; and (3) opinion as to the *one* thing that would most effectively alleviate the problem of rape in our society.

Defining Rape

Respondents were given a card with four definitions of rape printed on it; they were asked to read the definitions and to select the one that came the closest to describing their own view of rape. Although no numbers or labels appeared on the card, the four definitions are labeled here for purposes of discussion as (1) feminist, (2) legal, (3) stereotypic, and (4) feminist revision. Briefly, these definitions differ in that 1 and 4 are seen as comparatively liberal or feminist because they require fewer criteria in the definition of rape (that is, defining rape simply as nonconsenting sex; see note 12, Chapter 3). Definition 4, which allows for prosecution of husbands, has been offered in some states as a revision of the existing law. Definition 1 is still more inclusive; not only does it remove the husband's protection against culpability, but it also includes sexual acts other than intercourse (defined in most states as penile penetration of the vagina). Definition 2 was the legal definition of rape in Texas at the time of the research and varies only slightly from that in effect in most states. Definition 3 is a stereotype of what is generally labeled as "street rape," or what we have referred to earlier as a stereotypic or a "good rape." It is associated with a view of the rapist as a stranger who accosts his victim unexpectedly, forcing her, by threat or violence, to have sex with him. Victim and public responses, as well as the specific definitions, are presented in Table 11.

The stereotypic definition of rape was selected by more victims than any other, though not by a majority (46 percent). However, for both Black and Mexican American victims, the stereotypic definition was the majority choice (55 and 72 percent, respectively). In comparison, Anglo victims failed to select any definition by a majority, and they selected the stereotypic definition in considerably smaller numbers than the feminist definition. In the public attitude samples, the stereotypic definition shows up as the most frequent choice of Mexican Americans (49 percent for females, 38 percent for males) and Black females (30 percent), but only Mexican Americans approached a majority selection of this definition. Black males selected the stereotypic definition less frequently than any other group, while for Anglos it was the second most common choice. Overall, the rape victims were more inclined to select the stereotypic definition of rape than were any of the groups in the public attitude survey. This is particularly interesting since the majority of the victims experienced a stereotypic rape themselves, and having been exposed to the criminal justice system seemingly did little to cause them to adopt a legal definition of rape as their own (87 percent had at least initially reported their assault to the police).

Further analysis indicates that thirty-six victims (50 percent Anglo, 50 percent minority) were involved in what has been referred to here as stereotypic rape; within this subgroup, eighteen victims (50 percent) selected the stereotypic definition. However, comparisons between specific subgroups reveal the following: (1) although 67 percent of the minorities who were themselves victims of stereotypic rape selected the stereotypic definition, 70 percent of the minorities who were *not* victims of stereotypic rape chose this definition; and (2) while 33 percent of the Anglos who were victims of stereotypic rape selected that definition, 30 percent who were *not* such victims chose the stereotypic definition. To examine this matter further, statistical tests of association were made. Results indicate that the only significant association is between race-ethnicity (majority-minority) and

TABLE 11. Definitions of Rape as Selected by Samples (A, B, MA) and Victims (V)

DEFINITIONS[a]		ANGLO			BLACK			MEXICAN AMERICAN			ALL			
		M	F	V	M	F	V	M	F	V	A	B	MA	V
Feminist. Rape is when a man forces a woman to have sexual intercourse and/or some other sexual act.	N	59	66	14	63	46	3	37	29	2	125	109	66	19
	%	35	40	44	40	27	27	22	18	11	38	34	20	31
Legal. Rape is sexual penetration of a woman by a man who is not her husband, without the woman's consent.	N	22	14	5	36	37	1	38	17	0	36	73	55	6
	%	13	9	16	23	22	9	23	10	—	11	22	17	10
Stereotypic. Rape is when an unknown man attacks a woman and forces her (by threat or violence) to have sexual intercourse and/or some other sexual act.	N	56	43	9	35	50	6	64	79	13	99	85	143	28
	%	34	26	28	22	30	55	38	49	72	30	26	44	46
Feminist Revision. Rape is sexual penetration of a woman by a man, without the woman's consent.	N	30	41	4	24	36	1	28	37	3	71	60	65	8
	%	18	25	13	15	21	9	17	23	17	22	18	20	13
Percent[b]		100	100	101	100	100	100	100	100	100	101	100	101	100
Totals: Number of valid cases		167	164	32	158	169	11	167	162	18	331	327	329	61
Missing data		2	2	0	9	0	0	0	11	0	4	9	11	0

[a]Labels did not appear on the card given to respondents.
[b]Percentages do not always add to 100 because of rounding errors.

definition (stereotypic-other); proportionately more minority victims selected the stereotypic definition than did Anglo victims.[1] Therefore, it seems clear that the majority-minority group differences uncovered here cannot be attributed to whether victims were themselves involved in stereotypic assaults.

Ironically, both the Anglo and Mexican American samples as well as the victims selected the legal definition of rape less frequently than any other definition. Among the Black sample, just slightly fewer selected the feminist revision definition. In general, one of the feminist definitions (1 or 4) was the most frequent choice of all respondents except victims. The victim responses do not approximate (proportionally) the attitudes represented by their respective communities or the female segment of those communities; they are, by and large, more conservative in their definitions of rape. There is no way of knowing if the experience of rape predisposes one to a more conservative definition—perhaps as a defensive response to the controversy and skepticism that surround rape—or if these victims are simply not representative of their communities. Among victims, however, there is a clear majority-minority difference in the selection of a definition of rape. Only 31 percent of the minority victims (Black and Mexican American combined) selected either of the feminist definitions compared with 56 percent of the Anglo victims, and while the stereotypic definition was selected by 65 percent of the minority victims, it was chosen by only 28 percent of the Anglo victims. Since these differences are apparently not a function of their own rape experiences (stereotypic-other), these data offer some support for the argument that the feminist perspective on rape has yet to be assimilated by minority females. This view is further supported by the fact that minority females in the public samples were more inclined than Anglo females to choose the stereotypic definition of rape as the one best approximating their own view. If all responses are viewed on a feminist-conservative continuum, there is a consistency between victim and public attitude data. When selections of both feminist defintions (1 and 4) are combined to represent a liberal response to rape, Anglo respondents are the most feminist, Mexican Americans the least, with Blacks in between. Victim responses, grouped by racial-ethnic categories along this same liberal-conservative continuum, follow the same pattern.

Rape: Its Cause and Prevention

The Perceived Cause of Rape

Responses to an open-ended question, "In your opinion, what is the main cause of rape?", fell into six general categories (see Table 12). The modal response suggests that the perceived cause of rape rests with the mental or emotional problems of the rapist. The majority opinion apparently is that

TABLE 12. Opinions as to the Main Cause of Rape by Samples (A, B, MA) and Victims (V)

PERCEIVED CAUSE OF RAPE		ANGLO			BLACK			MEXICAN AMERICAN			ALL			
		M	F	V	M	F	V	M	F	V	A	B	MA	V
Rapist mentally ill or "crazy"	N	75	68	14	48	103	2	62	16	5	143	151	78	21
	%	46	42	45	29	62	20	38	10	29	44	45	24	36
Women's behavior/appearance	N	27	37	5	51	33	3	40	69	4	64	84	109	12
	%	16	23	16	30	20	30	25	43	23	20	25	34	21
Societal problems	N	10	20	5	10	4	0	17	38	2	30	14	55	7
	%	6	12	16	6	2	—	11	23	12	9	4	17	12
Sex-role problems	N	16	26	2	25	0	3	8	5	1	42	25	13	6
	%	10	16	7	15	—	30	5	3	6	13	8	4	10
Male sex drive	N	36	8	4	17	8	2	12	10	3	44	25	22	9
	%	22	5	13	10	5	20	7	6	18	13	8	7	16
Drugs and/or alcohol	N	1	4	1	16	18	0	23	24	2	5	34	47	3
	%	—	2	3	10	11	—	14	15	12	2	10	15	5
Percent[a]		100	100	100	100	100	100	100	100	100	101	100	101	100
Totals: Number of valid cases		165	163	31	167	166	10	162	162	17	328	333	324	58
Missing data		4	3	1	0	3	1	5	11	1	7	3	16	3

[a]Percentages do not always add to 100 because of rounding errors.

men would not rape women if they (men) were not mentally ill or emotionally disturbed. The open-ended question, however, lost a great deal in translation into categories for the purpose of coding. There was no way, for example, to semantically separate responses suggesting the rapist was mentally ill from those indicating the rapist was "crazy," even though these terms may represent different concepts. There were no small number of respondents who attributed the cause of rape to the rapist's mental or emotional health only on the next question (dealing with the alleviation of the problem) to suggest that rapists should be put to death or castrated, a response hardly congruent with a clinical view of mental illness. There were also some very explicit responses such as "rapists are crazy SOBs and should be shot." For coding purposes, all responses such as "crazy," mentally ill, or emotionally disturbed were grouped together. Although the respondents' precise meanings are unknown, they can perhaps be best understood as attributing the cause of rape to some kind of deviant or aberrant behavior on the part of males, rather than to mental illness in the more sophisticated, clinical sense.

The most pervasive belief as to the cause of rape for all Anglos (sample and victims) was that the rapist is sick or emotionally disturbed. Black victims split their responses equally between attributing the cause to women's behavior and/or appearance and to sex-role problems. In the Black sample, a majority of females were inclined to attribute rape to the rapist's mental state, while Black males very closely divided their responses between this cause and that of women's behavior and/or appearance. Mexican American victims were most likely to attribute the cause of rape to the rapist's mental illness, although a tendency to blame women ran a close second. Among the Mexican American sample, males were likely to attribute rape to mental illness. However, this "cause" held little credibility for Mexican American females who were inclined to blame female behavior and/or appearance for rape.

It is probably not surprising that so many respondents perceive mental illness as the main cause of rape since this phenomenon is so often used to explain a myriad of socially unacceptable, incomprehensible forms of behavior in contemporary society. It is disturbing, however, that most respondents, including victims, saw women's behavior and/or appearance as the second most frequent cause of rape. In particular, this perceived cause suggests a view that may be supportive of the victim-precipitation perspective or, in the vernacular of the day, the "she asked for it" syndrome. This view generally includes some (if not all) of the following elements: (1) the way in which women dress (provocatively); (2) that women may go to "questionable" places such as bars; (3) that women may exercise poor judgment (by being out late at night or by hitchhiking); or (4) that women may "tease" and flirt with men and thereby "lead them on."

These responses indicate that there is a strongly held belief that women have a "place" and a role and that when they step outside of certain boundaries, they are "asking for it." The relative frequency of this response is disturbing not only because it may reflect a tendency toward victim-blaming, but, on the part of victims, it may also be an indication of how they see their role in the context of their own rape experience. However, since the question asked for an opinion about the cause of rape in general, rather than the cause of one's own rape, it is possible that victims' responses reflect the degree to which the victim-blaming ideology has been internalized and should not necessarily be interpreted as a self-indictment. Other data from the victim interviews, as well as the public attitude data, would tend to support this latter interpretation. The rapist being "crazy" or mentally ill was the most frequently cited cause by all ethnic-sex subgroups except Black males and Mexican American females. All groups except Anglo males cited women's behavior frequently enough for it to rank first or second as the cause of rape. Against this backdrop of public opinion then, these victim responses should not be surprising. Obviously, there is a strong tendency in the public mind (with minimal variations by ethnicity and sex) to blame rape on women's provocative or careless behavior and on the "sick" behavior of aberrant males. Apparently, the rape experience does little to alter these well-ingrained attitudes.

The meaning of the other four response categories—none of which contains more than 30 percent of the responses of any group—requires some explanation. The third most frequently cited cause of rape was the male "sex drive"; responses here represent the view that men innately have a strong sex drive which, in certain circumstances, may get "out of control." Both victims and sample respondents, for example, expressed the opinion that a man will get it (sex) whenever, wherever, and however he needs to when the "urge" hits him. However, only Anglo males and the rape victims cited this cause with any degree of frequency. "Societal problems" includes a range of responses suggesting that the cause of rape lies within the contemporary sociocultural context of America. Examples include inequality, violence, crime, and the declining influence of "law and order" and of the family. The category of "sex-role problems" refers to the pressures placed on men in society, especially with regard to expectations vis-à-vis women. Respondents were likely to suggest two general areas: (1) that men just do not understand or know how to relate to women and/or that they have no respect for women; and (2) that the male sex role is problematic because of the emphasis placed on "being a man," on proving one's masculinity. If the feminist anti-rape movement has served a consciousness-raising function for the public at large, this category should reflect some degree of feminist awareness. Obviously, this is not the case. Only 3 to 16 percent of the sample subgroups cited this cause, although, interestingly, Anglo females and

Black males were considerably more likely than other groups to attribute rape to sex-role problems. Among victims, only Blacks attributed much importance to sex roles in relation to rape. Finally, the last group of responses attributes the cause of rape to stimuli external to the assailant; that is, had the rapist not been drinking, smoking marijuana, or using "dope," he would not have done such a thing. This response category is comprised almost exclusively of minority responses, especially those of Mexican Americans.

Alleviating the Rape Problem

On another open-ended question, respondents were asked, "In your opinion, what is the one thing that would reduce rape the most?" Responses were collapsed into five categories as shown in Table 13. By far, the majority of responses fell into two "solution" categories: a "law-and-order" approach and a perceived need for women to change their behavior. The former includes the predictable pleas for better police protection, stricter laws, harsher punishment, capital punishment, and even castration. Responses relating to women's behavior are basically of two kinds: (1) women exercising caution ("being more careful") with regard to their appearance, their behavior toward men, their mobility, and the places they frequent, and (2) suggestions that women should learn self-defense tactics in order to protect themselves against would-be assailants. Of the two kinds of responses, the latter were too small (2 to 6 percent) to warrant a separate category and therefore were combined with the other responses pertaining to women's behavior. Among victims, 40 percent cited "women being more careful" as the best way to reduce the rape problem compared with 31 percent who cited a law-and-order solution. While Mexican American victims were more likely to rely on a law-and-order approach, Black victims, by a majority, said women being more careful was the most effective solution. However, nearly a third of the Anglo and Mexican American victims also cited this "solution."

The remaining three solutions combined account for less than one-third of any given group (victims or public). There is, however, an interesting contradiction in relation to one of these responses. Specifically, public education refers to the perceived need for increased awareness and understanding of the rape problem, and treatment programs refer to the need for more and better ways to work (therapeutically) with men who have sexual problems. Yet, ironically, despite the fact that the problem was defined as one of mental illness by a majority of respondents, there were too few responses related to treatment alone to justify a separate category. In fact, only Anglo victims (by 26 percent) tended to identify public education *or* treatment programs as the best way to alleviate the rape problem.

In view of the perceived cause of rape, the most frequently cited solutions appear to be either empty rhetoric and/or incongruent. While just under

TABLE 13. Opinion on Most Effective Means of Alleviating the Rape Problem by Samples (A, B, MA) and Victims (V)

SUGGESTION TO ALLEVIATE PROBLEM		ANGLO			BLACK			MEXICAN AMERICAN			ALL			
		M	F	V	M	F	V	M	F	V	A	B	MA	V
Law-and-order approach	N	97	57	8	84	98	2	101	59	7	154	182	160	17
	%	58	35	26	51	59	22	61	38	47	46	55	49	31
Women changing their behavior	N	27	54	10	45	51	7	21	46	5	81	96	67	22
	%	16	33	32	27	30	78	13	29	33	25	29	21	40
Public education/treatment	N	19	15	8	29	16	0	17	8	1	34	45	25	9
	%	11	9	26	17	10	—	10	5	7	10	14	8	16
Better family life and/or religion	N	8	24	2	5	0	0	19	28	0	32	5	47	2
	%	5	15	6	3	—	—	12	18	—	10	2	15	4
Fundamental societal changes	N	16	14	3	3	2	0	7	16	2	30	5	23	5
	%	10	8	10	2	1	—	4	10	13	9	1	7	9
Percent[a]		100	100	100	100	100	100	100	100	100	100	100	100	100
Totals: Number of valid cases		167	164	31	166	167	9	165	157	15	331	333	322	55
Missing data		2	2	1	1	2	2	2	16	3	4	3	18	6

[a]Percentages do not always add to 100 because of rounding errors.

half of all Anglo and Black samples saw rape as a product of mental illness, 46 to 55 percent, respectively, proposed a law-and-order solution to the problem and only 10 to 14 percent suggested education and/or treatment as a "solution." While 24 percent of Mexican Americans saw rape as a product of mental illness, and 34 percent as a product of female behavior and/or appearance, almost half resorted to a law-and-order solution, while only 21 percent said that women should change their behavior. In short, close to half of all respondents in all three public samples proposed a law-and-order solution to the rape problem. While this may appear illogical and an unlikely solution on the surface, it is very typically American. Regardless of cause or the nature of the problem, our voluminous criminal codes attest to the fact that we want "the law" to handle our problems. In terms of these *ideal* expectations, minorities are little different from the dominant group. Other data suggest, however, that they are distrustful of the *reality* of the criminal justice system (as it works for them).

The "solutions" proposed by victims appear equally unrealistic and inconsistent on the surface. If women's behavior and/or appearance are *not* believed by most to be the main cause of rape, then why would so many cite "women being more careful" as the one thing that would reduce rape the most? There are several possible explanations for this, the most obvious being that victims made no attempt to link perceived causes with logically consistent solutions. However, a more likely explanation is that, regardless of the cause(s) of rape, victims may pragmatically feel that only they—women—can prevent rape. To say that women must bear the responsibility for preventing or reducing rape may suggest a firm grasp of reality, particularly since these women have experientially "been there." If the cause of rape is mental illness, what is to prevent the mentally disturbed man from becoming aggressive or violent? Who is responsible for protecting women from these "crazy" men? Or, if some men infer sexual invitations from the way women dress, where they go, and how they relate interpersonally, who has control over this imputation of meaning? Perhaps the victims who stated that women should be more careful, that they should learn self-defense, were simply saying that, given the state of contemporary society, women had best look out for themselves. This can be further supported given that this solution was cited more frequently (by victims) than the law-and-order approach, which has traditionally been the predictable response to the issue of crime prevention. It is also quite possible that these women have no illusions about the criminal justice system following their experience as rape victims. It may be of special interest that over three-fourths of the Black victims selected the "women being more careful" solution. Since Blacks, more than any other group, have a unique, though unenviable, history relative to law enforcement agencies, support for this perceived solution may represent a pragmatic statement that advocates taking care of one's own business. This attitude is, of course, role-restrictive for the female since it disallows freedom in movement, dress, and interpersonal relationships. That such a role-restriction may, in fact, be a result of having experienced rape is given some support by the public attitude data. Specifically, the public attitude responses on this item differ (from those of victims) in terms of the perceived solution to the rape problem. The most frequent response from all six ethnic-sex subgroups was related to law and order, and with the exception of Anglo and Mexican American females, a majority of all groups tended to rely on this solution. Women changing their behavior was cited second by all groups, but by females more than males. Among males, only Blacks approximated the female response. These findings would seem to suggest that women may be more aware than men that they (women) are responsible for preventing rape, and it seems that the rape experience simply exacerbates this awareness.

Summary

Victims tend toward a stereotypic definition of rape which reflects a greater degree of conservatism in relation to defining rape than is apparent in their respective racial-ethnic communities. However, victims and the public samples are similar in their placement on a feminist-conservative continuum vis-à-vis their definitions of rape; Anglos are the most feminist or liberal in their definitions, Mexican Americans the least, with Blacks in between. Despite certain variations by race-ethnicity and sex and victim-nonvictim status, these findings clearly suggest that the vast majority of respondents view rape as a behavior problem—primarily that of the rapist (mental illness) and secondarily that of the victim (inappropriate behavior and/or appearance). Few respondents of any group saw societal (macro-level) problems as causally related to rape, and fewer yet saw sex-role problems as causal. Perceptions of cause obviously preclude certain solutions or interventions. A majority of respondents resorted to law-and-order clichés or admonitions for women to change their behavior as their best suggestion on how to reduce the rape problem. The perceived need for women to accept responsibility for alleviating rape is consistent with perception of the problem as "caused" by female behavior. However, the same kind of consistency is not apparent between the most frequently cited "cause" and the most frequently voiced "cure." If rape is caused by mental illness, it would follow that its solution lies in the field of mental health rather than in the realm of law and order. Since efforts to remediate rape have largely been legal-judicial and the problem continues to grow, the attitudes of rape victims should be thought of as pragmatic rather than as nonfeminist. Until society demonstrates a better understanding of fundamental cause and moves to attack the problem in more than a symptomatic way, women must be responsible not only for their own behavior, but for that of men as well.

The San Antonio research has profiled a rape victim not unlike the victims of other studies and has added descriptively to the existent knowledge base with regard to support systems and the needs of victims. We have also quantitatively assessed the impact of rape and have examined whether certain differences among the victims and/or their experiences act to alleviate or exacerbate that impact. We have established that victims are only somewhat more conservative (or perhaps realistic) than their respective racial-ethnic communities with regard to how they define rape and perceive its cause and remediation. The next two chapters deal with the extrinsic aspect of rape, first in an effort to describe the social context of rape and then as we attempt to examine causation in terms of linkages between attitudes about rape and attitudes emanating from a system of racial-sexual stratification.

Note

1. Three chi-square tests of association were computed: Definition by Race-Ethnicity, Definition by Rape, and Rape by Race-Ethnicity. Only Definition by Race-Ethnicity was statistically significant with $X^2 = 7.13$, 1 df, $p \leq .01$.

COMMUNITY ATTITUDES—
COMMUNITY JUDGMENTS:
THE SOCIAL CONTEXT
OF RAPE

7

It seems apparent from the data presented in the preceding chapters that part of the impact of rape is a function of *who* one is in a social sense, specifically, that cultural-structural difference which results from being Black, White, or Mexican American. Women who become victims of rape, like everyone else, carry with them certain attitudes and experiences internalized from their respective environments and from their positions in society at large. Following a rape, they must deal with the varying reactions of family, friends, and their communities as these, too, become a part of their rape experience. This brings us to consider the other side of rape—its extrinsic quality. Rape as a social phenomenon neither begins nor ends with sexual assault. Rape as one woman's personal trouble is shaped by who she is and by all of the attitudes, judgments, and experiences that surround her daily, and these, we contend, are structured by a system of racial-sexual stratification. When research is guided by a theoretical framework such as that of racial-sexual stratification, it dictates what questions will be asked and predetermines certain kinds of findings. As indicated in Chapter 3, questions were designed to measure attitudes about rape, sex roles, male-female sexuality, and minority-related rape risks. Here, we describe some of these data which subsequently become the basis for an analysis of causal relationships.

Judging Forced Sexual Encounters as Rape

The scenarios used to elicit specific judgments about rape yielded a variety of data, including a three-dimensional measure of general Attitudes

About Rape and a Credibility Measure. The Attitudes About Rape Measure consists of three composite scores for each respondent: a Rape (R) Score, Fault (F) Score, and Court (C) Score. These scores "average out" responses on each dimension across all nine scenarios in that the composite score is inclusive of responses to nine diverse rape situations, some of which are controversial and some of which are no doubt perceived as "good rapes." The more specific and discriminating Credibility Measure, on the other hand, makes it possible to compare responses to these diverse rape situations. Comparing the Credibility Measure on all nine scenarios, one can assume that the scenario with the lowest numerical value has the most credibility in the mind of the public—that is, it is seen as the "best rape" or the most "real."

General Responses to Rape

If the mean composite Rape, Fault, and Court Scores are examined by race-ethnicity (sample), the findings are very consistent with those reported in Chapter 6. On two of the three dimensions (Rape and Court), Anglos are the most feminist; that is, they are more likely to define the situation as rape and are more willing to prosecute than are Blacks and Mexican Americans. Mexican Americans are the least feminist on these two dimensions, and Blacks are midway between. On Fault Scores, the minority pattern is reversed, with Blacks showing a greater tendency than Mexican Americans to blame the female for the rape. All differences between samples on these three dimensions are significant (see Table 28, Appendix C).

Table 14 shows the mean composite, R, F, and C Scores broken down into ethnic-sex subgroups and arrayed from feminist (low scores) to non-feminist. There are no significant differences between males and females on the definement of sexual encounters (Rape), and the response pattern for the samples as a whole is again that Anglos are the most feminist and Mexican Americans the least. On assessment of Fault, the sex-ethnic subgroups also follow the pattern shown by the samples as a whole; Anglos are the least likely to blame the female for the rape, followed by Mexican Americans and then Blacks. There are, however, significant differences between males and females in the Anglo and Black samples, with Anglo males and Black females being less likely to assess female fault than their cohorts of the opposite sex. When Court Scores are examined by sex and race-ethnicity, there is considerable variation in comparison with scores for the entire sample. This change stems from the significant differences between males and females in the two minority samples. The greatest disparity is between Blacks where females are the most willing to prosecute, while Black males are second only to Mexican American males in their unwillingness to prosecute.

Several other observations can be made from the table. The array of

TABLE 14. Rank-Order of Group Means on Composite Rape, Fault, and Court Scores

RANK	RAPE		FAULT		COURT	
	GROUP	*MEAN*	*GROUP*	*MEAN*	*GROUP*	*MEAN*
Feminist 1	Am	14.8	Am	20.0	Bf	14.9
2	Af	15.2	Af	21.4	Am	15.0
3	Bf	16.1	MAf/MAm	21.7	Af	15.8
4	Bm	16.7			MAf	16.8
5	MAf	17.6	Bf	22.0	Bm	17.4
6 Nonfeminist	MAm	18.1	Bm	22.9	MAm	18.1

Notes: Am = Anglo males   Bf = Black females
        Af = Anglo females   MAm = Mexican American males
        Bm = Black males   MAf = Mexican American females

Means have a possible range of 9 to 36. Low scores reflect definement of forced sexual encounters as rape, low assessment of female fault, and willingness to prosecute the assailant. Therefore, lower scores are viewed as indicating comparatively feminist attitudes about rape.

scores reveals a similarity in attitudes on definement of rape and willingness to prosecute, both in terms of the group means and the pattern of group responses. However, the fact that the lowest Fault Score is approximately two points above the highest Rape and Court Scores suggests a tendency among all groups to assess some degree of fault to the victim. Anglo males are the low scorers (most feminist) on all of the composite measures except Court where Black females score just slightly below them in willingness to prosecute. Minorities, particularly minority males, are comparatively more conservative on all three dimensions of Attitudes About Rape than are Anglos. Mexican American males are the least inclined to define sexual encounters as rape and are the least willing to prosecute, while Black males are the most inclined to view the victim as at fault.

The Credibility of Rape

The composite measures just presented are useful because they allow for a massive amount of data reduction, and they incorporate responses to a range of life-like situations that reflect (on a group level) the diversity masked in what is referred to as the "rape problem." However, they do not reflect the variation in responses to different "kinds" of rape—that is, responses to stereotypic street rapes versus responses to rapes resulting from hitchhiking or from bar pickups. While it would be too tedious to discuss each of the scenarios in terms of definitions, assessment of fault, and willingness to prosecute, a review of these data indicates that respondents tended to vary their judgments with regard to components of the particular scenario—for example, the relationship between the victim and assailant, the reputation and/or activity of the victim, use of a weapon and injury. In Table 15, data from all the scenarios are summarized using the Credibility Measure (the sum of Rape, Fault, and Court responses on each scenario). The table shows the scenarios in rank-order, from the one perceived as most credible (low scores) to the one perceived as least credible (high scores) by ethnic and sex subgroups.

Although there is considerable variation in scores, S1—the street rape involving both a weapon and victim injury—was perceived as the most credible rape by all groups. Clearly, this scenario includes all the components of a "good rape" (the assailant was a stranger; the victim's activity/behavior was not in question; a weapon was involved; the victim was injured). All groups ranked either S2 (street rape: no weapon) or S8 (date-rape: weapon) as second or third in credibility. This suggests that while the stranger-to-stranger rape may be "preferred" by the public, the use of a weapon, even when the victim and assailant are dating, may be an overriding variable in determining credibility.[1] The importance of a weapon and injury is also demonstrated by the fact that S2 varied from S1 only in the absence of a weapon and injury. Yet, on the average, scores on S1 are almost one point higher than on S2. Four groups placed S7 (prostitute: stranger, weapon, injury) as the fourth most credible scenario; the two subgroups differing from this pattern were minority males who saw the rape of the bar pickup with a weapon (S5) as more credible. Beyond the fourth rank-order, there is little consensus on the credibility of the remaining scenarios except for those judged to be the least credible.

While the stereotypic street rape with weapon and injury was seen as the most credible by all racial-ethnic and sex subgroups, at the low end of the credibility continuum we find the husband-wife assault and/or one of the bar pickups. Except for Mexican American and Black females, all groups judged the husband-wife assault and one of the bar pickups as the least or next-to-least credible rape. Women who allow themselves to be "picked up" in bars apparently have little credibility as rape victims, perhaps because they are seen as engaging in risk-taking and/or role-violating behavior. A wife, on the other hand, may have little credibility when she is seen as having violated traditional role-stratification by refusing to be compliant. The

TABLE 15. Rank-Order of Rape Scenarios from Most to Least Credible by Ethnic Group and Sex

RANK	ANGLO		BLACK		MEXICAN AMERICAN	
	M	F	M	F	M	F
Most Credible						
1	S1 3.27	S1 3.48	S1 4.30	S1 3.30	S1 3.87	S1 3.31
2	S8 3.98	S2 4.43	S2 4.91	S8 4.11	S2 4.69	S2 4.67
3	S2 4.31	S8 4.62	S8 4.96	S2 4.14	S8 5.01	S8 4.91
4	S7 4.50	S7 4.86	S5 5.17	S7 5.42	S5 6.25	S7 5.72
5	S5 5.23	S3 5.34	S3 5.62	S9 5.82	S7 6.23	S9 5.75
6	S3 5.30	S5 5.96	S4 5.67	S4 5.93	S3 6.42	S3 6.10
7	S4 5.70	S4 6.03	S7 5.94	S3 6.01	S4 6.44	S5 6.60
8	S6 5.92	S6 6.07	S9 7.27	S5 6.12	S6 6.59	S4 6.61
9	S9 6.75	S9 6.34	S6 7.42	S6 6.74	S9 7.02	S6 7.01
Least Credible						

Notes:

S1 - Street rape: weapon, injury
S2 - Street rape: no weapon, no injury
S3 - Hitchhiker: stranger, weapon
S4 - Hitchhiker: acquaintance, no weapon
S5 - Bar pickup: weapon
S6 - Bar pickup: no weapon
S7 - Prostitute: stranger, weapon, injury
S8 - Date rape: weapon
S9 - Husband-wife assault

Mean scores for each scenario had a possible range of 3 to 11. The lower the score, the more credible the scenario, as determined by definement, assessment of female fault, and willingness to prosecute the assailant.

response of Mexican American and Black females on the husband-wife assault (placing it in the middle position in terms of credibility) is especially interesting. While Black females have tended to be somewhat feminist in their responses all along, Mexican American females have not. That Mexican American females gave a comparatively high degree of credibility to the husband-wife assault is a reflection of a more feminist or liberal response, a clear departure from their otherwise conservative response pattern. There may, however, be a very simple explanation for what appears to be a deviant response for them. That is, the Mexican American wife commands respect in her home; the home is her power-base where she has acknowledged control. Indeed, it may well be the male in this scenario who is guilty of role-violation because he has failed to show her the respect due a good woman.

On Tradition and Liberation in Sex Roles

As explained in Chapter 3, four indices (see Appendix A.2) were designed to measure traditional versus nontraditional Sex Role Beliefs and Behavior and high versus low support of Women's Liberation Beliefs and Behavior. Sample findings undifferentiated by sex indicate that on both of the Sex Role indices, Anglos are the most nontraditional, Mexican Americans the most traditional, with Blacks between, but closer to Mexican Americans than to Anglos. On the Women's Liberation indices, the pattern varies. Blacks demonstrate the strongest attitudinal support for Women's Liberation Beliefs; they are followed by Anglos and Mexican Americans who differ significantly from Blacks, but not from each other. Anglos and Blacks are equally supportive of Women's Liberation Behavior and differ significantly from Mexican Americans who are less supportive of such behavior.

When responses are broken down into ethnic-sex subgroups, there is no consistent pattern for any subgroup. However, racial-ethnic and sex differences are very apparent, as can be seen in Table 16 where mean scores on the four indices are arrayed from low (traditional sex-role attitudes and low support of women's liberation) to high (nontraditional sex-role attitudes and high support for women's liberation). Mexican American females are the most traditional in their attitudes about Sex Role Behavior and are the least supportive of Women's Liberation Behavior. Mexican American males demonstrate significantly less traditionality (in comparison with females) on the two Sex Role indices, but are low in support of Women's Liberation (Beliefs and Behavior). Black males are the most traditional of any subgroup in their Sex Role Beliefs. At the other end of the continuum, Anglo females are the most nontraditional in their attitudes about Sex Role Beliefs and Behavior, and Black females are the most supportive of

TABLE 16.   Sex Role-Women's Liberation Measures: Mean Score Array
and Significance of Group Contrasts

INDEX	NONFEMINIST LOW		MEAN SCORE ARRAY			FEMINIST HIGH
SR Beliefs	Bm 17.2	MAf 18.0	MAm 18.4	Am 19.1	Bf 19.9	Af 20.8
SR Behavior	MAf 17.0	Bm 17.7	MAm 17.9	Bf 20.2	Am 20.6	Af 21.5
WL Beliefs	MAm 19.2	Am 20.5	Af 20.9	MAf 21.2	Bm 21.4	Bf 21.7
WL Behavior	MAf 21.5	MAm 21.6	Am 22.9	Bm 23.0	Af 23.2	Bf 23.3

GROUP CONTRASTS BY RACE-ETHNICITY AND SEX:
SIGNIFICANCE OF *t*-VALUES

	MALES			*FEMALES*		
	A-B	A-MA	B-MA	A-B	A-MA	B-MA
SR Beliefs	.001	.01	.001	.01	.001	.001
SR Behavior	.001	.001	ns	.001	.001	.001
WL Beliefs	.01	.001	.001	.01	ns	ns
WL Behavior	ns	.001	.001	ns	.001	.001

Notes: ns = not significant. Mean scores have a possible range of 8 to 32. The higher the score on the two Women's Liberation indices, the more positive or feminist are attitudes supportive of women's liberation. The higher the scores on the two Sex Role indices, the more feminist or nontraditional are attitudes about male-female sex roles.

Am = Anglo males	Bf = Black females
Af = Anglo females	MAm = Mexican American males
Bm = Black males	MAf = Mexican American females

Women's Liberation, although not significantly more so than Black males and Anglo females on the same indices.

Much of the feminist literature relating to the women's movement points to a conflict between attitudes supportive of women's liberation and traditional male-female sex roles. An examination of the San Antonio data reveals that all respondents generally tend toward attitudes supportive of

Women's Liberation (Beliefs and Behavior) in that scores tend to cluster in the upper half of the possible range. Somewhat contradictorily, attitudes also appear to be supportive of traditional male-female Sex Roles (Beliefs and Behavior) in that scores tend to cluster in the lower half of the possible range. Consequently, a given subgroup found to evidence nontraditionality in sex-role attitudes might not predictably show strong support for women's liberation. Nor were those groups weak in support of women's liberation always the most likely to show strong traditionality in sex-role attitudes. For example, the scores of Anglo females place them as the most nontraditional on Sex Role Beliefs. However, they demonstrate low support for Women's Liberation Beliefs when compared with some other subgroups. The scores for Black males suggest that they are the most traditional of all subgroups on Sex Role Beliefs. Yet, they are surpassed only by Black females (from whom they do not differ significantly) in support of Women's Liberation Beliefs, two seemingly incompatible response patterns. As can be seen in Table 16, Mexican Americans tend, more than other groups, to follow the predictable pattern of sex-role traditionality and low support for women's liberation.

There appears to be a degree of ambivalence in these responses, or perhaps we have simply tapped a generation in transition as evidenced by adherence to traditional beliefs and behavior in relation to sex roles and simultaneous attitudinal support for women's liberation. The data suggest that the traditional sex role-women's liberation dichotomy or continuum may be a conceptualization that does not "fit" empirical reality. This possibility, in addition to questions about reliability and content validity across the three samples (see Appendix A.5), led us to discard the four indices, except for descriptive purposes, and to pool the twenty-five sex role-women's liberation items for factor analysis. To accommodate the sampling procedure, the three samples were factor analyzed separately; sex was disregarded in this procedure in order to develop measures of community attitudes about sex roles and women's liberation.[2] The resulting factors represent underlying attitudinal dimensions for each of the samples, and they have been given labels that reflect their content themes (as determined by examining the relative weights of factor loadings; see Table 29 in Appendix C). The first three factors extracted for each sample are described below. It should be kept in mind that these labels do not represent a quantitative measure of the attitudinal dimensions represented in the samples. This quantification will come later when, for the purpose of inferential statistical analysis, the factors are converted to factor scores which denote, to a greater or lesser degree, the presence of this factor.

ANGLOS

Factor One for Anglos is labeled *Liberation* because it appears to represent unidimensional attitudinal support for both beliefs and behavior associated with women's liberation. Factor Two is most appropriately labeled *Freedom-Equality* since it deals with freedom from traditional feminine role restraints and with support for certain rights on a par with males. Factor Three represents sex-role *Stereotypes* because it is comprised of items describing the stereotypic sex-role attributes of male toughness and female nurturance.

BLACKS

Factor One for Blacks is labeled *Traditionality* and is comprised of attitudes that attribute both stereotypic male-female behavior and attributes to gender. Factor Two apparently represents a form of *Modified Liberation* as it includes a mix of attitudinal support of women's liberation with some lesser but accompanying support of traditional sex-role stereotypes. Factor Three has a more unidimensional theme of *Liberation* and is comparable to Factor One for Anglos, representing definitive support for women's liberation beliefs and behavior.

MEXICAN AMERICANS

Factor One for Mexican Americans is labeled *Male Role* because the items describe an authoritarian conceptualization of the male role in relation to the female. Factor Two represents female *Equality* since it is comprised of attitudinal support for behavioral equality of males and females. Factor Three is labeled *Female Role* and clearly represents the placement and restriction of women in traditional family and work-related roles.

In using these factors as descriptive data, it is important to note that the factoring procedure produced a similar attitudinal dimension for all three samples—one that is descriptive of women's liberation and/or equality in sex roles (Factors One and Two for Anglos, Factor Three for Blacks, and Factor Two for Mexican Americans). In addition, a factor descriptive of traditional, stereotypic sex-role behavior and/or attributes was extracted for both Anglos and Blacks (Factor One for Blacks, Factor Three for Anglos). This same phenomenon is also manifested in a somewhat more exaggerated form among Mexican Americans in Factors One and Three, representing stereotypic male and female roles and attributes. These factors appear to describe the communality and uniqueness of community attitudes about sex roles to a greater degree than the four Sex Role-Women's Liberation indices, and they will be collectively referred to as measures of sex-role attitudes for each of the three samples.

Men, Women, and Rape

Respondents were asked to agree or disagree with thirteen statements designed to elicit the degree to which rape is perceived as integral to male and/or female sexuality or behavior. Specifically, seven items deal with beliefs (or myths) about women, and six deal with beliefs about men in relation to rape (see Appendix A.3). Not all of these items are examined individually. However, some of the findings seem to establish certain patterns in relation to men and women and their sexuality in relation to rape.

Beliefs About Male-Female Sexuality and Rape

As can be seen in Table 17, the range of responses on most of the items pertaining to female behavior-sexuality seems to reflect ambivalence and lack of consensus with regard to rape. The findings also suggest a strong tendency on the part of some groups to fix responsibility for rape—both its cause and prevention—with women. For example, there was majority support among all respondents except Black females that women should "fight and resist" a rapist. A substantial proportion of three groups—Black males and Mexican Americans of both sexes—agrees that "a woman cannot be raped by her husband." Only Black males demonstrated strong support for the belief that women are "curious and excited" about rape. Interestingly, responses on item 2 suggest a rejection of the tactic of trying the victim's reputation in rape cases; yet, item 5 indicates that Black males and Mexican Americans of both sexes feel that a woman's reputation will be damaged as a result of a rape experience.

The six items pertaining to males in relation to rape are shown in Table 18 along with the proportion of respondents who agreed with each. As with the data pertaining to females and rape, these findings reveal contradictions, ambivalence, and lack of consensus. The most agreement across all groups is on items 2 and 4: men can rape and get away with it, and men who commit rape are mentally ill. Perhaps this is tacit acknowledgment that many rapes go unreported and/or unacknowledged and that known rapists are more likely than others to be mentally ill; or perhaps the findings simply represent dissonant beliefs. The belief that rapists are mentally ill mitigates the fear of rape and makes it more tolerable because it negates the view that all men are potential rapists. Five of the six ethnic-sex subgroups (Anglo males are the exception) expressed, by a majority, the belief that men sometimes have sex urges they cannot control. A smaller proportion of respondents saw "most men as capable of committing rape." Some of the significant differences on these items are majority-minority in nature, relating, no doubt, to the unique experience of minorities with regard to rape. In particular, it is of interest to note that minority males (by 73 and 92 percent) were more likely than other groups to agree that "men are often falsely accused of rape."

These data reveal some systematic findings with regard to group beliefs about male-female sexuality and have some discomforting implications for minority communities vis-à-vis rape. With few exceptions, on both sets of beliefs, Anglo respondents appear to be more moderate or, comparatively

TABLE 17. Beliefs About Women and Rape by Ethnic Group and Sex

ITEM		PERCENT AGREEING[a] *ANGLO* M	F	*BLACK* M	F	*MA* M	F
1. Rapes could be avoided if women did not provoke.	N	31	41	112	39	51	116
	%	19	25	73	23	32	70
2. A woman's past has nothing to do with rape.	N	129	135	99	157	125	103
	%	76	81	63	94	77	71
3. Women are afraid but curious and excited about rape.	N	43	28	106	12	38	48
	%	27	17	84	7	24	32
4. A woman cannot be raped without a weapon.	N	16	7	84	14	27	21
	%	10	4	55	9	17	13
5. Once a female is raped, her reputation is ruined.	N	13	25	79	20	67	79
	%	8	16	51	12	41	50
6. Women should fight, resist a rapist.	N	87	77	113	32	140	121
	%	52	52	70	21	89	85
7. A woman cannot be raped by her husband.	N	42	47	112	51	77	69
	%	25	29	76	34	49	43
N[b]		166	161	151	161	161	156
Missing data		3	5	16	8	6	17

[a]Percentages are based on combined strongly agree and agree responses; for the exact wording of these items see Appendix A.3.
[b]N = the average number of valid responses on all seven items.

speaking, more feminist in their views than the other samples, although Black females (when considered separately) are frequently more feminist in their views than Anglos. Differences between Anglo males and females are statistically significant on eight of the thirteen items and, where differences are significant, males and females are about equally divided between what appear to be feminist versus more conservative responses. Black males and females differ significantly on all thirteen items, with females providing the more feminist responses. Their differences are of considerable magnitude and could raise many questions with regard to the treatment of rape victims in the Black community and, more generally, with regard to the day-to-day

TABLE 18.   Beliefs About Men and Rape by Ethnic Group and Sex

ITEM		PERCENT AGREEING[a]					
		ANGLO		BLACK		MA	
		M	F	M	F	M	F
1. Most men are capable of committing rape.	N	73	55	113	50	78	106
	%	43	34	72	33	49	65
2. Men can commit rape and get away with it.	N	155	162	97	150	141	125
	%	93	98	65	92	88	77
3. Men have sex urges they can't control.	N	58	91	119	82	92	144
	%	35	56	74	50	55	87
4. Men who commit rape are sick.	N	152	152	127	164	146	102
	%	91	92	83	98	87	63
5. Men who commit rape hate women.	N	46	94	87	29	68	56
	%	29	62	60	20	47	38
6. Men are often falsely accused of rape.	N	64	98	142	63	107	74
	%	40	63	92	41	73	57
N^b		164	160	153	157	157	155
Missing data		5	6	14	12	10	18

[a]Percentages are based on combined strongly agree and agree responses; for the exact wording of each item, see Appendix A.3.

[b]N = the average number of valid responses on all six items.

dynamics of male-female relationships among Blacks. Black males appear to be especially skeptical with regard to the validity of rape. While this is understandable in light of Black history, these findings suggest that Black males have coped with their threat at female expense. A belief system which holds that women provoke rape; that they are "curious and excited" about rape; and that a woman cannot be raped without a weapon, makes rape into something less than a crime of violence and more a part of the dynamics of male-female sexuality. Such attitudes have negative implications for rape victims in the context of the Black community; they suggest a lack of support and a failure to grant credibility to the experience of rape.

Mexican Americans present yet another response pattern to male-female sexuality and rape. Males and females differ significantly on six of the thirteen items, indicating greater consensus than the other two samples. The response pattern of Mexican American females suggests ambivalence, acceptance of female responsibility for rape, and some degree of resignation to the possibility of rape as a component of male-female sexuality. For example, the majority of Mexican American females agreed that most rapes could be avoided if women did not provoke them, but less than a third of the males shared this view. Mexican American females agreed by 77 percent that men can commit rape and get away with it; males supported that view by 88 percent. They agreed by 87 percent that men have sex urges they cannot control, while only 55 percent of the Mexican American men shared that belief. They agreed by 65 percent that most men are capable of committing rape; only 49 percent of males agreed. These females further evidenced their assumption of blame-responsibility for rape by an 85 percent agreement that women should fight and resist a rapist, a view supported by 89 percent of their male cohorts. Half of the women agreed that when a woman is raped her reputation is ruined, but only 41 percent of male respondents agreed with this assertion. By comparing the responses of all females in Tables 17 and 18, it appears that Mexican American females may be vulnerable to rape in more ways than one. Should they become victims, these data suggest that they would not only have to cope with the objective consequences of rape, but with their own subjectively perceived guilt and self-blame as well. Hence, they might be expected to have comparatively greater difficulty in coping with rape than Black or Anglo females. Indeed, our data on Mexican American victims show them to have suffered comparatively more from the experience of rape than either Black or Anglo victims.

The Dynamics of Male-Female Sexuality and Rape

To use the term *feminist* in discussing these findings related to beliefs about male-female sexuality can only be a generalization based on some very obvious myths (for example, "most rapes could be avoided if women did not provoke them or secretly want to be raped" is a blatant, nonfeminist stereotype) or on subjective judgments. On some of the thirteen items, however, there is no predictable feminist response (inferable from theory). Rather, some items are subject to idiosyncratic interpretation or to controversy.[3] For this reason (and in order to reduce the data), these thirteen items were factor analyzed for each of the three samples. The resulting factors represent underlying attitudes about male-female sexuality vis-à-vis rape (see Table 30, Appendix C for factor loadings).

ANGLOS

Factor One for Anglos is labeled *Male-Female Sexuality* and results from a bipolar acceptance/rejection of the view that rape is the product of the dynamics of normal male-female sexuality versus acceptance/rejection of rape as a result of emotional disturbance among males. Factor Two, labeled *Skepticism,* is also comprised of bipolar dimensions, acceptance/rejection as to the reality of rape (women may "ask for it") versus male responsibility (they frequently "get away with rape"). Factor Three clearly reflects concern with *Female Responsibility* in relation to rape, specifically with provocation, resistance, and the victim's reputation.

BLACKS

Factor One for Blacks is similar to Factor One for Anglos, but because it seems to represent a more strident theme, it was labeled *Sexual Conflict.* Not only does this factor include the view that rape is just another part of the interplay of male-female sexuality, but it also goes further by depicting a distrust and dislike for women in general. Factor Two, labeled *Blame-Skepticism,* expresses both a tendency toward victim-blaming and skepticism with respect to rape. Factor Three is difficult to interpret but apparently encompasses a concern that normal men (those who are not mentally disturbed) may be labeled rapists by disreputable females. The overriding theme of the factor seems to be the reputation of the victim; therefore it is labeled *Victim-Defined Rape.*

MEXICAN AMERICANS

Factor One for Mexican Americans appears to depict rape as an integral part of the dynamics of male-female sexuality. *Male-Female Sexuality* suggests that "women want to be raped" and that in response, "men will be men." Factor Two clearly suggests the belief that women harbor some kind of *Rape Wish.* Factor Three, *Sick Rapist,* is equally clear in representing rapists as emotionally disturbed woman-haters.

These factors will be collectively referred to as attitudes about male-female sexuality, and, again, the factoring procedure produced some common attitudinal themes across samples as well as some ethnic-specific factors. It is somewhat disconcerting to find attitudes perceiving rape as integral to the dynamics of "normal" male-female interaction (Anglos-Factor One, and Mexican Americans-Factor Two) or as a part of a built-in conflict between the sexes (Blacks-Factor One). Further, the thematic content of these three factors does not reflect or support the feminist assertion that all men are rapists (see Table 30, Appendix C). Rather, these factors represent a common thread of attitudes which not only suggest that it is the nature of men to rape, but that it is the nature of women to *want* to be victims. Skepticism, blame, and assessment of female responsibility are prevalent themes for both Anglos and Blacks. In terms of ethnic-specific factors, *Victim-Defined Rape* for Blacks no doubt reflects a skepticism about rape that has been compounded over the years as Whites have used rape as a tactic of social control. In essence, this factor represents a withholding of judgment on an alleged rape until the victim's reputation and background can be scrutinized. Factors Two and Three for Mexican Americans (*Rape Wish* and *Sick Rapist*) are particularly interesting when considered together. They suggest that both rapists and victims are subject to uncontrollable forces: females may be predisposed to rape because of some "rape wish," and men commit rape because they are mentally ill.

On Rape and Minority Risks

The comparisons we have drawn among the three samples, as well as of male-female responses within those samples, give some indication of how race-ethnicity, sex, and different experiences and life chances shape attitudes about rape, sex, and male-female sexuality. While the findings are generally consistent with the theoretical framework of racial-sexual stratification, an effort was made to inject some more direct measures of the ways in which race-ethnicity intervenes in relation to attitudes about rape. Specifically, an effort was made to quantify (1) the extent to which rape is perceived as an intergroup phenomenon, (2) perceived and/or experienced discrimination against minority rape victims and minority males as accused rapists, and (3) direct victimization experience with rape and/or other violent crimes.

Intergroup Versus Other Kinds of Rape

Statistics reveal that most reported rapes are intragroup (White-White or Black-Black). However, rape is frequently sensationalized by the media and feared by the public as an intergroup crime, especially a Black-White crime. In an effort to determine the extent to which persons would acknowledge a perception of rape as race-related, respondents were asked the following forced-choice question:

When men rape women, do you think they rape women who are:
(1) from their own race or ethnic group (for example, both the rapist and the victim are White, or both are Black, or both are Mexican American); or do you think men rape women . . .
(2) from a race or ethnic group different from their own (for example, Black men raping White women, or White men raping Mexican American or Black women)?

Table 19 shows the responses to this question by sample and sex. As is evident, some people refused to be forced into a choice because they insisted that a woman's color or ethnicity would not matter once a man decides to rape.

TABLE 19.   Beliefs About Intergroup Rape by Ethnic Group and Sex

Belief expressed that:		ANGLO		BLACK		MA	
		M	F	M	F	M	F
Men rape women of their	N	94	51	67	72	65	29
own race-ethnic group.	%	56	31	40	43	39	17
Men rape women from	N	32	80	66	64	93	53
different race-ethnic group.	%	19	48	40	38	56	31
It does not matter.	N	26	16	0	0	4	45
	%	15	10	—	—	2	26
No response/ don't know	N	17	19	34	33	5	46
	%	10	11	20	19	3	26
Totals	N	169	166	167	169	167	173
	%	100	100	100	100	100	100

With the exception of Anglo males, approximately one-third to one-half of all respondents saw rape as primarily *Intergroup*. Mexican American males (56 percent) and Anglo females (48 percent) were most likely to identify rape as intergroup. Mexican American males were the only ones for whom intergroup responses outnumbered all other responses combined. Black males were equally divided in viewing rape as inter- as opposed to intragroup (or other). Mexican American females were the most likely to see the inter- versus intragroup dichotomy as irrelevant; that is, if a man is going to commit rape, he will not be deliberately selective. This question may be one to which people had simply never given much thought, or it could be a question respondents were reluctant to answer honestly. For whatever reason, a substantial number of respondents said they did not know. If these ("don't know") responses are taken out of the tabulations in Table 19, close to half (42 to 57 percent) of the remaining respondents (except Anglo males) expressed the opinion that rape is an intergroup phenomenon. Since statistics on known rapes indicate that the majority are intragroup, these attitudes indicate a disjunction with reality that could be indicative of some degree of racism, some awareness of majority-minority conflict, or the fact that the media coverage of rapes may be slanted toward those of an intergroup nature.

Perceived or Experienced Discrimination and Rape

Four agree-disagree items dealt specifically with the respondent's perception (in some cases experience) of the "official" (medical, legal, judicial) treatment proferred minority rape victims and whether minority males are perceived as "unfairly accused" of raping White women. The questions dealt with Blacks and Mexican Americans separately, but responses on all four were summed for a composite score used as a measure of perceived or experienced minority *Discrimination*. As can be seen in Table 20, Black males were the most inclined to perceive minority victims and suspects as treated unfairly. Following Black males in descending order of perceived discrimination were: Black females, Anglo females, Mexican American males, Mexican American females, and Anglo males. Differences between the sexes are significant only for Anglos, while significant differences among the three samples are between Blacks and the other two ethnic groups. As shown in the lower part of Table 20, all males differ significantly, but differences among females are significant only for Blacks in comparison with Anglos and Mexican Americans. The mean scores represent perceptions of minority discrimination, as might be expected in view of the history of racism and sexism in America. Blacks perceive the greatest degree of discrimination, and Anglo males the least.

Victimization Experience-Knowledge

Near the end of the interview, respondents were asked if they had ever been a victim of rape (females) or sexual assault (males). Only seventeen Anglos (5 percent), six Blacks (2 percent), and eleven Mexican Americans (3 percent) admitted such victimization experience. The reported incidence of rape appears to be very low—a total of thirty-four victims out of a total of 1,011 interviews. Since the question was asked of both males and females (four males did report themselves as victims of sexual assault), this amounts to a rape victimization rate in the adult population of the city of approximately fifty-one Anglos, eighteen Blacks, and thirty-two Mexican Americans per 1,000 population. In addition to the question about rape/sexual assault, two other questions provide some further indication of experience with or knowledge about violent crime: "Have you ever been a victim of robbery, mugging, assault or any other violent crime?" and "Has any member of your family or any friend or acquaintance ever been a victim of rape, attempted rape, or sexual assault?" Responses to all three questions were summed to form a *Victimization* Score, ranging from 1 to 3 (reflecting the number of "yes" responses), and were taken as a measure of the respondent's knowledge and/or experience with regard to violent crime. As shown in Table 21, Black males reported greater exposure to, or experience with, violent crime than any other group, although they were followed closely by

TABLE 20.   Perceptions of Minority Discrimination by Ethnic Group and Sex

MINORITY DISCRIMINATION	ANGLO		BLACK		MEXICAN AMERICAN	
	M	*F*	*M*	*F*	*M*	*F*
Mean score	10.7	11.9	13.7	13.3	11.8	11.4
SD	3.0	2.6	2.8	1.9	2.4	2.2
Sig. by sex	.001		ns		ns	
Number	169	166	167	169	167	173

GROUP CONTRASTS BY RACE-ETHNICITY AND SEX: SIGNIFICANCE OF *t*-VALUES

	ANGLO-BLACK	ANGLO-MA	BLACK-MA
All	.001	ns	.001
Males	.001	.001	.001
Females	.001	ns	.001

Note: ns = not significant. Mean scores have a possible range of 4 to 16. High scores indicate perceived unequal (unfair) treatment of minorities.

Anglo females and then by Mexican American females. Black females and Mexican American males accrued the lowest Victimization Scores of the six groups. Anglo and Mexican American females were more likely than their male cohorts (for Mexican Americans the difference is significant) to have had victimization experience or knowledge. Black males have significantly higher Victimization Scores than Black females. All males differ significantly on Victimization, with Blacks ranking first and Mexican Americans last in terms of mean scores. The reported incidence of Victimization knowledge-experience was low for Black females in comparison with Anglo and Mexican American females. Consequently, Victimization Scores for Black females differ significantly from those of Anglos and Mexican Americans.

These findings, which show Anglos to be more familiar with violent crime than minorities, are contrary to other victimization data. Aside from some informal (and speculative) interviewer feedback, there are no explanations of why Anglos may have reported victimization experience more or minorities less than on other surveys, or why experience in the city of San Antonio may be different. Interviewers suggested that they "sensed" that some women were rape victims but did not want to admit it; in some cases,

TABLE 21.   Mean Victimization Scores by Ethnic Group and Sex

SCORES	ANGLO			BLACK			MA		
	ALL	*M*	*F*	*ALL*	*M*	*F*	*ALL*	*M*	*F*
Mean	.44	.36	.52	.38	.56	.21	.32	.15	.48
SD	.68	.66	.70	.68	.77	.51	.57	.39	.67
Sig. by sex		ns			.001			.001	
Number	335	169	166	336	167	169	340	167	173

GROUP CONTRASTS BY RACE-ETHNICITY AND SEX:
SIGNIFICANCE OF *t*-VALUES

	A-B	*A-MA*	*B-MA*
All	ns	.01	ns
Males	.01	.001	.001
Females	.001	ns	.001

Note: ns = not significant. Mean scores have a possible range of 1 to 3. The higher the score, the greater the experience with or knowledge about rape/sexual assault, or other crimes of violence.

they suspected the reason was related to incest. Male interviewers suggested that some men have difficulty admitting victimization experience to another male. One other possible contributing factor in these findings is that Whites may be more vulnerable—or they may subjectively feel more vulnerable—to crime in a city where they are a numerical minority, even though they are very much the dominant group in a sociological sense.

Summary

These data suggest that public responses to rape vary significantly across ethnic-racial groups and between males and females within groups. They also suggest that attitudes toward rape are not unidimensional but vary to some degree in terms of how rape is defined, the assessment of female fault, and willingness to prosecute the assailant. The findings also show that respondents seem to vary their judgments of forced sexual encounters in terms of the components of these situations—for example, relationship between assailant and victim, reputation and/or activity of victim, and use of a weapon and injury. However, beyond the stereotypic "good rape," there is little consensus in public judgments.

Respondents, regardless of race-ethnicity or sex, show support for both traditional sex roles and women's liberation. Perhaps related to the largely White, middle-class makeup of the women's movement, minorities (with the exception of Black females) appear to favor traditional male-female sex roles more than Anglos. This cannot be generalized, however, to a rejection of women's liberation because Blacks tend to be similar to Anglos in their approval of women's liberation behavior and stronger than Anglos in their agreement with beliefs consistent with women's liberation. While Mexican Americans are the least supportive of women's liberation, their support is greater than might be expected in light of their support of traditional sex roles. Of the underlying attitudinal dimensions extracted by use of factor analysis, the samples appear to share a dimension descriptive of some aspect of women's liberation-equality, while other dimensions are more ethnic-specific.

Measures of attitudes pertaining to male-female sexuality vis-à-vis rape reveal contradictions, ambivalence, and lack of consensus between samples (ethnic groups) and within samples (by sex). However, there was majority agreement on some items. For example, over half of all respondents (except Black females) indicated that women should fight and resist a rapist. Over half of all respondents agreed that a woman's reputation or past sexual history should have nothing to do with the question of rape. A majority of respondents indicated that rapists are mentally ill, but even greater proportions said that men can rape and get away with it. Some minority-related themes also emerge from these data. Among Blacks, responses from males and females on items relating to female sexuality are so far apart as to suggest a lack of understanding and even conflict between the sexes. Among Mexican Americans, a self-blame, guilt theme clearly emerges from females. The factors extracted from each sample help to clarify these ethnic-specific attitudinal dimensions about male-female sexuality and rape.

Several minority, race-related variables seem to reflect some of the most acute areas of racial inequality in relation to rape. However, operationalization and instrumentation of these measures are still unrefined and require additional work before they can become more than crude indicators of discrimination and victimization. Tentatively, the minority-related data suggest the following: just under one-fifth to over one-half of all respondents perceive rape as primarily an intergroup phenomenon. Black males are the most likely to perceive or to have experienced discrimination in relation to rape (directed toward victims or toward accused rapists). Anglo males perceive or have experienced less discrimination than other groups. Black males also reported the highest incidence in relation to violent crime victimization, but if the samples are taken as a whole, Anglos show the highest victimization experience, followed by Blacks and then by Mexican Americans.

Little effort has been made to interpret or explain these data. They "speak" and are descriptive of some of the judgments, attitudes, and beliefs that surround rape as a complex social phenomenon, no doubt shaped by experience and position in a racially-sexually stratified social system. In Chapter 8, we attempt to establish some causal, empirical linkages between attitudes about rape and the sex and race-related attitudes and beliefs described here.

Notes

1. Several additional scenarios (other than the nine included) were pretested and dropped from the final interview schedule in order to reduce the number to a more manageable level. Among those dropped was a *date-rape which involved no weapon*. It was overwhelmingly rejected as a credible rape by pretest respondents. Another scenario which described *hitchhiking with a stranger with no weapon* was dropped for the same reason.

2. Factors are underlying dimensions. In this case, they were rotated and extracted via the varimax procedure using iterations. They are, therefore, linear and orthogonal factors. For a description of this particular procedure, see Norman H. Nie, et al., *Statistical Package for the Social Sciences*, 2d ed. (New York: McGraw-Hill, 1975), pp. 468-514. For a more general discussion of factor analysis, see Jae-On Kim and Charles W. Mueller, *Factor Analysis: Statistical Methods and Practical Issues* (Beverly Hills, Calif.: Sage Publications, 1978).

3. For example, the statement, "Once a female is raped, her reputation is ruined . . . ," is subject to individual interpretation, and responses may vary in terms of reality versus what "ought to be." The statement that women should "fight and resist a rapist" is very controversial, even among the ranks of feminists. It is complicated by arguments that resistance may increase the likelihood of serious injury or death and, on the other hand, by some state laws which still require a show of resistance to meet the legal criteria of rape. Statements about male sexuality are equally subjective and/or controversial. For example, one could reason from a feminist perspective that the masculine socialization process builds in a propensity for hating women; on the other hand, some respondents might see such hate as a function of mental illness.

PREDICTING THE SECOND ASSAULT

8

It has been argued in Chapter 2 that rape, and some attitudes about rape, represent a convergence of racism and sexism in a system of racial-sexual stratification. Obviously, only a few of the propositions which this theory suggests can be tested here. However, several key theoretical relationships between variables derived from the theory and attitudes about rape can be examined. At the exploratory level, we were interested in determining whether attitudes about sex roles and/or women's liberation, beliefs about male-female sexuality, and race-related experiences/perceptions are empirically linked with attitudes about rape. We described some of these attitudes in Chapter 7 and now move on to the task of identifying variables with the power to predict and/or explain attitudes about rape for each of the three ethnic groups and for males and females within each.

The dependent variable which is the focus of this chapter is Attitudes About Rape. Since such attitudes were conceptualized and operationalized as three-dimensional, there are in reality three dependent variables—Rape, Fault, and Court Scores—derived from responses to the nine research scenarios. A tendency to define the incidents in the scenarios as rape, not to blame the victim, and an inclination toward willingness to prosecute the assailant were labeled feminist attitudes about rape. From the theoretical framework of Chapter 2, fourteen independent variables were selected and examined in terms of the contribution each might make toward explaining and/or predicting the three attitudinal dimensions of rape. Prediction and explanation are separate but interrelated questions. Explanation has to do with how powerful the independent variables are in explaining the variation in the dependent variable(s). This is, of necessity, a quantitative question. For example, if the independent variables were found to explain 25 percent of the variation in either Rape, Fault, or Court Scores, we would still have left 75 percent unexplained, even though we may have moved closer to explaining this phenomenon than has ever before been done. The question of prediction, on the other hand, can be translated into what variables we should look for among Anglos, Blacks, and Mexican Americans if we want some reliable indication of whether their attitudes about rape will tend to be comparatively feminist or nonfeminist. This is also a quantitative question in the sense of attending to *significant,* independent predictors—that is, those which are statistically associated at a certain level of probability (in this case, .05 or beyond) with attitudes about rape. Such variables can thus be said to have significant predictive power and can be utilized to formulate models with inferential value so that, given a similar research design, these models should work to predict attitudes about rape.

The fourteen independent variables comprise four categories (subsets): demographic characteristics, sex-role attitudes, beliefs about male-female sexuality, and minority-related rape risks. Before presenting our findings, these variables will be reviewed briefly, and some theoretical hypotheses will be offered with specific predictions as to the direction independent variables are expected to take relative to the dependent variables.

The Independent Variables

Demographic Characteristics

Because we wanted to be sure that our sex and minority-related at-titudinal variables were not simply disguised socioeconomic differences, we used demographic characteristics statistically as control variables. However, based on a general assumption that "liberal" (as opposed to conservative) attitudes are likely to be associated with high socioeconomic characteristics and young age, and based on some specific knowledge of the feminist, anti-rape movement and its supporters, we were able to theoretically predict the direction of relationships between demographic variables and attitudes about rape as follows:

1. Low (young) age is expected to be associated with feminist attitudes about rape (low Rape, Fault, and Court Scores).
2. High education is expected to be associated with feminist attitudes about rape.
3. High income is expected to be associated with feminist attitudes about rape.
4. Female sex is expected to be associated with feminist attitudes about rape.
5. Non-Catholic (dichotomized from Catholic) is expected to be associated with feminist attitudes about rape.

Sex-Role Attitudes

Three factors (quantified as factor scores) for each sample (the derivation of which was explained in Chapter 7) were used as measures of attitudes about sex roles. The theoretical hypothesis is that (for all samples) *attitudes reflective of nontraditionality in sex roles and/or supportive of women's liberation will be associated with feminist attitudes about rape; conversely, attitudes supportive of traditional sex roles will be associated with nonfeminist attitudes about rape.* It is not expected that all factors will be significant predictors of Attitudes About Rape, but it is expected that at least one will be significant on one or more dimensions (R, F, C Scores) for each sample, and such a finding can be viewed as support for the hypothesis. The direction each sex-role factor is expected to take in relation to the Rape, Fault, and Court Scores is expressed in the research hypotheses below in terms of feminist-nonfeminist attitudes about rape.

ANGLOS
1. High support for women's *Liberation* (SR1) is expected to be associated with feminist attitudes about rape (low R, F, C Scores).
2. High support for *Freedom-Equality* (SR2) in sex roles is expected to be associated with feminist attitudes about rape.
3. High adherence to *Stereotypes* (SR3) about male-female sex roles is expected to be associated with nonfeminist attitudes about rape (high R, F, C Scores).

BLACKS
1. High *Traditionality* (SR1) in sex roles is expected to be associated with nonfeminist attitudes about rape.
2. High *Modified Liberation* (SR2), combining liberation and traditionality in sex-role attitudes, is expected to be associated with feminist attitudes about rape.
3. High *Liberation* (SR3) in relation to sex roles is expected to be associated with feminist attitudes about rape.

MEXICAN AMERICANS
1. High support for an authoritarian *Male Role* (SR1) is expected to be associated with nonfeminist attitudes about rape.
2. High *Equality* (SR2) in sex roles is expected to be associated with feminist attitudes about rape.
3. High support for a traditional *Female Role* (SR3) is expected to be associated with nonfeminist attitudes about rape.

Beliefs About Male-Female Sexuality and Rape

Three factors for each sample were used as measures of the dynamics of male-female sexuality vis-à-vis rape. The theoretical hypothesis is that *beliefs which attribute rape to the nature and/or behavior of females or to the dynamics of "normal" male-female sexuality are expected to be associated with nonfeminist attitudes about rape; conversely, beliefs which attribute rape to the nature and/or behavior of males are expected to be associated with feminist attitudes about rape.* On a more specific level, research hypotheses were formulated for each sample. Again, the theoretical hypothesis can be accepted if any of the following significantly predicts at least one dimension of Attitudes About Rape for a given sample.

ANGLOS
1. High *Male-Female Sexuality* (MF1), the belief that rape is part of normal male-

female interaction, is expected to be associated with nonfeminist attitudes about rape (high R, F, C Scores).

2. High *Skepticism* (MF2) about the reality of rape is expected to be associated with nonfeminist attitudes about rape.
3. High *Female Responsibility* (MF3), the tendency to blame women for rape, is expected to be associated with nonfeminist attitudes about rape.

BLACKS

1. High *Sexual Conflict* (MF1), where rape is perceived as built into the conflictual relationship between males and females, is expected to be associated with nonfeminist attitudes about rape.
2. High *Blame-Skepticism* (MF2), the tendency to doubt that rape is real and, if it is, to blame the female, is expected to be associated with nonfeminist attitudes about rape.
3. High *Victim-Defined Rape* (MF3), the tendency to define rape in terms of the reputation of the victim, is expected to be associated with nonfeminist attitudes about rape.

MEXICAN AMERICANS

1. High *Male-Female Sexuality* (MF1), viewing rape as a part of normal male-female interaction, is expected to be associated with nonfeminist attitudes about rape.
2. High *Rape Wish* (MF2), the belief that women harbor a need or desire to be raped, is expected to be associated with nonfeminist attitudes about rape.
3. High *Sick Rapist* (MF3), the tendency to see rape as a product of mental illness, is expected to be associated with feminist attitudes about rape (low R, F, C Scores).

Minority-Related Rape Risks

The three measures used to represent minority-related rape risks require further work before they can be taken as adequate measures of racism in relation to rape. However, it is expected that at least one of the three will be significantly associated with one or more dimensions of Attitudes About Rape for each sample. The inclusion of these race-related variables assumes a minority-majority difference, and hypotheses are in some cases differentiated by sample and by one of the three dependent variables. For example, based on what is known about minority attitudes toward the criminal justice system, some theoretical differences can be hypothesized with regard to willingness to prosecute alleged rapists (as opposed to the other two dimensions of attitudes about rape).

VICTIMIZATION

Given the fact that minorities, as groups, have typically been more victimized by violent crime than the majority population, this measure was conceptualized as minority-related, and its theoretical association with the dependent variables is expected to vary by samples as follows:

For Anglos, high Victimization is expected to be associated with feminist attitudes about rape. That is, to have some experience as a victim will predispose one toward victim-oriented, low Rape, Fault, and Court Scores.

For the minority samples, high Victimization is expected to be associated with feminist attitudes on definement of rape and assessment of female fault, but nonfeminist attitudes with regard to prosecution. That is, experience as a victim will cause more victim-orientation, resulting in lower Rape and Fault Scores, but experience with the criminal justice system will negatively influence willingness to prosecute, resulting in higher Court Scores.

DISCRIMINATION

This is a measure of the respondent's perception of the treatment given minority rape victims and the perception of minority males as falsely accused of raping White women. For two reasons, it is likely that this measure represents something different for Anglos compared with minority respondents: (1) Minority discrimination can only be perceived by Anglos, whereas Blacks and Mexican Americans have experienced it directly or indirectly. (2) Minority discrimination vis-à-vis rape is perceived by minorities almost entirely as minority males falsely accused of raping White women. These expected differences, particularly the latter, are the rationale for the following hypothesized relationships between Discrimination and attitudes about rape.

For Anglos, high Discrimination is expected to be associated with feminist attitudes about rape. That is, high perceived Discrimination will be associated with low Rape, Fault, and Court Scores.

For minorities, high Discrimination is expected to be associated with nonfeminist attitudes about rape. That is, high perceived/experienced Discrimination will be associated with high Rape, Fault, and Court Scores.

INTERGROUP

This nominal variable represents a dichotomized perception of rape as intergroup versus other (intragroup, neither, or both). Since the facts about known rapes show them to be predominantly intragroup, to view rape primarily as intergroup may indicate a lack of substantive knowledge or a denial of reality, perhaps suggesting some degree of racism.

For Anglos, high Intergroup perception is expected to be associated with nonfeminist definement of rape and assessment of female fault, but with high willingness to prosecute alleged assailants (presumably of another race or ethnicity). Perception of rape as an intergroup phenomenon will predispose persons toward high Rape and Fault Scores, but toward low Court Scores, thus revealing a convergence of both sexism and racism.

For minorities, high Intergroup perception is expected to be associated with nonfeminist attitudes about rape. That is, perception of rape as intergroup will be associated with high Rape, Fault, and Court Scores, in essence denying the reality of rape, placing blame on the victim, and refusing to prosecute the alleged assailant. Again, from the minority perspective, these relationships represent a convergence of sexism and racism.

Data Analysis and Procedure

While most readers are no doubt less concerned with the minute details of data analysis than with the substantive findings, it is important that some information be provided. Too many research efforts have been discounted on the basis of poorly designed and executed data analysis. For example, we found that we had a problem with the dependent variables which needed to be resolved before the data were analyzed. Specifically, although attitudes about rape were conceptualized as three-dimensional, we found that Rape, Fault, and Court Scores were not independent of one another and, in fact, were significantly correlated for all three samples. Based on some substantive knowledge relating to attitudes about rape and use of logical inference with regard to the direction certain cause-and-effect relationships might take, statistical procedures were used to remove the interrelatedness of the dependent variables. That is, the influence of Fault Scores was removed from Rape Scores, and the influence of both Rape and Fault Scores was removed from Court Scores *before* any statistical relationships between independent and dependent variables were examined.[1] On another matter in relation to statistical procedure, we decided to consider the power of demographic variables *before* the more theoretically relevant sex and race-related variables. This was done for two reasons: (1) there is evidence that attitudes conceptualized as liberal-conservative are consistently associated with some socioeconomic characteristics; and (2) in order to more rigorously test race and sex-related variables, demographic variables were first allowed to explain as much variation in Attitudes About Rape as possible. Finally, the statistical procedure used to test the relationship between the fourteen independent variables and the three Attitudes About Rape measures was multiple regression analysis. (For specific details, see Appendix D.)

Findings

Tables 22, 23, and 24 summarize the variables that were found to be *significant predictors* of Attitudes About Rape (by sample and by sex) and show the amount of variance explained in Rape, Fault, and Court Scores by all independent variables working together. Tables 31 through 39 in Appendix D should be consulted for complete statistical findings, plus a listing of all the variables that survived each regression analysis with the significant

TABLE 22. Variables that Predict Attitudes About Rape and Explained Variance by Ethnic Group

ANGLOS	BLACKS	MEXICAN AMERICANS
DEFINEMENT OF RAPE		
Fault Scores	Fault Scores	Fault Scores
Female Responsibility (MF3)	Victim-Defined Rape (MF3)	−Age
Skepticism (MF2)	Modified Liberation (SR2)	Rape Wish (MF2)
	Discrimination	Female Role (SR3)
	Income	Sick Rapist (MF3)
		Education
		Sex
Explained variance = 31%	33%	27%
ASSESSMENT OF FEMALE FAULT		
−Sex	Sexual Conflict (MF1)	Female Role (SR3)
Female Responsibility (MF3)	−Age	−Rape Wish (MF2)
Male-Female Sexuality (MF1)	Victim-Defined Rape (MF3)	
Liberation (SR1)	Traditionality (SR1)	
	Modified Liberation (SR2)	
	−Victimization	
Explained variance = 13%	13%	6%
WILLINGNESS TO PROSECUTE		
Rape Scores	Rape Scores	Rape Scores
Fault Scores	Sex	Sex
−Sex	Discrimination	Female Role (SR3)
Victimization	−Income	−Equality (SR2)
		−Education
Explained variance = 71%	57%	57%

Note: The minus sign (−) denotes relationships that were not in the predicted direction.

TABLE 23. Variables that Predict Attitudes About Rape and Explained Variance for Males by Ethnic Group

ANGLOS	BLACKS	MEXICAN AMERICANS
	DEFINEMENT OF RAPE	
Fault Scores	Fault Scores	Fault Scores
Female Responsibility (MF3)	Modified Liberation (SR2)	Income
Skepticism (MF2)	Discrimination	Rape Wish (MF2)
Discrimination		
Intergroup		
Explained variance = 30%	39%	33%
	ASSESSMENT OF FEMALE FAULT	
Female Responsibility (MF3)	−Vicitmization	Female Role (SR3)
Intergroup	Traditionality (SR1)	Equality (SR2)
		Religion
Explained variance = 9%	22%	12%
	WILLINGNESS TO PROSECUTE	
Rape Scores	Rape Scores	Rape Scores
Education	Liberation (SR3)	Rape Wish (MF2)
Fault Scores	Discrimination	
−Income	−Age	
Intergroup		
Explained variance = 67%	65%	65%

Note: The minus sign (−) denotes relationships that were not in the predicted direction.

TABLE 24. Variables that Predict Attitudes About Rape and Explained Variance for Females by Ethnic Group

ANGLOS	BLACKS	MEXICAN AMERICANS
	DEFINEMENT OF RAPE	
Fault Scores Female Responsibility (MF3) Skepticism (MF2) Freedom-Equality (SR2)	Fault Scores Victim-Defined Rape (MF3)	Fault Scores Religion Equality (SR2) Sick Rapist (MF3)
Explained variance = 35%	29%	28%
	ASSESSMENT OF FEMALE FAULT	
Female Responsibility (MF3) Liberation (SR1) Male-Female Sexuality (MF1)	Income	Female Role (SR3)
Explained variance = 14%	9%	7%
	WILLINGNESS TO PROSECUTE	
Rape Scores Fault Scores	Rape Scores Fault Scores −Income −Liberation (SR3)	Rape Scores Fault Scores Female Role (SR3)
Explained variance = 74%	40%	50%

Note: The minus sign (−) denotes relationships that were not in the predicted direction.

predictive *and* explanatory variables noted. As shown in Table 22, the independent variables jointly explain (on a sample level) from 27 to 33 percent of the variance in Rape Scores, 6 to 13 percent of the variance in Fault Scores, and 57 to 71 percent of the variance in Court Scores. When the sexes are considered separately (Tables 23 and 24), in most cases the explained variance is somewhat lower than for the samples as a whole. While the proportion of explained variance is respectable for exploratory survey work, the largest proportion in any of the three dimensions of Attitudes About Rape is attributable to another dependent variable: definement of Rape in willingness to prosecute (Court Scores) and assessment of Fault in definement of Rape. Nonetheless, the remaining sex and minority-related variables were significant in their contributions to the explained variance in all but one instance (based on Subset F; see Tables 31–33 and 37–39, Appendix D).

These findings provide a moderately satisfactory explanation of the kinds of attitudinal and demographic characteristics that are significant determinants of how rape is defined. Furthermore, they provide an adequate explanation of the kinds of variables that are involved in decision-making with regard to prosecution of alleged rapists. However, the findings are very weak in explaining the kinds of attitudes and characteristics that account for the tendency to assess fault or blame to the victim in rape situations. Moving from explanation to prediction, the variables shown (in order of predictive power) in Tables 22, 23, and 24 are perhaps of more interest because they are significantly and independently associated with the dependent variables. These predictors of attitudes about rape are used in examining four basic research questions upon which our discussion is based.

Do Specific Demographic Characteristics Predict (1) Definement of Sexual Encounters as Rape; (2) Assessment of Female Fault; and/or (3) Willingness to Prosecute Alleged Rapists?

Definement of Rape and Demographic Characteristics

Anglos: No demographic characteristics predict Rape Scores.

Blacks: Income predicts Rape Scores; high income is associated with feminist definitions of sexual encounters as rape.

Mexican Americans: Sex, Age, and Education predict Rape Scores. Females (more than males), older (more than younger) persons, and those of high education are associated with feminist definitions of rape. Among males, high Income is associated with feminist definitions of rape and among females, Catholics are less inclined than non-Catholics toward feminist definitions of rape.

Conclusion: Demographic characteristics predict how minorities will define rape situations, but they are not predictive for Anglos. In at least one instance, all demographic variables were found significantly associated with definement of rape for either Blacks or Mexican Americans (or for males or females within these samples). Except for Age, all vary in the predicted direction.

Assessment of Female Fault and Demographic Characteristics

Anglos: Sex is a predictor of Fault Scores; males are more likely than females to assess low female fault in rape situations.

Blacks: Age predicts Fault Scores; older persons are less likely than younger ones to blame the female for her rape. For females, high Income is associated with low assessment of female fault.

Mexican Americans: No demographic variables predict Fault Scores for the sample as a whole, but for males, Catholics are inclined toward high assessment of female fault.

Conclusion: Few demographic variables are significant predictors of assessment of female fault, and they are either ethnic or ethnic-sex specific: Sex for Anglos; Age for Blacks; Income for Black females; and Catholic religion for Mexican American males. Two of the four variables that predict fault do not work in the predicted direction—Sex for Anglos and Age for Blacks.

Willingness to Prosecute and Demographic Characteristics

Anglos: Sex is a predictor of Court Scores for Anglos; males are more willing than females to prosecute alleged rapists. For males considered separately, both high Education and low Income are associated with high willingness to prosecute alleged rapists.

Blacks: Sex and Income predict Court Scores; females are more willing than males to prosecute alleged rapists, and persons of low income are more willing than those of higher income to prosecute. When the sexes are considered separately, older Age for males and low Income for females predict high willingness to prosecute.

Mexican Americans: Sex and Education are significantly associated with Court Scores. Females are more willing to prosecute than males, and persons of low education are more willing to prosecute than those of high education.

Conclusions: Demographic variables appear to be more important as predictors of willingness to prosecute than of definement of rape and assessment of female fault. As often as not, however, the direction of the relationship is contrary to that predicted. (1) Sex is consistently associated with willingness to prosecute across all samples; however, it works in different directions. Minority females are more willing than minority males to prosecute alleged rapists, while among Anglos, the males are more willing to prosecute. (2) Of six other significant relationships between demographic variables and willingness to prosecute, only one (Education for Anglos) is in the predicted direction.

Do Attitudes About Sex Roles Predict (1) Definement of Sexual Encounters as Rape; (2) Assessment of Female Fault; and/or (3) Willingness to Prosecute Alleged Rapists?

Definement of Rape and Sex Roles

Anglos: No significant relationships are found for Anglos as a whole, but for females, high support of *Freedom-Equality* (SR2) in sex roles is associated with feminist definitions of rape.

Blacks: For all Blacks (and males in particular), support for *Modified Liberation* (SR2) is associated with feminist definitions of rape.

Mexican Americans: For all Mexican Americans, high support of a traditional *Female Role* (SR3) is associated with nonfeminist definitions of rape, and for females, high support for *Equality* (SR2) in sex roles is predictive of feminist definitions of rape.

Conclusions: The theoretical hypothesis for sex-role attitudes and definement of sexual encounters is supported. Attitudes reflective of nontraditionality in sex roles and/or supportive of women's liberation are associated with feminist definitions of rape, while traditionality in sex roles is associated with nonfeminist definitions. (1) Attitudes supportive of women's liberation-sexual equality cut across racial-ethnic lines to predict feminist definitions of rape situations for females in all samples and for Blacks of both sexes. (2) Attitudes supportive of a traditional female role among Mexican Americans are associated with nonfeminist definitions of rape situations.

Assessment of Female Fault and Sex Roles

Anglos: High *Liberation* (SR1) is associated with low assessment of female fault for the sample as a whole and for females in particular.

Blacks: High *Traditionality* (SR1) in sex roles predicts high assessment of female fault for all Blacks and for males in particular. High support for *Modified Liberation* (SR2) is associated with low assessment of female fault for the sample as a whole.

Mexican Americans: Adherence to a traditional *Female Role* (SR3) is associated with high assessment of female fault for the sample as a whole and for both males and females separately. For males, support for sex-role *Equality* (SR2) is linked with low assessment of female fault.

Conclusions: The theoretical hypothesis is supported for sex-role attitudes and assessment of female fault. (1) Attitudes supportive of liberation and/or sex-role equality cut across racial-ethnic and sex categories to predict low assessment of female fault for all Anglos, all Blacks, and Mexican American males. (2) Traditionality in sex roles for Blacks and adherence to a traditional female role for Mexican Americans are both associated with high assessment of female fault in rape situations.

Willingness to Prosecute and Sex Roles

Anglos: No sex-role variables predict willingness to prosecute.

Blacks: No sex-role variables are associated with willingness to prosecute for Blacks as a whole, but high *Liberation* (SR3) is associated with willingness to prosecute for both males and females considered separately. However, the relationship works in different directions. For males, high Liberation predicts high willingness to prosecute alleged rapists, while for females (contrary to prediction), it is associated with low willingness to prosecute.

Mexican Americans: High support for *Female Role* (SR3) and for *Equality* (SR2) are both associated with low willingness to prosecute; the latter relationship is contrary to that predicted. High support for Female Role is also associated with low willingness to prosecute for females considered separately.

Conclusions: The theoretical hypothesis regarding sex-role attitudes and willingess to prosecute alleged rapists is given support only for Mexican Americans. (1) Attitudes supportive of a traditional female role predict low willingness to prosecute among Mexican Americans as a whole, as well as for females considered separately. (2) Attitudes about women's liberation-sex role equality predict willingness to prosecute for both minority samples. However, the direction of the relationships for Black females and for Mexican Americans as a whole is contrary to that predicted.

Do Beliefs About Male-Female Sexuality Predict (1) Definement of Sexual Encounters as Rape; (2) Assessment of Female Fault; and/or (3) Willingness to Prosecute Alleged Rapists?

Definement of Rape and Male-Female Sexuality

Anglos: For Anglos as a whole, as well as for both males and females considered separately, *Skepticism* (MF2) and *Female Responsibility* (MF3) are associated with nonfeminist definitions of rape situations.

Blacks: For Blacks as a whole, and for Black females in particular, *Victim-Defined Rape* (MF3) is associated with nonfeminist definitions of rape.

Mexican Americans: Those who believe that women harbor a *Rape Wish* (MF2) are likely to be nonfeminist in their definitions of rape situations, while those who believe that rapists are sick (MF3) are likely to be feminist in their definitions of rape. For males considered separately, *Rape Wish* (MF2) predicts nonfeminist definitions of rape, while for females, *Sick Rapist* (MF3) is still predictive of feminist definitions of rape.

Conclusions: These findings lend support to the theoretical relationship hypothesized between beliefs about male-female sexuality and definement of sexual encounters as rape. The beliefs that predict how rape situations are defined are apparently ethnic-specific, but all work in the predicted direction. (1) For Anglos, a tendency toward skepticism and assignment of female responsibility in rape situations predict nonfeminist definitions of rape. (2) For Blacks, a concern with the victim's reputation is linked with nonfeminist definitions of rape situations. (3) For Mexican Americans, belief in the existence of a rape wish is associated with nonfeminist definitions of rape situations, while belief that rape is perpetrated by sick, emotionally disturbed males is associated with feminist definitions of rape.

Assessment of Female Fault and Male-Female Sexuality

Anglos: High support for *Male-Female Sexuality* (MF1) and *Female Responsibility* (MF3) are associated with high assessment of female fault for the sample as a whole and for males and females considered separately.

Blacks: High *Sexual Conflict* (MF1) and *Victim-Defined Rape* (MF3) are associated with high assessment of female fault.

Mexican Americans: Belief in the existence of a female *Rape Wish* (MF2) is associated with low assessment of female fault; the direction of this relationship is contrary to that predicted.

Conclusions: These findings lend support for the theoretical relationship hypothesized between male-female sexuality and assessment of female fault in rape situations, and with one exception, all relationships are in the predicted direction. (1) Viewing rape as an integral part of male-female sexuality, or sexual conflict, predicts high assessment of female fault for Anglos and Blacks and especially for Anglo females. (2) Other male-female sexuality factors which predict assessment of female fault are ethnic-specific, but all relate to the nature or behavior of women: (a) for Anglos, a tendency to hold females responsible for rape is associated with high assessment of female fault; (b) for Blacks, judging rape in terms of the victim's reputation predicts high assessment of female fault; and (c) for Mexican Americans, belief in a rape wish predicts low assessment of female fault.

Willingness to Prosecute and Male-Female Sexuality

Anglos: No beliefs about male-female sexuality predict willingness to prosecute alleged rapists.

Blacks: No beliefs about male-female sexuality predict willingness to prosecute alleged rapists.

Mexican Americans: Belief in a female *Rape Wish* (MF2) predicts low willingness to prosecute for Mexican American males.

Conclusion: These findings provide little support for the theoretically hypothesized relationship between beliefs about male-female sexuality and willingness to prosecute alleged rapists. Only for Mexican American males does one of the male-female sexuality factors predict willingness to prosecute. That is, Mexican American males who believe that women want to be raped are unwilling to prosecute those assailants.

Do Perceptions of Minority-Related Rape Risks (Victimization, Discrimination, and Intergroup) Predict (1) Definement of Sexual Encounters as Rape; (2) Assessment of Female Fault; and/or (3) Willingness to Prosecute Alleged Rapists?

Definement of Rape and Victimization

Victimization is not independently linked with definement of rape situations for any of the samples or sex subgroups.

Conclusion: Victimization does not predict the definement of sexual encounters as rape.

Assessment of Female Fault and Victimization

Anglos: No relationship was found between Victimization and assessment of female fault.

Blacks: High Victimization experience is associated with high assessment of female fault in rape situations for the sample as a whole and for males in particular.

Mexican Americans: No relationship was found between Victimization and assessment of female fault.

Conclusion: Only for Blacks, and especially for Black males, was a relationship found between Victimization experience and assessment of female fault in rape situations. Blacks who have experience as victims are likely to assess high female fault; the direction of this relationship is contrary to that predicted.

Willingness to Prosecute and Victimization

Anglos: High Victimization experience is associated with willingness to prosecute alleged rapists.

Blacks: No relationship was found between Victimization experience and willingness to prosecute alleged rapists.

Mexican Americans: No relationship was found between Victimization experience and willingness to prosecute alleged rapists.

Conclusion: Only for Anglos was a relationship found between victimization experience and willingness to prosecute. The direction is as predicted; victimization experience increases one's willingness to prosecute alleged rapists.

Definement of Rape and Discrimination

Anglos: Discrimination is significantly associated with definitions of rape for Anglo males in a classical kind of liberal-conservative linkage. Males who perceive high minority discrimination are inclined toward feminist definitions of rape situations.

Blacks: Discrimination is significantly associated with definement of rape for all Blacks, and Black males in particular. Blacks who perceive or have experienced high minority discrimination tend toward nonfeminist definitions of rape situations.

Mexican Americans: There was no relationship found between Discrimination and definement of rape situations.

Conclusion: As predicted, perceived or experienced discrimination against minorities as victims or as suspected rapists influences Anglo males toward feminist definitions of rape, but influences Blacks toward more nonfeminist definitions.

Assessment of Female Fault and Discrimination

Discrimination is not associated with assessment of female fault for any of the samples or subgroups.

Conclusion: Discrimination does not predict assessment of female fault.

Willingness to Prosecute and Discrimination

Anglos: No relationship was found between Discrimination and willingness to prosecute alleged rapists.

Blacks: High Discrimination is associated with low willingness to prosecute alleged rapists for all Blacks and for Black males in particular.

Mexican Americans: No relationship was found between Discrimination and willingness to prosecute alleged rapists.

Conclusion: Blacks who have experienced or perceived discrimination vis-à-vis rape tend to be unwilling to prosecute alleged rapists. The direction of this relationship is as predicted.

Definement of Rape and Intergroup

Anglos: Intergroup is linked with definement of rape for Anglo males only; those who perceive rape as an intergroup phenomenon are inclined toward nonfeminist definitions of rape.

Blacks: There was no relationship found between Intergroup and definement of rape situations.

Mexican Americans: No relationship was found between Intergroup and rape definitions.

Conclusion: Where rape is perceived as primarily an intergroup phenomenon, Anglo males are comparatively nonfeminist in defining sexual encounters as rape.

Assessment of Female Fault and Intergroup

Anglos: Anglo males who perceive rape as primarily an Intergroup phenomenon are more likely to assess female fault in rape situations than those who perceive rape as intragroup or other.

Blacks: No relationship was found between Intergroup and assessment of female fault.

Mexican Americans: No relationship was found between Intergroup and assessment of female fault.

Conclusion: The perception of rape as primarily an intergroup phenomenon is associated with a tendency to assess high female fault in rape situations for Anglo males, but not for other groups.

Willingness to Prosecute and Intergroup

Anglos: Anglo males who perceive rape as Intergroup are more willing than others to prosecute alleged rapists.

Blacks: No relationship was found between Intergroup and willingness to prosecute alleged rapists.

Mexican Americans: No relationship was found between Intergroup and willingness to prosecute alleged rapists.

Conclusion: The perception of rape as primarily as intergroup phenomenon is associated with high willingness to prosecute alleged rapists for Anglo males, but not for other groups.

Summary—Discussion

Demographic Characteristics and Attitudes About Rape

In twenty-seven regression runs (see Tables, Appendix D), the five demographic variables were found to be significant predictors of the three rape measures a total of nineteen times, fifteen times involving the minority samples. In almost half of these cases, however (nine out of nineteen), the demographic variables worked in a direction contrary to that predicted. In two findings, males were more feminist in their attitudes than females; in three cases, higher income respondents were less feminist than lower income respondents; in three findings, older respondents proved more feminist than younger ones; and in one case, more highly educated respondents were less feminist in attitudes than those with lower education. Six of these nine negative findings involve the dependent variable of willingness to prosecute, and six involve minority samples or sex subgroups.

Predictions with regard to the association between demographic characteristics and Attitudes About Rape were made on the basis of previous research (establishing a link between "liberal" attitudes and high socioeconomic characteristics) as well as an educated guess based on the impact of the women's movement on women, the young, and the middle classes. Apparently, this may not have been a good basis for prediction where minorities are concerned, at least in relation to one dimension of Attitudes About Rape—willingness to presecute. It seems clear that willingness to prosecute alleged rapists is problematic for Blacks and Mexican Americans, although this should come as no surprise given the perspective of Chapter 2. Still, it is important to point out that, while predictions involving minorities were in the "wrong" direction six times, they were significant and in the "right" direction nine times. Only two of those "right" predictions, however, involve the question of prosecution, and both of these have to do with sex—that is, females were more willing to prosecute than males.

These findings related to demographic characteristics and Attitudes About Rape suggest that risk, perceived or real, which amounts to a kind of vested interest in rape, may be the best predictor of attitudes about rape. The higher the vested interest of certain groups (or categories) of people, the greater the tendency to react defensively. Such defensiveness may be manifested in the form of conservative or nonfeminist attitudes about rape which shift to more feminist or liberal attitudes as the risks diminish or as potential victimization is reduced.

SEX

Sex was significantly associated with the dependent variable proportionately more than any other demographic characteristic (five out of nine possibilities). Obviously, the greatest impact of sex on any of the three measures of Attitudes About Rape was that of willingness to prosecute. It was significantly associated with Court Scores for all three samples. However, while minority females were more willing than their male counterparts to prosecute alleged rapists, among Anglos, males were more willing to prosecute. Anglo males were also less likely than Anglo females to assess female fault in rape situations.

Apparently, minority males perceive a sufficiently high degree of threat in relation to rape cases that they represent a kind of anti-prosecution force working counter to the vested interest of minority females as potential victims. This perceived risk may represent a tendency among minority males to see themselves as the accused, or it may represent a more generalized distrust of the criminal justice system (for both victims and the accused). Anglo males, on the other hand, were more feminist than Anglo females on two of the three rape measures (assessment of female fault and willingness to prosecute). There are several viable explanations for these sex and racial-ethnic differences: (1) While the findings suggest that Anglo females are inclined toward "victim-blaming," this may be their way of dissociating themselves from culpable females in order to provide some insulation against the threat of rape. (2) By comparison, Anglo males may be more feminist than females because rape poses little threat to them. As suspects or as potential victims, Anglo males have less reason than females *or* minority males to react defensively. Middle-class Anglo males do not have a history which leads them to distrust the criminal justice system or to view the charge of rape as a means of keeping them in their "place" in a racially stratified society; minority males do have such a history. (3) Given that Anglo males were the only group for whom there was a significant association between perception of rape as an intergroup phenomenon and all three dimensions of Attitudes About Rape, there is some support for the view that rape is symbolic of both racism and sexism for some White males.

INCOME AND EDUCATION

Next to Sex, Income was the demographic variable most frequently linked with Attitudes About Rape. It was significantly associated with the dependent variables six times, but in three cases it took a direction contrary to that predicted, always in relation to willingness to prosecute (for all Blacks, for Black females, and for Anglo males). Again, vested interest in the form of perceived risk is suggested as an explanation. Higher income males may feel that they are vulnerable to false and vindictive accusations of rape, and higher income Black females could suffer the loss of reputation and/or community support should they choose to prosecute a rape case. A similar negative finding is the relationship between Education and willingness to prosecute for Mexican Americans. Contrary to prediction (and other associations between Education and Attitudes About Rape), high education for Mexican Americans is associated with low willingness to prosecute alleged rapists. This may suggest that better educated persons perceive more risk in relation to prosecution of a rape case, or it may simply reflect a high level of distrust for the criminal justice system.

AGE

The findings with regard to age are perhaps the most interesting and unexpected of the relationships between demographic variables and Attitudes About Rape. Age was significantly and independently linked with one of the dependent variables only three times. All three cases involve minorities, however, and the direction is contrary to that predicted. For Blacks, older age was significantly associated with low assessment of female fault; for Black males, older age predicted willingness to prosecute; and older Mexican Americans were more inclined than younger ones to define sexual encounters as rape. While the prediction regarding Age and feminism was based on the rationale that young people are more "liberal" in their attitudes and have been influenced to a greater extent by the women's movement than older persons, this logic does not take into account diminishing vested interest. Specifically, rape is traditionally a crime perpetrated by young men against young women. Young people of both sexes—and especially young minorities—have a vested interest in rape: females as potential victims and males as the high-risk suspect group. Young minorities who are conservative in defining rape and who are prone to victim-blaming are perhaps being defensive and self-protective; whereas, older persons are further removed from the risk and threat of rape and, therefore, can better afford to be "liberal" or feminist in their judgments. Young Black males, with their history of oppression via the charge of rape, certainly have enough vested interest and distrust of the system to be unwilling to prosecute rape cases even on a hypothetical level as presented in the research scenarios.

Sex Roles and Attitudes About Rape

In relation to sex roles, there are two themes or attitudinal patterns which consistently predict Attitudes About Rape: that of women's liberation-sexual equality, and the other, a traditionality in male-female roles and relationships. However, only the sex-role factors depicting women's liberation or sexual equality cut across ethnic-sex differences to predict definitions of rape and assessment of female fault for all three samples and willingness to prosecute for both minority samples. Traditionality in sex roles also emerges as an important predictor of Attitudes About Rape for minorities. A general traditionality in sex roles was associated with how Blacks assessed female fault in rape situations. For Mexican Americans, support for a very traditional role for women was associated with all three dimensions of Attitudes About Rape. In fact, this was the only single factor (SR3) to predict all three dimensions of Attitudes About Rape for any one sample.

There were also two interesting negative findings (that is, not in the predicted direction) in relation to sex roles and Attitudes About Rape. Again, some minorities deviated from the predicted response pattern on the dimension of willingness to prosecute. Mexican Americans and Black females who were high in support of women's liberation or sexual equality tended to be unwilling to prosecute alleged rapists. These findings, in addition to the negative findings on Income, Education, and Age for some minorities, suggest that a distrust for the criminal justice system may override other attitudinal and socioeconomic influences in predicting willingness to prosecute alleged rapists. Further study is necessary to determine whether unwillingness to prosecute rapists is associated with fear that the victim will be put on trial, awareness of past injustices to minorities of both sexes in the criminal justice system, or simply the belief that there are other options for dealing with rape.

Beliefs About Male-Female Sexuality and Attitudes About Rape

The beliefs about sexuality which were found to predict Attitudes About Rape represent underlying dimensions of attitudes ranging from a general skepticism about rape to the belief that women harbor a rape wish. Anglos tended to define rape situations with an attitude of skepticism or with some reservation about the reality of rape in general. Both their definition of rape situations and their assessment of female fault were to some degree a function of their underlying belief that women are responsible for rape. A similar finding among Blacks was the importance given the victim's reputation in defining rape situations and in assessing female fault. Two other dimensions found to predict assessment of female fault among Anglos and Blacks suggest that rape is no more than an extension (if not an integral part) of the dynamics of normal male-female sexuality or conflict between the sexes.

This same attitudinal frame of reference is seen in a more extreme form among Mexican Americans where the belief that women harbor a rape wish was associated with definement of rape and assessment of female fault, and for Mexican American males the belief was also associated with willingness to prosecute. However, belief in a female rape wish did not always work in the predicted direction in relation to Attitudes About Rape. While this belief was associated with nonfeminist definitions of rape and low willingness to prosecute as expected, it was also associated with low assessment of female fault. Apparently, the implication is that women have a natural proclivity toward rape; hence, they are not seen as responsible for their behavior, but neither is the male really culpable. If it is in the "nature" of women to want to be raped, it would follow that men who rape do the "natural" thing. Yet, the belief that rapists are sick was also associated with definement of rape for Mexican Americans. Examined together, the beliefs that women have a rape wish and that rapists are sick, emotionally disturbed men suggest a pathological web of male-female interaction for which neither sex is directly responsible.

While the male-female sexuality factors are more ethnic-specific, and perhaps more idiosyncratic than the sex-role measures, they were also more powerful and more frequent predictors of Attitudes About Rape. Some of the dimensions factored out of sample responses represent precisely the kinds of attitudes that feminists in the anti-rape movement have attacked in their ideological linking of sex roles-sexism and rape. In fact, the linkage is apparently more complex than simple sex-role socialization, although that certainly is a component. What these male-female factors appear to have tapped is a concept of *rape sexuality* which seems to vary more in degree than in kind from one sample to another. For example, some of the empirical linkages suggest that respondents were cautious in labeling sexual encounters as rape because women are seen by reputation and/or behavior as responsible and "men will be men." Other linkages suggest that there is an element of female sexuality and an element of male sexuality, the dynamics of which equal rape. But what appears to tip a finely honed balance of the "normality" of male-female interaction is perception of the female's behavior, nature, and/or reputation (and hence her degree of "fault").

Beliefs that constitute a kind of rape sexuality vary somewhat by race-ethnicity but offer a readily accessible frame of reference when persons are called upon to make day-to-day judgments in relation to sexual encounters. What is obviously important for each racial-ethnic community is *not only* these differences (for example, the difference between Female Responsibility, Victim-Defined Rape, and Rape Wish), but also the presence of other attitudes, particularly those related to women's liberation and sex-role equality, which may serve to mitigate some of the more negative implications of beliefs about male-female sexuality and rape.

Minority-Related Rape Risks and Attitudes About Rape

The three race-related variables were not as powerful in predicting Attitudes About Rape as were other measures. In fact, they were not significant predictors for Mexican Americans at all. This latter finding may reflect differences in the degree to which racism-inequality affects the lives of Mexican Americans and Blacks or, perhaps more likely, it may reflect a weakness in measurement. Findings for the Anglo and Black samples, however, are consistent with our theory of racial-sexual stratification. For Anglo males, high awareness or experience with minority Discrimination was associated with feminist definitions of rape, while, for Blacks, high Discrimination was associated with nonfeminist definitions of rape situations and an unwillingness to prosecute alleged rapists. Anglos with Victimization experience were more willing (than those without such experience) to prosecute rapists. For Blacks, on the other hand, high Victimization experience was associated with high assessment of female fault in rape situations. Intergroup was a significant predictive variable only for Anglo males, but on all three attitudinal measures. The direction indicates an interesting association with high assessment of female fault and conservative definitions of rape. Yet, perception of rape as Intergroup is also associated with willingness to prosecute. Although these three findings are inconsistent in a feminist-nonfeminist context as well as in a legal-judicial frame of reference, they are quite consistent with a theory of racial-sexual stratification.

Conclusions

The findings presented here answer some questions and elicit others. It is clear that there is considerable overlap in the three dimensions of Attitudes About Rape, but there is some independence in definement of rape situations, assessment of female fault, and willingness to prosecute which can perhaps be further clarified by improved measurement. It is also clear that assessment of female fault is a significant predictor of how rape situations are defined which, in turn, significantly predicts willingness to prosecute alleged rapists. Assessment of female fault remains the least satisfactorily explained dimension of this work. On the other hand, willingness to prosecute is obviously the most problematic dimension of rape for minorities. Their attitudes are no doubt a reflection of their unique history and present inequality in relation to the dominant group. Based on these data, we can surmise that the charge of rape (with both sexual and racial connotations) exacerbates an already well-established distrust of the White-controlled criminal justice system among Blacks and Mexican Americans. Finally, the findings provide some convincing support for the theory of racial-sexual stratification as stated in the following conclusions.

1. *Demographic variables apparently differentiate categoric risks vis-à-vis rape: specifically, the greater the perceived or actual risk of rape to certain age, sex, and racial-ethnic groups, the more conservative or nonfeminist their attitudes about rape will be.* Future work should focus more specifically on conceptualizing and measuring these risks as well as the mitigating effects of sex role-sexuality attitudes in relation to categoric risks.

2. *The theoretical hypothesis of a relationship between sex-role attitudes and attitudes about rape is supported for all three samples on two dimensions of attitudes about rape (definement and assessment of female fault) and is also supported for Mexican Americans on willingness to prosecute.* Attitudes reflective of nontraditionality in sex roles and/or supportive of women's liberation are associated with feminist attitudes about rape. Conversely, attitudes supportive of traditional sex roles are associated with nonfeminist attitudes about rape. It is clear that sex-role attitudes are not as important in determining willingness to prosecute as they are in determining how rape situations are defined and how female fault is assessed. Quite logically, willingness to prosecute seems largely a result of how rape situations are initially defined and, to a lesser extent, of how female fault is assessed. Perhaps a path analysis treatment in future work might help to clarify these sequential associations more fully for each group.

3. *The theoretical hypothesis of a relationship between beliefs about male-female sexuality and attitudes about rape is supported for Mexican Americans on all three dimensions of attitudes about rape and for Anglos and Blacks on two dimensions (definement of rape and assessment of female*

fault). Beliefs that attribute rape to the nature and/or behavior of females or to the dynamics of "normal" male-female sexuality are associated with non-feminist attitudes about rape, whereas beliefs that attribute rape to the nature and/or behavior of males are associated with feminist attitudes about rape. Again, it is clear that decisions regarding prosecution of alleged rapists are influenced less by beliefs about male-female sexuality than by definement of the situation and assessment of female fault.

4. *The findings tend to confirm the hypothesized relationship between minority-related rape risks and attitudes about rape for two of the three samples.* Discrimination, perceived or experienced, predicted two of the three dimensions of Attitudes About Rape for Blacks. Both Discrimination and Victimization predicted one dimension of Attitudes About Rape for Anglos. Perception of rape as an Intergroup phenomenon among Anglo males not only predicts nonfeminist definitions of rape situations and high assessment of female fault, but also high willingness to prosecute alleged rapists—a classical convergence of racism and sexism.

Note

1. To the degree that people behave logically, it can be assumed that a definition of the situation (Rape) precedes a decision with regard to prosecution (Court) of the alleged assailant. Therefore, it was assumed that Rape Scores would act in a causal way on Court Scores and that, in order to test whether willingness to prosecute is significantly influenced by the independent variables, it would first be necessary to partial out (remove statistically) the effect of Rape Scores on Court Scores. It is also possible that assessment of female fault in rape situations could influence willingness to prosecute. Thus, it was prudent to remove the influence of Fault Scores (in addition to Rape Scores) from Court Scores in order to test the significance of the independent variables on willingness to prosecute. Logic further suggests that the correlation between Rape and Fault should begin with assessment of female fault and move in a causal way to definement of rape. Therefore, the influence of Fault Scores was also removed from Rape Scores.

UNDERSTANDING RAPE: A HUMANISTIC APPROACH

9

In a very general sense, this work has been about the social problem of rape and the "personal trouble" of the rape victim. Our exploration into the extrinsic and intrinsic meaning of rape has been guided by a theory of racial-sexual stratification, coupled with an examination of crisis theory in relation to the victim's experience. Our macro-level theoretical perspective does not preclude the validation of crisis theory as a conceptual model for understanding victims' responses to rape, nor are these contradictory paradigms. Racial-sexual stratification is global, dealing with systemic sources of inequality that leave some groups comparatively more vulnerable as rape victims and as suspected rapists. If rape emanates from our social system and its race- and sex-based inequality, the problem will not be substantially alleviated without radical social change, and ultimately a more egalitarian social system must be the goal of the anti-rape movement. It would, however, be insensitive and inexcusable to ignore the plight of rape victims or to be remiss in searching for ways in which to more effectively meet their needs while we concentrate on ultimate, long-range social change. In essence, the anti-rape movement must perfect a bi-level strategy that will confront both the personal trouble and the social problem of rape.

The preceding chapters have been devoted largely to research findings that are, no doubt, subject to varying interpretations. In this final chapter, we attempt to integrate and interpret both "sides" of the phenomenon of rape as reflected in our findings. We have elected to highlight the public attitude data first because they describe the social or community context which utlimately gives extrinsic meaning to rape. Then, against this backdrop of social reality, the rape experience can be more thoroughly understood, not simply as the victim's "personal trouble," but as the interplay of both extrinsic and intrinsic forces that, working together, all too often seem to culminate as a "second assault." Our discussion is subsequently directed toward some implications for future research and some possible applications of our work in relation to services for victims, strategies for community change, and a more humanistic approach to the complex reality of rape.

The Social Reality of Rape

At the end of Chapter 2, we suggested some sex-role prototypes (sexual bargaining, sexual survival, and sexual differentiation) which represent variations of a sex-role script resulting from the experience of being Anglo, Black, or Mexican American in a system that is racially and sexually stratified. Our empirical analysis of the public attitude data helps to clarify and illuminate these suggested prototypes. In an attempt to construct models that will begin to predict community attitudes about rape and consequently help to place the victim-impact findings in perspective, we offer a brief review of those variables that were found to predict at least two of the three dimensions of Attitudes About Rape for each racial-ethnic group.

Anglos

For Anglos, only two variables meet our criteria of significant predictors of Attitudes About Rape: *Female Responsibility* and *Sex*. To judge rape in terms of a woman's behavior (that is, whether she provoked it, invited it, or just did not resist enough) is quite consistent with the theme of SEXUAL BARGAINING which we suggested as the essence of male-female sex roles for the White middle class. Much of sexual bargaining or male-female reward-seeking is done by a woman from a position of relative powerlessness because she has been socialized to believe that her body is her only (or at least her most valuable) resource—it is all she has to withhold or give. To the degree that women are seen as tempting, seducing, or teasing men as part of their normal behavior, they will be seen as responsible for rape. To the degree that women have been socialized to interact with men from this kind of role, they will not only feel responsible for their own rape, but they will also hold other women responsible for theirs.

With respect to *Sex* as a predictor of Attitudes About Rape, contrary to what we expected, Anglo males were found to be comparatively more feminist than females. However, we do not reject this finding as simply idiosyncratic or as a regional deviation, despite the fact that it is inconsistent with other findings (Feild, 1978; and Harris, 1977). Rather, from our perspective of racial-sexual stratification, we would suggest that White males are clearly the furthest removed from the risks of rape, and, therefore, they can best afford to take a liberal stance on the issue. Perhaps what is actually more surprising is that Anglo females have apparently been influenced *so little* by the feminist anti-rape movement as reflected in their comparatively nonfeminist Attitudes About Rape. When males and females were considered separately, we also found that *Female Responsibility* predicted nonfeminist Attitudes About Rape for both sexes. Among Anglo females, only support for the sex-role variables of *Freedom-Equality* or *Liberation* were found to predict feminist Attitudes About Rape. Among males, the perception of rape as *Intergroup* predicted nonfeminist attitudes across all three measures, clearly bringing the racial dimension to the forefront of Attitudes About Rape.

Blacks

Four variables predicted at least two of the three dimensions of Attitudes About Rape for the Black sample as a whole: *Victim-Defined Rape, Modified Liberation, Discrimination,* and *Income.* These variables lend credibility to the prototype we suggested as descriptive of the Black sex-role script—SEXUAL SURVIVAL—which places less importance on the protection of the masculine vis-à-vis the feminine role than on basic survival of the individual. The fact that judgments about rape among Blacks are to some extent a function of the victim's reputation should not be surprising since such attitudes are male-protective and female-defensive, making the daily risk of rape victimization somewhat more tolerable for all. High perceived/experienced minority *Discrimination* is associated with nonfeminist Attitudes About Rape, a finding that is male-protective and supports our assertion (and that of Brownmiller, 1975) that, in the Black community, rape means Black men accused of raping White women.

Although the themes reflected in *Victim-Defined Rape* and *Discrimination* are survival attitudes more protective of males than of females, a third variable in the Black model is *Modified Liberation,* a pragmatic combination of attitudes supportive of women's liberation and sex-role traditionality and associated with feminist Attitudes About Rape. While, at face value, this *Modified Liberation* may appear to represent ambivalence or inconsistent sex-role attitudes, it is consistent with the survival theme. Forced by the priority of survival needs to disregard the "ideal" masculine and feminine role expectations, many Blacks, nevertheless, tend to support some aspects of the sex-role stereotypes associated with the middle-class White world, giving them a mix of traditionality and pragmatic "liberation." Finally, *Income* was found to predict two dimensions of Attitudes About Rape, although it worked in a direction contrary to what we had expected on willingness to prosecute alleged rapists. We would suggest that Blacks still have a generalized distrust of the criminal justice system which is also a pragmatic position, again reflecting a survival theme that permeates the Black experience.

Few variables met our criteria of predicting two dimensions of Attitudes About Rape for males and females considered separately. Not unexpectedly, *Discrimination* is a significant predictor for Black males, as is either *Modified Liberation* or simply *Liberation.* Thus, while the rape risks which Black males perceive (as suspects) are strong, there is some amelioration of consequent antifeminist attitudes among men who hold some degree of sex-role liberation. *Income* is the only variable to meet our criteria of inclusion for Black females, and, as with the sample as a whole, it works in a direction contrary to that predicted in that higher income women are less willing to prosecute alleged rapists.

Mexican Americans

We suggested that SEXUAL DIFFERENTIATION characterizes the relationship between Mexican American males and females. Both sexes have explicit, clearly defined role responsibilities which together form the nucleus of the traditional family. The most powerful predictors of Attitudes About Rape for Mexican Americans seem to emanate from this role differentiation: attitudes supportive of a very traditional, restrictive *Female Role* and belief that women harbor a *Rape Wish*. While the latter apparently serves to ameliorate harsh assessment of female fault in rape situations, it is, paradoxically, a "feminist" judgment which originates from a sexist assumption. Judging from the strength of these two clusters of attitudes, for the Mexican American community, rape is encapsulated in role and gender expectations related to who women are and how they should behave.

Two demographic variables that meet our criteria of model inclusion are *Sex* and *Education*. As predicted, women are more feminist than men, and those with higher education are more feminist than persons with less education, except on willingness to prosecute where, once again, we encounter the same minority-criminal justice anathema we have described before. When males and females are considered separately, only *Rape Wish* (working in the predicted direction) predicts Attitudes About Rape for males, while *Female Role* predicts for females, further documenting the indisputable link between sex-role expectations for women and rape. Among Mexican Americans, rape seems to be endemic to the female role.

The Personal Reality of Rape

Victim-Impact and Community Attitudes

When our victim-impact findings are placed against the social backdrop of these models of community attitudes and sex-role prototypes, the potential for what amounts to a "second assault" is clearly illuminated. Although we acknowledge that this is something of a *post hoc* analysis, our original research objectives were to explore and examine the *compounded phenomenon* of rape which we see as comprised of both intrinsic (personal) and extrinsic (public) dimensions. Realistically, we feel that the findings "speak" for themselves, that some of the more obvious linkages between community attitudes and victim responses have already emerged and crystallized. Nevertheless, we recognize that our approach may be only one of many, and we hope that it will stimulate further discussion and investigation.

Our victim findings indicate that Mexican American women are the most adversely affected and perhaps the least adequately prepared to cope with the experience of rape. From the time immediately after the rape when their needs are unlikely to be satisfactorily met, to some point many months later, they experience a significantly greater degree of negative impact than Anglo or Black victims. To the extent that we have reliably and validly assessed impact, Mexican American victims evidenced the greatest degree of crisis response; the most negative changes in their feelings about men; the most definitive tendency to withdraw from their usual pattern of functioning; and (though not significantly different from Anglo or Black victims), the highest average number of assault-related health concerns. Given the kinds of public attitudes about rape found among Mexican Americans, we can see that these impact findings are predictable. However, what distinguishes the Mexican American community from that of the Anglos or Blacks is not so much the attitudes that *are* present (they differ only by degree), but those that *are not* present, at least not to a significant degree.

Based on our findings, there are no obvious mitigating forces working at the community level to diffuse or weaken the association between rape and female role-female sexuality which seems to dominate public attitudes among Mexican Americans. There are no strong feminist themes, or male support systems. Advanced education tends to work against nonfeminist judgments about rape, but the median education among Mexican Americans is low, and even this potential is convoluted by the negative attitude Mexican Americans hold toward the criminal justice system (as reflected by a general unwillingness to prosecute alleged rapists). The end result is that Mexican American victims suffer more negative effects from the rape experience than Anglo or Black victims. In relying so heavily on the strength of the family and its male-female role assignments in order to provide insulation against a racist dominant society, Mexican Americans have built in certain inequities in the responsibility assigned women. To the degree that the strength and security of the Mexican American family rests on the role(s) of women, they are highly vulnerable—to the rapist's assault, to their own subjective response, and to public reaction.

At the other end of the continuum, the Black victims we interviewed were, in a comparative sense, the most successful in coping with the impact of the rape experience. Although our data obviously cannot document what is historical supposition, our earlier analysis suggests that the identity of Black women is shaped less by their sex roles and sexuality than by racism. However, even if we acknowledged that Black women bring a different subjective sense of self to the rape experience (as to any life experience, positive or negative), our findings from the Black community would still predict a less severe impact relative to Anglo and Mexican American victims. Specifically, we found that there is an ameliorating theme related to women's liberation which counters nonfeminist attitudes about rape. There is also a pragmatism on the part of Blacks in judging rape via the victim's reputation. While this attitude is potentially unfair and discriminatory for all women, this "victim test" can work in two ways: if the woman is culpable, this is reflected in conservative attitudes about rape, but if her reputation stands up under scrutiny, this is reflected in attitudes supportive of victims. Attitudes such as those we see included in the "victim test" are protective of the vulnerable Black male, but also represent support for women who are adjudged innocent victims of rape.

For Anglo victims, the impact of the rape experience is somewhat "mixed." That is, our findings show them to be somewhere between the other two groups on our impact continuum, experiencing somewhat less severe impact than Mexican Americans, but a somewhat greater degree of impact than Blacks (see Figure 2). Once again, the public attitude data parallel this finding. Among Anglos, the predictors of attitudes about rape lie somewhere between those of the two minority communities in terms of the potential for mitigating or exacerbating the impact of the victim's experience. On the one hand, the prevalence of a mentality which holds women responsible for rape because they are thought to "control" male behavior by their own behavior does not reflect a supportive environment for rape victims. It actually promises some degree of blame (or at least doubt) regardless of who the victim is or what she was doing. In addition, among some Anglo males there is a convergence of racism and sexism that is likely to produce attitudes nonsupportive of victims and punitive toward alleged rapists. On the other hand, there are some mitigating supports in that, by and large, Anglo men are comparatively liberal or feminist in their judgments about rape. In addition, Anglo women who have some inclination toward support of women's liberation-sex role equality tend to hold feminist attitudes about rape, thereby providing some peer support for victims.

Resolution and Closure: Toward Relief from Anger

Thus far, we have attempted to highlight and integrate the victim-impact and public attitude data, along with some of our earlier historical suppositions. This allows us to understand impact within the social context in which women live and function and to take into account what they bring to the experience of rape. Although we believe that these components comprise the greater part of a holistic understanding of rape, there is yet another aspect which must be addressed—the importance of finding some positive means of closure on the rape experience. While we can bring little empirical evidence to document the importance of such closure, we suggest that the presence or absence of a viable means by which the victim is able to redress or avenge rape *becomes a part of the rape experience.* One clear and unequivocal emotion which every interviewer for this study sensed (and commented on) was anger in the form of unrequited rage. How does a woman, who is now all too aware of her powerlessness, resolve or achieve a sense of closure on this aspect of the rape experience?

Talking with only a few rape victims provided a gut-level understanding of some recent acts of violence, even murders (by women), to avenge rape. The person who has never been raped has limited understanding of what it means for a woman to be forced into submitting her sexual self—that which she has been socialized to believe is her most valuable quality. It is entirely possible that the impact of rape endures simply because there are no viable means to dispel this anger, this rage. While the victim data document such anger, they provide no definitive guidelines for moving beyond to some kind of satisfactory resolution.

In recent years, increased attention has been given to implementing various restitution and compensation programs for victims of crime. While such programs are long overdue, we doubt that any kind of financial payment can effectively compensate victims of rape, for the loss cannot be translated into monetary terms. Monetary compensation can alleviate the financial hardship resulting from rape-related medical costs, but it cannot repay the psychic cost of the victim's anger, nor can it help her achieve closure on this experience. Theoretically, some degree of closure can be achieved through the criminal justice system; yet, there are obstacles here as well. First, the victim must have her case "founded" and accepted for prosecution. But even if this happens, the victim's role as the complainant for the prosecution may leave her with the feeling that the interests of the "state" have taken precedence over her own. She will have the added burden of knowing that if her case goes to court, in fact, her reputation will be "on trial." Finally, the reality of "positive" closure through the criminal justice system (that is, conviction and incarceration of the assailant) is elusive. While we are inclined to believe that final, positive closure in this sense could help the victim regain her pre-crisis equilibrium, resolve her feelings about the rape, and get on with the business of living, our data do not include enough cases with closure—positive or otherwise—to test this proposition.

Of the sixty-one victims who participated in this study (more than one-fourth having been assaulted more than one year before the interview), only four reported that their cases had been disposed of judicially and only seven others stated that their cases were still in some stage of adjudication. Furthermore, of the four cases that had been disposed of judicially, only one resulted in a felony conviction. These figures are not encouraging, particularly considering the fact that these sixty-one cases were by and large "good rapes" by all legal-judicial criteria. In addition, nearly all of the victims we interviewed had some support from rape crisis center personnel and were, therefore, probably better informed about legal-judicial procedures than the "average" victim. It may well be that the prolonged crisis, suggested by our data, is sustained not only by public attitudes such as those we have documented for all racial-ethnic communities, but also by the absence of closure: the assailant was never apprehended; he was never indicted; he pled guilty to a lesser offense; *or* he was acquitted of the charge altogether. For the victim, these outcomes make her rape unfinished business; they reveal rape to be a crime without justice; and they leave the victim with no sanctioned means to resolve her feelings of having been assaulted a second time.

While we believe that justice under the law is the least any victim has the right to expect, we do not advocate a law-and-order response to rape. It is a "solution" which, in effect, is no solution because of built-in problems: (1) unreported rapists are never apprehended; (2) police and prosecutor bias enter into the acceptance/rejection of cases; (3) it disproportionately affects minority males who are accused of raping majority females; and (4) it treats the symptoms, not the underlying causes, of rape. Although at present there is no viable alternative to criminal processing of rapists, at least a more representative processing can be achieved. While some of the public attitude data support a "get tough," law-and-order approach to rape, judgments on specific rape situations suggest that this view applies only to "real rapes" and that there is a strong public defensiveness against innocent men being trapped in rape charges by vindictive or disreputable women. Our public attitude data clearly indicate that willingness to prosecute rapists is a function of how rape situations are defined, and assessment of female fault is highly interrelated with the initial judgment of whether the incident was "really" a rape. Justice remains elusive precisely because it is our attitudes about rape, and not the law, which predict our judgments in relation to specific rape cases. We must work to alleviate the root causes of rape, for reliance on "justice" in a racially-sexually stratified society is a logical contradiction. Until at least some of the root causes are eliminated, a rape victim must continue to live with her anger which, unresolved, changes not only her life, but also her total sense of self.

Rape Risks: Who Has a Vested Interest?

If one potentially productive hypothesis emerges from this work, it is that vested interest—probably emanating from rape risks or perceived threat—is associated with attitudes about rape. Rape risks, however, apparently work in different ways for different groups, depending on how they are perceived and/or experienced, and what resources can be garnered to alleviate them. The public attitude data suggest that a relationship exists between attitudes about rape and certain categoric (age, sex, and perhaps socioeconomic) risks in the form of vested interest, but it is a complex association because of the dynamics of minority-majority threat superimposed on male-female threat. For example, the data indicate that Anglo females are generally more conservative than males in their attitudes about rape. There are some exceptions, however, specifically those White males who perceive rape as an intergroup phenomenon. For these men, rape apparently represents more than a threat to significant others (females); it is also a threat to one's exclusive control over *all* White females. It is therefore too simplistic to say that females are more threatened by rape than males and that their relatively conservative attitudes about rape are defensive; men, too, can be defensive.

The question of vested interest is still more complex in relation to minorities *and* to males and females. In terms of today's reality, it is probably safe to assume that Black females are more at risk in relation to rape (as potential victims) than are Black males (as potential suspects). However, this assumption is based on statistical fact and the knowledge that society is less racist today than in the past when Black males were not infrequently lynched for allegedly raping White women. But from another perspective, every Black male who has been socialized to survive in a racist society "knows" that White women are still the property of White men, that the Black man is still a "nigger," and that "niggers" are "known" to rape White women. Thus, for Black males, rape is a different kind of risk; in effect, it has become an internalized threat. Meanwhile, Black females are in the unenviable position of being subjected to multiple threats. As with all females, they are threatened in a physical sense by rape, but they must also be aware that any charge of rape they make against White males is suspect (and likely to bring them more trouble than justice). On the other hand, any charge of rape made against Black males will compound their image as "sexual animals" and thrust them into the White-controlled criminal justice system (with consequent risks for all Blacks).

Feminist attitudes about rape which Black females, by and large, demonstrated in the public attitude data are defensive. Whereas White females may deny that rape can happen to them, Black females know that rape can and does happen in their neighborhoods, and anti-rape attitudes are their best protection. However, these attitudes on the part of Black females do not mean they will join, or even support, the feminist movement. To Black women concerned with the basics of day-to-day living, the movement may be something of a luxury which they cannot yet afford. It is too ideological, too anti-male, too White, and too middle class to be relevant for them. Some Blacks are even antifeminist because they object to what they consider a ludicrous analogy (coming from White, middle-class women) that women, like Blacks, are an oppressed minority. Black females are, by necessity, pragmatic, as reflected in the victim data. They are likely to try to reduce rape risks by altering their own behavior and by surviving an attack if it does occur. Realistically, they tend to be self-reliant in dealing with rape risks.

Racism and sex are perhaps less interwoven for Mexican Americans and Anglos than for Blacks and Whites. For Mexican American males, rape constitutes a threat to one's honor, to protective and proprietarian responsibilities. For Mexican Americans, rape is an in-group threat whereas, for Blacks, it is an out-group threat. For Mexican American females, in addition to the obvious physical risk, rape may symbolize a role violation. If, as suggested in Chapter 2, a Mexican American female derives respect, status, and some measure of power by fulfilling the traditional female roles in relation to her family, then any violation of prescribed role behavior—albeit against her will via rape—could represent a real, and not simply a perceived, threat to her honor and status. The consequences of rape as role violation are evident for Mexican American victims in the impact data. In addition, it may also be of interest to note that Mexican Americans had the lowest refusal rate for interviews among the public attitude samples; yet, as victims, they had the highest refusal rate of any group. Although it cannot be documented with hard data, we might speculate that the comparatively high refusal rate for Mexican American victims is indicative of some degree of guilt, shame, and/or self-blame resulting from violation of the female role by having been raped. Furthermore, the relatively conservative attitudes about rape demonstrated by Mexican American females in the public attitude data reinforce this contention. If women in one's own community tend to accept rape as valid only when it fits the stereotypic definition, and if they cite women's behavior/appearance more frequently than any other "cause" of rape, then Mexican American victims may be left with few options in terms of how they will react to the rape experience.

Both the victim and public attitude data suggest a number of associations between rape risks (or perceived threats) and attitudes about rape. We have discussed only some of these associations, treating perceived threats or risks in relation to rape as vested interests for certain groups or categories of respondents. We are convinced of this emergent theme in our data and submit that the next logical step in empirical understanding of the phenomenon of rape must be a careful conceptualization, differentiation, and measurement of risks, perceived threats, and vested interests.

Knowledge for What? Some Implications

Our findings carry far too many implications for us to deal adequately with all of them here. Therefore, our discussion is limited to some of the most inclusive and pragmatic—that is, those that have the greatest potential for short-term payoff in service delivery for victims and for alleviation of the rape problem at the community and, ultimately, at the societal level.

Implications for Service-Delivery: Some Help for Counselors and Victims

As noted before, our victim sample was relatively small, and we do not know to what extent our findings can be generalized. Nevertheless, we feel that there are some issues related to service-delivery that deserve consideration in light of the victim study. First, our systematic examination of the rape-as-crisis assumption led us to suggest a reconceptualization that has direct implications for use of the crisis intervention model with rape victims. Second, we uncovered a continuum of impact which includes a consistent pattern of response variations among Anglo, Black, and Mexican American victims, a finding that leads us to discuss the values and attitudes of majority group service-delivery persons vis-à-vis minority victims. Finally, linking some of the victim and public attitude findings, we offer a few suggestions for helping victims manage the institutional bureaucracy.

CRISIS INTERVENTION WITH RAPE VICTIMS

Findings from our empirical examination of rape-as-crisis can be summarized as follows: (1) victim responses to rape are more accurately conceptualized as a prolonged crisis; (2) during this prolonged crisis, the impact of the rape experience persists in the form of residual crisis effects; and (3) if crisis resolution is defined as the reestablishment of pre-rape equilibrium, we still do not know when, or if, victims achieve it. In view of these findings, we have developed some guidelines for the use of the crisis intervention model with rape victims, a model that takes into account the existence of residual crisis effects. The framework for this service-delivery model is primarily that of an on-call, around-the-clock rape crisis program, simply because most victim services continue to be provided in this manner. Based on the literature regarding victim services (see, for example, Brodyaga, et al., 1975; Abarbanel, 1976; and McCombie, et al., 1976) and our own first-hand experience, this model can be incorporated into existing programs and implemented by trained staff members or volunteers.

Crisis intervention with rape victims should begin as soon as possible following the initial contact or request for services. In the framework of a rape crisis program, this usually means that the victim is first seen at the hospital emergency room, often before she has been examined by a physician (assuming that she has not suffered injuries requiring immediate medical attention). In most cases, victims require specific information about medical treatment, particularly in relation to the risk of pregnancy and venereal disease. They often require information about police procedures, such as whether and how to report the offense, file a formal complaint, and make a statement to the investigating detectives. In addition, as reflected in our findings, victims often want and need the emotional support of an understanding person who will literally remain with them as the medical and police procedures are carried out. In this phase immediately after the rape, we feel there is no question as to the adequacy and appropriateness of the crisis intervention model. Both the immediacy of service-delivery and the specific kinds of services provided—structure, information, and support—are clearly congruent with the situation.

When the medical examination has been completed and at least some initial decisions have been made about reporting the offense to the police, the focus of intervention may need to change. That is, the victim's subjective response to the current situation now needs more specific attention. What are her immediate concerns? What kinds of reactions does she anticipate from significant others, and how does she see herself responding to their reactions? What is her perception of the rape? What are the primary affective themes in her perception (for example, anger, grief-loss, anxiety)? A basic assessment at this time, though tentative, will not only help to anticipate the victim's subsequent attempts to cope with the rape, but should also be used in formulating a working contract.[1] Specifically, by the end of this first meeting, a mutually agreed-upon contract should be made with the victim, including (1) delineation and partialization of the specific issues that are of primary concern to her; (2) identification of the significant and generalized others who may be engaged as support systems; (3) review of the relevant institutionalized medical, legal-judicial processes (that is, planned medical followup and subsequent steps in pursuing prosecution, if she wishes); and (4) determination of the time and place of the next meeting/interview.

If we remain true to the crisis model, intervention continues for approximately six weeks and is guided by the substance of the contract (the specifics of which may be adjusted to remain current with the victim's needs). During this time, the victim's affective and behavioral functioning are continually assessed in an attempt to help her regain her pre-rape equilibrium. Further attention is given to her decisions regarding prosecution and to the reactions of significant others. The overall focus remains directed toward the rape incident and what it means to the victim in the context of her social world. Our question vis-à-vis the crisis model emerges only at this point. Our impact findings clearly suggest that there are residual effects of the rape experience which, in many cases, persist, certainly beyond six or eight weeks. If our reconceptualization of rape as a prolonged crisis is valid, then the most realistic approach may be to discuss the possibility of residual effects candidly, hopefully not to the degree that a self-fulfilling prophecy is set, but in the sense of providing anticipatory guidance. In our view, it would be more reassuring for the victim to know something about (potential) longer term impact than to complicate her adjustment process by having her wonder "what's wrong with me that I haven't gotten over this yet"? Although the decision to continue with formal intervention beyond this six-week point will depend primarily on the victim, we suggest that some followup contacts be planned, if only to keep interventive options open for several months. This may be especially critical for the victim who pursues prosecution because (although we have no hard supporting data) each time she is called to identify a suspect or is subpoenaed to court (often several months after the assault), she may, to some degree, "relive" the rape experience, including all the discomfort that has been resolved previously.

Finally, we recognize the argument that victims who receive "quality" crisis intervention services should not experience the kinds of residual effects documented among our sample. This argument suggests that victims in our sample may have suffered prolonged crisis because the services that they received were inadequate. Since we did not focus on service evaluation, we cannot refute this argument.[2] An equally viable explanation, however (and the one we have adopted in suggesting that rape be reconceptualized as a prolonged crisis), is that the impact of rape does not simply "fade" or end within a matter of weeks or even months, regardless of the nature and quality of crisis intervention services. We feel that the public attitude data provide too many clues as to the community environment (support or nonsupport for victims) to attribute our victim-impact findings solely to the quality-of-services argument.

CAVEATS FOR COUNSELORS

In light of our findings that different racial-ethnic groups experience comparatively greater or lesser degrees of negative impact as a result of the rape experience, we think that the issue of values and attitudes of majority group service deliverers merits consideration. Although we tend to focus on staff and volunteers of rape crisis programs, our discussion is certainly no less relevant for the medical, law enforcement, and legal-judicial personnel with whom rape victims must interact. Somewhat ironically, "helping relationships" may hold as much potential for inflicting harm as good, and, in this situation, the presenting problem of rape is so controversial and value-laden that the knowledge, values, and attitudes of the helping persons take on even greater importance than they normally do. We do not question the "good intentions" of rape crisis personnel, but we are concerned with the pervasive influence of mainstream-society values and attitudes that may be translated into culture and class-bound expectations vis-à-vis minority victims. Our concern is that minority rape victims may find themselves "victimized" again as they encounter well-intended, but uninformed, service deliverers.

Since most rape crisis programs have evolved in response to the feminist anti-rape movement, not surprisingly staff and volunteers are largely female, White, and middle class, well-entrenched in the mainstream society.[3] Despite protests to the contrary, the socialization process lays the foundation for what later emerge as certain preconceived notions about rape, about how victims (should) feel, and how they (should/will) react to this experience. To the degree that these subtle, preconceived notions are translated into expectations, all rape victims are placed in jeopardy. What happens, for example, when the counselor is confronted with a victim who seems relatively unperturbed by the rape incident? What kind of interpretation does the counselor make when the victim says she feels no need for continued help? Or, at another point in the range of responses, what kind of assessment is made of the victim who seems relatively powerless to regain control of her feelings, who seems to be overly concerned with "what other people will think"? The first two questions are raised because of findings related to Black victims in this study; inappropriately, the counselor might conclude that the victim either was not "really" raped or that being raped is not especially upsetting to Black women. The other questions are raised because of findings related to Mexican American victims, and, inappropriately, the counselor might decide that the victim is overly dependent, neurotic, and even a bit paranoid.

Ideally, minority counselors should work with minority victims, but this is probably unrealistic in terms of present, short-term reality. Moreover, it is overly simplistic to assume that same race-ethnicity equals same life experiences, hence, "instant rapport." Still, some steps can be taken to prevent misunderstanding and misinterpretation. Initially, it is important to recognize that each person, counselor and client alike, enters the helping relationship as a unique composite of values, attitudes, and life experiences. Women from different racial-ethnic groups will bring their identity—shaped both by historical experience and contemporary inequality—to bear on the definition of the problem, its meaning and its resolution. For example, given the history of race relations in America and the exploitation (sexually and otherwise) of Black women, rape may represent just one part of a constellation of trouble, especially for the poor. Therefore, while rape is by no means an inconsequential event to a Black woman, it may not, in fact, be the worst thing that has ever happened to her, and because her identity has been shaped more by color than by sex, it will not likely destroy her. Should a Black victim evidence relatively minor trauma or little disruption in life-style as a consequence of rape, one counselor might conclude that she is "acting like nothing happened," while another could describe her as "coping adequately, all things considered." Both are perceptions of the same reality, but one carries a judgmental connotation, suggesting that there is something not quite "right" about the victim's response. The other demonstrates a more value-free acknowledgment of the possibility that there is a broader reality for that victim.

At the other end of the continuum, based on our findings, Mexican American women seem to be the most adversely affected by the rape experience. When the victim seems unable to regain control and is disproportionately concerned with "what people will think," the same dilemma may emerge with respect to attitudinal and cultural differences between the mainstream counselor and Mexican American victim. For example, most of the Mexican American victims in this study indicated their religious preference as Roman Catholic. The Catholic church has traditionally supported and maintained a stringent view that a woman should resist rape in order to protect the conjugal rights of her husband. Any violation of these rights, with or without the woman's consent, is likely to result in shame and dishonor to one's self, one's husband, and/or one's family. While it would be far too simplistic to suggest that religious preference might "explain" the comparatively severe impact of rape among Mexican Americans, it is a valid illustration of how knowledge of just one variable can help the counselor better assess the victim's response.

We have tried to demonstrate the importance of two points in relation to majority counselor-minority victims. While a general awareness of, and sensitization to, racial-ethnic and cultural diversity is a necessary first step toward building more effective helping relationships, the second step must involve expanding our knowledge with respect to specific client groups. Admittedly, this is no small task. Nonetheless, we strongly advocate (and both sets of research findings support) the development and implementation of comprehensive attitudinal *and* substantive training programs for persons who work with victims of rape. Service-delivery persons, especially those referred to as mainstreamers, must become sensitized to their own values, attitudes, and biases in relation to the phenomenon of rape. Although the act of rape may represent objective reality, it is subjectively experienced, and victims must be allowed to use their coping skills within the social context as they perceive it. In addition, service-delivery persons must be given a sound knowledge base in relation to their potential client populations (preferably from representatives of those populations), specifically with respect to sociocultural variations and the uniqueness of particular racial-ethnic groups.

While our data clearly document racial-ethnic differences in response to rape, thereby confronting the fallacy of holding to a common expectation of how victims should and will respond, a word of caution must be added. It would be fatuous, and detrimental, to adopt rigid expectations of how someone will respond to rape because of skin color, surname, or religion. Our position is that service-delivery persons must understand the range of possible responses to rape associated with racial-ethnic (and class) differences while remaining open to providing support, counseling, and related services to the victim as her needs are presented. There are, no doubt, rape crisis centers and other victim-oriented programs already attuned to these issues. However, perhaps for the first time, there is research evidence which not only underscores the need for comprehensive training, but also offers some guidelines as to its substance. The time and energy invested in developing and implementing such training should improve the quality of interventive efforts and ultimately result in more humanized services for all.

MANAGING THE INSTITUTIONAL BUREAUCRACY

Rape crisis center personnel (in their short history) have generally mounted a bi-level service approach: providing emotional support, counseling, and referrals; and helping victims through the institutional maze of medical, law enforcement, and legal-judicial bureaucracy. Our data indicate that not only in the area of counseling must attention be given to racial-ethnic differences, but also in the area of institutional service-delivery. Black and Mexican American victims voiced proportionately more complaints about disrespectful treatment than Anglos, and they were more likely to encounter judgmental attitudes and/or to have felt that their needs were ignored by institutional personnel. Our findings further allow us to project that, while Black victims (on the whole) may need less in the way of emotional support and counseling, they may, in fact, require more support and monitoring of institutional service-delivery. Our public attitude data, for example, indicate that Black females were more willing than any other group to prosecute rapists. Yet, other data show that they are frequently frustrated in their efforts to secure justice for the crime of rape.

All too frequently, neither the Black nor the Mexican American victim is taken seriously in the institutions that must officially validate rape. Mainstream rape crisis counselors can perhaps provide their most valuable service to Black victims by helping them to "work the system," by serving as advocates with medical personnel, the police, and prosecutor. These counselors, the majority of whom are White, middle class, and knowledgeable about how the system works, cannot be as easily "pushed aside" or ignored as a minority victim who may be less adept at working the system and has already expended a good part of her emotional and psychic energy in coping with the rape experience. To carry this concept of individualized services a step further, rape crisis personnel will likely find that Mexican American victims require a full measure of *both* counseling and institutional advocacy, but they may not want the latter. In fact, Mexican American women may withdraw from any public identity as rape victims, accepting only counseling and emotional support. Compared with Anglo and Black females, Mexican American females in our public attitude survey tended to be unwilling to prosecute alleged rapists. The difficulty Mexican American victims seem to have in coping with rape apparently leads them to withdraw, to become more passive in their general level of functioning. They may not want to report a rape and to carry their case through the judicial process; rape crisis counselors must ultimately allow them this option. While some counselors see their role as that of an advocate on behalf of *all* rape victims (and we obviously support advocacy as a legitimate function), the needs and desires of the individual victim must be respected.

Strategies for Change: Society and Community

The public attitude data suggest two levels where interventive strategies aimed at alleviating the rape problem are appropriate: the societal (or macro-) level and the community (or meso-) level. On the macro-level, the data provide substantial empirical support for the feminist position that rape emanates from sexual inequality, but the data combined with the history of certain minority-dominant relationships indicate that racial-ethnic inequality is also a causal factor. In fact, this work suggests that rape represents an imbroglio of both kinds of stratification. This is not to assert that rape is always directly traceable to racial-sexual conflict but, rather, that it is a predictable product of a social system which has set male over female, White over Black, and Anglo over Mexican American, and has institutionalized the structure of dominance. In such a system, rape is the ultimate tool of social control: a continual assertion of male dominance; a minority imitation of majority dominance; a weapon of retaliation for minority males; and a technique of power-maintenance for White males.

This work does not fully document the assertion that rape is symbolic of a system of racial-sexual stratification. It does, however, break new ground in this direction—enough to support the claim that alleviation of the rape problem requires radical social change. Strong, macro-level efforts directed toward this goal must be maintained in the forseeable future. Simultaneously, however, some directives in the public attitude data for meso-level community change can help alleviate the rape problem on a local level. The data further direct that these community efforts be pragmatic rather than ideological.

SOCIETAL CHANGE

A substantial decrease in both racial and sexual inequality is required to reduce the rape problem to one of infrequent incidents of aberrant behavior. The feminist movement has, thus far, mounted the only macro-level attack on rape, and it is imperative that this effort continue and expand to include racial-ethnic stratification as well as sexual stratification. Although societal changes are in progress today, it is evident that the kinds of fundamental social changes that will ultimately result in a more egalitarian society come very slowly. We must not sit back and relax simply because things appear to be "getting better." Racial-ethnic and sexual inequality are not eased simply because history propels us toward some illusion of "progress" or because each generation is presumably more egalitarian than the previous one. Reduction in inequality between the sexes and in minority-majority group relations has come about only because of organized social action—continual pressure on economic, social, and political institutions—emanating from the civil rights, women's, and Chicano movements. Nor does society automatically move ahead toward equality even after change is set in motion. Reactionary movements and attitudinal backlashes can threaten progress. It is absolutely essential to maintain the feminist momentum which has produced the beginning of male-female equality and to renew and strengthen efforts—which seem to be waning—toward racial-ethnic equality.

The public attitude data clearly show that rape means different things to different racial-ethnic and sex subgroups. Of nine scenarios (eight of which constituted rape by legal definition), respondents approached consensus on the different dimensions of rape on only one—a stereotypic street rape involving both a weapon and victim injury. The findings also show disparity between abstract definitions and opinions about rape versus judgments on real-life situations. However, neither in the scenario data nor in unstructured responses relating to the cause and prevention of rape is there any strong indication of feminist ideology in the public's perception of the rape problem. In short, despite the anti-rape movement and the feminist politicalization of rape, there is no ground swell of feminist, anti-rape ideology among any segment of the public as represented by these data. It should not be concluded, however, that, while only relatively small segments of the population are feminist in attitudes about rape, the impact of the anti-rape movement has been totally lost on the public.

There have been political (institutional) responses to the feminist ideology of the anti-rape movement. There are also indications (largely as a result of the mass media) that the public has become somewhat better educated to the fact that rape is a crime of considerable magnitude and increasing frequency and that rape victims have needs which have heretofore been ignored, if not exacerbated, by our institutional responses. Media attention given the anti-rape movement may also have resulted in an increased number of known rapes, although it is impossible to determine how much of this increase stems from more reporting and how much comes from an increase in the actual incidence of rape. These short-term payoffs from the anti-rape movement have most likely benefited majority more than minority victims.

COMMUNITY INTERVENTION

Although not by design, rape crisis centers, staffed largely by White, middle-class feminists, are appealing to and serving victims much like themselves. Hence, our suggestions for community intervention are aimed primarily at the minority communities we studied. This is not to ignore the rape problem of majority females, but existing rape crisis centers are believed to be reaching this group and meeting their needs relatively well. The general directives provided here are very clear and apply across the board: more public education about rape crisis centers, establishment of centers in all communities, and adequate funding to have paid staff in addition to volunteers. Given the present state of knowledge, such centers appear to be the most viable means of serving rape victims regardless of race-ethnicity or social class. Yet, findings from this research suggest that, at the present time, service-delivery systems for victims of rape are not geared to meet the needs of minority victims and that some action is called for at the community level.

The public attitude data provide some basis for support of anti-rape strategies tailored to the needs of minority communities, but we feel strongly that these data should be utilized (perhaps expanded and their validity checked) by persons indigenous to these communities. Some of our research findings related to Blacks and Mexican Americans may be used to provide some substantive suggestions for community-based education programs about rape. For example, one focal point may be the need to develop programs that will (1) encourage open dialogue between men and women, focusing on their respective vested interests in rape; (2) support and encourage rape victims (by use of minority communications media, institutions, and leadership) to report rapes and to utilize the services of rape crisis centers (some of which should be community-based) and health care facilities; (3) overcome biases and unsubstantiated myths about rape (particularly in relation to female behavior); (4) sensitize and train health care, law enforcement, and legal-judicial personnel to some of the unique aspects of the rape problem which may be manifested by specific client groups; and (5) monitor dominant institutions (medical, legal-judicial) to ensure the quality of services to the minority community. Again, it should be stressed that specific details regarding the form and substance of community-level interventive strategies are best formulated by the communities themselves. However, a few examples will serve to suggest some possible applications of our data.

One of the primary findings that emerged in relation to the Black community is the wide disparity of attitudes between males and females, presumably because of conflicting vested interests in rape. This knowledge could be the key to community intervention because it is clear that any anti-rape campaign in the Black community must deal with the attitudes of males as well as with those of females. Considering the present attitudes about rape, appeals to rape victims to report rapes and/or media campaigns that encourage utilization of rape crisis centers will likely increase the threat rape poses for Black males. Such a reaction will, of course, broaden the schism between males and females, and thwart the development of a community of support for victims of rape (including, certainly, support for prosecution of rapists). How such community education is to be undertaken and what agencies, groups, or local institutions should be involved are questions that are best addressed by persons who know their communities, their leadership, and the institutional support networks that can best ensure the success of their efforts.

Among Mexican Americans, it is not so much male-female disparity in attitudes about rape which must be dealt with, but the similarity in prejudicial attitudes, with females in some cases having more nonfeminist attitudes than males. Our data indicate a need for the Mexican American community to redefine rape, to move it away from its apparent connotation as a female role violation, or in some cases, the product of mentally ill men or of women who harbor a "rape wish." Rape needs to be confronted for what it is—a crime and a violation of individual freedom. It is ironic that the strongest Mexican/Mexican American institution, the family, has, along with support from the Catholic church, unwittingly propagated the belief that rape does not happen to "good women" who attend to their traditional responsibilities in socially acceptable places. This "definitional injustice" is compounded by the fact that the major support systems in the Mexican American community (where a person would normally go for help) are themselves threatened by rape. Consequently, because of their having defined rape as role-violating behavior, the church and family are, at best, impotent to help victims of rape. At worst, their reactions become a part of rape. It is, therefore, time to reexamine the rape problem, and, in view of the strength of the Mexican American community and its institutions, action must come from within. Chicana women in some communities are carving out their own unique feminism, integrated with strong familial and cultural themes. These and other indigenous groups must take the initiative in building community support and in (1) bringing rape into the open and dealing with it definitively as a crime, as a violation of individual freedom; (2) cultivating family and church support for community education about rape and other sexual offenses; and (3) providing community-based services for meeting the needs of rape victims within a family counseling context.

The interventive strategies presented here are clearly more pragmatic than ideological because the data indicate little evidence of feminist ideology in minority communities. Currently, there are community-based minority groups (some of them women's groups) concerned about rape and interested in building support for public education and victim services. However, these groups are more likely motivated by ther own pragmatic concerns than by identification with, or support of, feminist ideology.

Thus, feminists (largely White and middle class) may have to sacrifice their ideology for pragmatism in order to achieve short-term goals, attract minorities to the anti-rape movement, and effectively increase services to these communities. For those of us intent on seeing a more egalitarian society, one free of sexism and racism, we must allow these differences. For whatever we perceive as its source, rape is a human restriction from which we all seek liberation. Until such time as macro-level strategies achieve the long-term goal of sexual-racial equality, programs are needed on the local level to meet the needs of rape victims, to raise community consciousness about rape, and to require accountability of social institutions.

No More Savage Discovery

Several years ago, William Ryan caused White, middle-class, liberal-thinking social scientists to take a new look at old paradigms and the value judgments that produced them. He caused us to look with chagrin at what he termed the "art of savage discovery"—the art of victim-blaming—the process of defining those who are in reality victims of poverty, discrimination, and inequality as deviants or as victims of their own cultural deprivation.[4] We are acutely aware that one possible response to this work will be that of victim-blaming. Some will find support here for what have become facile sociological models—subcultural explanations for social problems. Substantial racial-ethnic variations in public attitudes about rape and about sex roles have been documented. Congruent with these attitudes, significant variations in victim responses to rape have been documented. It will be all too easy to find causal explanations for these data in the Black poverty subculture thesis where the dominant figure is the indomitable Black matriarch. It will be equally simplistic to interpret the Mexican American data by use of a stereotypic *barrio* family where the female is a submissive, nonperson completely dominated by the male and his *machismo*. We reject these subcultural explanations of the rape problem because they ignore the core culture and the dominant social system which are White, male-dominated, and structured to keep *both* women and minorities in their places. There is nothing in the minority communities or subsocieties which is not found (to a greater or lesser degree) in the dominant society *or* which is not a direct result of minority-dominant realtionships—sexual and/or racial—past and present. If there is a savage discovery in relation to the problem of rape, it should not be minority subcultures or victims of rape who are "discovered," and perhaps not rapists either, but rather the system which has written and propagated the sex-role scripts for male and female and which has institutionalized the powerlessness of women and minorities. Until these inequities are eradicated or at least alleviated, we are all members of a savage system which has predetermined that certain groups will be victims—a structured inequality in which we all lose as human beings.

Notes

1. In social work practice, and particularly as part of the crisis intervention model, a contract is an *explicit, mutual agreement* between the worker and client which sets out the framework for the helping relationship. That is, the focus of intervention, immediate goals, roles, and expectations of the participants are discussed and clarified. For more detail, see Anthony N. Maluccio and Wilma D. Marlow, "The Case for the Contract," *Social Work* 19 (1974): 28–36.

2. Although we did not attempt to evaluate service-delivery (other than the ratings by victims), our personal knowledge of service-delivery through AAVAP (in San Antonio) is that "crisis intervention" was limited, in most cases, to the initial contact in the hospital emergency room and to one followup contact. While there were exceptions where extensive followup services were provided, for the most part AAVAP service-delivery did not closely adhere to the "ideal" crisis intervention model. With regard to this matter, there is a need for research into service-delivery from an evaluative perspective. Specifically, the crisis model should be examined in terms of its relative effectiveness in mitigating the impact of rape.

3. Here the term *mainstream society* connotes the White, middle-class dominant group. A mainstream counselor is therefore thought of as White and middle class, a person who basically holds the values and attitudes of the dominant group. Our discussion tends to focus on mainstreamers simply because they comprise the majority of service-delivery persons who work with rape victims. Ideally, we would hope to see more minorities (in this case, Blacks and Mexican Americans) who are indigenous to their respective communities involved in both planning and implementing victim-oriented services.

4. For an elaboration of the victim-blaming ideology, see William Ryan, *Blaming the Victim* (New York: Vintage Books, 1976), pp. 3–30.

OPERATIONAL DEFINITIONS AND MEASUREMENT

APPENDIX A

A.1 Victim Research: Independent Variables

Age-at-assault was operationally defined as respondents' self-reported ages (in years) at the time of the rape, then grouped into three categories: (1) 14–21; (2) 22–29; (3) 30 and older. These categories were viewed as approximating the developmental stages of adolescence, young adulthood, and adulthood in an attempt to explore the theoretical linkage between maturational crises (that is, developmental stage) and situational crises (that is, rape).

Time-since-assault was operationally defined as the number of months that had elapsed between the rape and the research interview, then grouped into four categories: (1) up to 8 weeks; (2) 2–6 months; (3) 7–18 months; (4) more than 18 months. If the crisis theory tenet that crises are time-limited is valid in the case of rape, the most recent victims (group 1) would be the most likely to evidence a significantly higher degree of crisis.

Victim race-ethnicity was operationally defined as the respondents' self-identification as Anglo, Black, or Mexican American, or synonymous terms.

Inter- versus intragroup rape refers to rapes committed by an assailant of one race-ethnicity on a victim of a different (intergroup) or the same (intragroup) race-ethnicity. As a dichotomous variable, it was created to explore whether the impact of inter- versus intragroup rape differs. Operationally, the variable was created by pairing the race-ethnicity of the victims with that of their assailants.

Stereotypic versus nonstereotypic rape refers to rapes that seem to fit a "popular" or common stereotype of a "real" rape. A stereotypic rape was operationally defined as one in which (1) the victim did not know the assailant; (2) the victim was accosted without warning; and (3) the assailant had a weapon. Since this was a dichotomous variable, any rape that failed to include one or more of these elements was defined as nonstereotypic.

Institutional support systems refers to individuals representing institutions, agencies, or groups that are available to assist rape victims (for example, police, medical personnel, rape crisis counselors, clergy, and professional counselors). This variable was operationally defined as the number of institutional support systems sought out or encountered by victims. For descriptive purposes, ratings were obtained which reflect the degree to which victims perceived these persons as helpful or not helpful.

Personal support systems refers to individuals who relate to victims as family members, friends, or significant others. This variable was operationally defined as the number of such persons with whom victims discussed the rape. For descriptive purposes, ratings of relative "helpfulness" were obtained. Both institutional and personal support system variables were created in an attempt to see if their presence or absence would serve to mitigate or exacerbate the impact of rape.

A.2 Public Attitude Study: Sex Role-Women's Liberation Indices

Scoring of each of these items was on a four-point scale of strongly agree to strongly disagree, with values ordered so that low scores indicate support for traditional sex roles (beliefs and behavior index) and lack of support for women's liberation (beliefs and behavior). High scores suggest more feminism or nontraditionality in sex roles and support for women's liberation.

TRADITIONAL SEX-ROLE BELIEF INDEX (SR BELIEFS)
1. Men are more inclined to be intellectual than women.
2. Men are more aggressive or forceful than women.
3. Women are more moral than men.
4. Women are more sympathetic than men.
5. Women are more artistically inclined than men.
6. Women are more emotional than men.
7. Men are better leaders than women.
8. Men are better able to reason logically than women.

TRADITIONAL SEX-ROLE BEHAVIOR INDEX (SR BEHAVIOR)
1. In marriage, the husband should make the major decisions.
2. One of the most important things a mother can do for her daughter is to prepare her for the duties of being a wife.
3. Secretarial work, nursing, or teaching are better jobs for a woman than engineering or business.
4. In marriage, the major responsibility of the wife is to keep her husband and children happy.
5. For a woman, looks or personality are more important than intelligence or education.

WOMEN'S LIBERATION BELIEF INDEX (WL BELIEFS)
1. A woman does not have to have a man around to be happy.
2. Men and women are born with the same human nature; it is the way they are brought up that makes them different.
3. Taking care of a home and raising children is not as fulfilling (or satisfying) as having a job or a career.
4. In America, women as a group have been taken advantage of by men.
5. There is almost no job a man can do that a woman cannot do just as well.

WOMEN'S LIBERATION BEHAVIOR INDEX (WL BEHAVIOR)
1. Women should have as much sexual freedom as men.
2. A woman has a right to go anywhere she wants to and do anything she wants just as much as a man.
3. Women should involve themselves more in politics and business.

4. A woman has a right to put her own self-fulfillment or happiness ahead of her obligations to her husband and children.

5. Women should receive equal pay for equal work with men.

6. A woman—whether she is married or not—has a right to control her own body and to decide whether or not to have a child.

7. The Equal Rights Amendment to the Constitution should be passed by all states to insure that women share equally in all privileges and responsibilities of American life.

A.3 Public Attitude Study: Beliefs About Male-Female Sexuality

These items were scored on a four-point scale of strongly agree to strongly disagree.

BELIEFS ABOUT FEMALE SEXUALITY AND RAPE

1. Most rapes could be avoided if women did not provoke them or secretly want to be raped.

2. A woman's past sexual history or reputation should have nothing to do with the question of rape.

3. Even though women are terrified of being raped, somewhere in the back of their minds there is a curiosity and excitement about rape.

4. A woman cannot really be raped unless a weapon is used.

5. Once a woman or girl is raped, her reputation is ruined as far as men are concerned.

6. Women should fight and resist a rapist rather than give in to him out of fear.

7. A woman cannot be raped by her husband.

BELIEFS ABOUT MALE SEXUALITY AND RAPE

1. Given the right situation, most men are capable of committing rape.

2. Men can commit rape and get away with it.

3. Men sometimes have sex urges they can't control, especially when they see women dressed in sexy clothing.

4. Men who commit rape are sick, emotionally disturbed people.

5. Men who commit rape usually hate women in general.

6. Men, regardless of race or ethnic group, are often falsely accused of rape.

A.4 Public Attitude Study: Demographic-Background Characteristics

Race-ethnicity was determined by the three samples—Anglo, Black, and Mexican American. Since interviewers could interview only persons of their own sex and race-ethnicity, these attributes were determined at the time of the interview. Race-ethnicity was not entered into the analysis as a social attribute. Rather, each sample was analyzed separately, and comparisons were made among the three.

Age was measured and coded as the number of years attained at last birthday.

Education was measured and coded as the last year completed in a system of formal education.

Income was recorded for the respondent and for the spouse where both worked or had income. Subsequently, a *family income* was computed by adding the two.

Religion was coded in terms of prevalent Protestant groups in the city, Catholic, and no preference or "other." These categories were subsequently collapsed in order to dichotomize religion into *Catholic* and *Other* for statistical analyses of the data.

Sex was dummy-coded for the purpose of statistical analyses as Male=0, Female=1.

A.5 Reliability-Validity of Public Attitude Measures

Little effort has been directed toward development of cross-cultural additudinal measures, and no previous effort has been made to quantify cross-cultural attitudes about rape. Hence, an attempt was made to test the reliability of some of the measures we employed. Specifically, Chronbach's Standardized Alpha was used to test the reliability of the three measures of Attitudes About Rape and the four Sex Role-Women's Liberation indices. The reliability coefficients for these seven measures are shown in Table 25. Coefficients for the three measures of Attitudes About Rape show a moderate reliability with only one of the nine coeffecients below .50. Reliability of the Sex Role-Women's Liberation indices is also moderate with two of the twelve scores falling below .50.

These reliability coefficients suggest that (1) there is an ethnic bias working in the Mexican American sample where reliability is the lowest on four of the seven measures; and (2) the reliability of the Women's Liberation Beliefs Index is weak for all groups. The latter problem could, no doubt, have been alleviated by the inclusion of more items of comparable kind and quality (only five were included). However, we had learned from pretesting that the length of the interview schedule, and the number and complexity of questions involved in measuring Attitudes About Rape were potentially problematic if we included every item of interest. Therefore, we decided it was necessary to hold the number of Sex Role-Women's Liberation items to a minimum. Realistically though, ethnic-racial bias appears to be the more critical question in relation to these measures.

Since there are inherent dangers of ethnic-racial bias in this kind of research, care was taken to control the conditions of measurement (pretesting and translation of the interview schedule into Spanish, matching interviewers and respondents on race-ethnicity and sex). Despite these precautions, interviewers reported that Mexican American respondents, particularly females, did not seem to "relate" to the Sex Role-Women's Liberation items and in some cases could not respond to them. For this sample then, the question of reliability is, no doubt, tied to an interrelated and/or underlying question of content validity. That is, items used as measures of Sex Role-Women's Liberation may not have represented these phenomena among Mexican Americans as well as they did among Blacks and Anglos. The Fault Score reliability for Blacks is also low, perhaps reflecting cultural bias, perhaps simply reflecting the idiosyncratic nature of Black responses. The topic of rape is fraught with ambivalence in the Black community. The term conjures up very different images of victimization for both males and females, in which case their diverse responses may limit the validity of any one attitudinal measure.

Because the reliability coefficients shown in Table 25 raised questions about the reliability and validity of cross-cultural measures of sex-role related variables, the Sex Role-Women's Liberation items and the Beliefs about Male-Female Sexuality items were factor analyzed for each sample independently. This procedure helped not only to reduce the data, but also to extract the most representative dimensions of attitudes relating to sex-role attitudes and sexuality for each of the three samples. Finally, while we do not discount our findings or the conclusions to which they lead, we do caution that cross-cultural research relating to sex roles, sexuality, race, and rape is new. Consequently, our instrumentation and measurement must be viewed as exploratory.

TABLE 25. Chronbach's Standardized Alpha Reliability Coefficients for Sex Role-Women's Liberation Indices and Attitudes About Rape Measures

INDICES AND COMPOSITE SCORES	ANGLOS	BLACKS	MEXICAN AMERICANS
Sex-Role Beliefs	.71	.74	.62
Sex-Role Behavior	.61	.75	.52
Women's Liberation Beliefs	.49	.58	.45
Women's Liberation Behavior	.74	.60	.60
Rape (R) Score	.77	.62	.65
Fault (F) Score	.71	.48	.52
Court (C) Score	.72	.68	.68

SAMPLING

B.1 Sampling Victims

The initial respondent population from which the victim sample was drawn included all female rape victims who had received services from the Alamo Area Volunteer Advocate Program, Inc. (in San Antonio, Texas) between February 1975 (when the program began) and December 1977. A decision to include victims fourteen years of age or older (at the time of the assault) was made before any contacts were attempted. As noted earlier, we had elected to exclude cases involving the rape of a child, and some lower age limit had to be established. In view of these considerations, and given the length and demands of an in-depth interview, the minimum inclusion age of fourteen was set somewhat arbitrarily. As of June 1977 when this phase of the research was being initiated, only 154 victim files were available, and it seemed doubtful that we would be able to locate and secure agreement to participate from a high proportion of that number. Consequently, we sought the help of the Austin Rape Crisis Center (in Austin, Texas) in order to ensure a larger sample size.

An initial review of the 154 AAVAP files resulted in the loss or exclusion of over one-third of the original population for the following reasons: (1) insufficient information to initiate contact (N=15); (2) the victim was under the age of fourteen at the time of the assault (N=17); (3) no rape had occurred (N=5); (4) the victim did not reside in the area (N=9); and (5) the victim was handicapped (for example, severely retarded) so that an in-depth interview was not feasible (N=6). The result of this review was that the original population had been reduced by fifty-two before we had even begun to make contacts. When contacts were initiated with the remaining 102 victims, the following outcome categories evolved: (1) thirty victims were known to have moved; (2) ten victims could never be located, even though we had no evidence that they had moved; (3) in four cases, there was no such address as that listed in the file; (4) five persons denied they had been raped, or said they were the "wrong" person; (5) fourteen victims were contacted but refused to be interviewed; and (6) thirty-nine victims agreed to participate and were interviewed. Most of the other twenty-two respondents were victims who had received services from the Austin Rape Crisis Center during the same time period as the AAVAP population, although a few were "mushroom referrals" from victims we had interviewed in San Antonio. For additional details, see Karen A. Holmes and Joyce E. Williams, "Problems and Pitfalls of Rape Victim Research," *Victimology* 4 (1979): 17–28.

B.2 Public Attitude Sampling Procedure

To increase the probability of selecting respondents of the desired race-ethnicity, census tracts were ranked in terms of their ethnic proportion. Those tracts 90 percent or more Black, 90 percent or more Mexican American, and 85 percent or more Anglo were defined as the population from which the sample was to be drawn. The 1970 U.S. Census was used in this ranking process. Three tracts were identified as Black, eleven as Anglo, and sixteen as Mexican American. Individual residences included in the 1976 Polk City Directory were identified for interviewing, using the systematic probability technique. Assuming a 50 percent loss in the sample as a result of refusals, wrong ethnicity, and wrong sex, and attempting to compensate for over-representativeness among single females, female head of households, and females as primary adults within the household, the following samples were drawn: 762 addresses from the Anglo tracts, 1,060 from the Black census tracts, and 954 from the Mexican American tracts. In order to match sex of interviewer and respondent, half of the sample was assigned male and half female, alternating addresses after a random start. The sample error for samples of this size (N = 334) is .05 at the .05 level of confidence. Thus, the results obtained can be expected to vary within a range of plus or minus 5 percent. The sampling error for male and female samples (N = 167) is .08; results from these samples can thus be expected to vary plus or minus 8 percent. Table 26 provides a summary of the contact outcomes from this sampling procedure.

TABLE 26. Summary Outcome of Three Sample Pools

DISPOSITION	ANGLO		BLACK[a]		MA	
	N	%	N	%	N	%
Totals						
Contacts-Attempted Contacts	762	100.0	581	54.8	808	84.7
Sampled Pools	762	100.0	1060	100.0	954	100.0
Respondent Contacts	468	100.0	330	100.0	427	100.0
Interviews Completed	335	71.6	212	64.2	340	79.6
Refusals	132	28.2	117	35.5	78	18.3
Interviews Terminated	1	0.2	1	0.3	9	2.1
Attempted Contacts	294		251		381	
Percent of Total Contacts		38.5		43.2		47.1
Invalid Numbers[b]	148	19.4	117	20.1	150	18.6
Not Home[c]	146	19.1	134	23.1	231	28.6

[a]The Black sample data are based on incomplete records because the contact record sheets of three interviewers were not available for inclusion in the final tabulation. Two interviewers worked on the project for several weeks and were forced to quit because of a job transfer and family illness. Their completed interview schedules were turned in without their contact record sheets. Another interviewer had his car burglarized while he was doing an interview, and all of his contact record sheets (in his briefcase) were stolen. The incomplete data are presented here with the assumption that they do not differ substantially from that which was not retrieved. A total of 336 Blacks were interviewed.

[b]Invalid numbers were the result of: wrong sex, wrong race-ethnicity, no such address, business address, no soliciting allowed, or a vacant house.

[c]Potential respondents were classified as "not home" after two contacts at different hours of the day, or weekend and weekday contacts failed to find anyone home.

TABLES 27–30

APPENDIX C

TABLE 27. Race-Ethnicity of Rape Victims and Offenders as Compared with Composition of General Population in Selected Cities (Percentages)

CITY	VICTIM A	VICTIM B	VICTIM MA	OFFENDER A	OFFENDER B	OFFENDER MA	POPULATION A	POPULATION B	POPULATION MA
Seattle	80	14	1	34	59	2	85	7	2
Detroit	25	74	1	10	89	—	54	44	2
Kansas City	52	47	—	31	65	2	71	20	8
New Orleans	43	57	—	15	81	—	50	45	4
Phoenix	64	15	16	45	38	14	79	5	14
Denver	63	16	21	35	30	34	72	9	17
San Antonio	61	16	21	35	26	35	39	9	52
Austin	61	21	9	na	na	na	67	14	19

Notes: These data were compiled from several different sources as follows: Seattle, Detroit, Kansas City, New Orleans, and Phoenix data are from Donna Schram, *Forcible Rape: Final Project Report* (Washington, D.C.: National Institute of Law Enforcement Assistance Administration, 1978). The Denver data are from John MacDonald, *Rape Offenders and Their Victims* (Springfield, Ill.: Charles C. Thomas, 1971, pp. 51 and 76). The San Antonio data were collected by the authors from Police Offense Reports (June 1974-June 1975); and the Austin data were supplied by the Austin Rape Crisis Center (1977). The racial-ethnic composition of cities was compiled from the 1970 census reports for each city.

A = Anglo   B = Black   MA = Mexican American
na = not available   — = under 1 percent

TABLE 28. Composite Measures (and Group Contrasts) of Definement of Rape, Assessment of Female Fault, and Willingness to Prosecute Assailant by Ethnic Group and Sex

SCORES	ANGLO			BLACK			MEXICAN AMERICAN		
	ALL	M	F	ALL	M	F	ALL	M	F
Rape									
Mean	15.0	14.8	15.2	16.4	16.7	16.1	17.9	18.1	17.6
SD	3.4	3.0	3.7	2.9	3.4	2.3	2.9	2.8	3.0
N	335	169	166	336	167	169	340	167	173
Sig. by sex		ns			ns			ns	
Fault									
Mean	20.7	20.0	21.4	22.4	22.9	22.0	21.7	21.7	21.7
SD	4.0	3.6	4.3	3.4	4.0	2.8	3.2	2.8	3.6
N	335	169	166	336	167	169	340	167	173
Sig. by sex		.001			.01			ns	
Court									
Mean	15.4	15.0	15.8	16.1	17.4	14.9	17.4	18.1	16.8
SD	3.2	2.6	3.6	3.3	3.6	2.3	3.1	3.3	2.7
N	335	169	166	336	167	169	340	167	173
Sig. by sex		ns			.001			.001	

GROUP CONTRASTS BY RACE-ETHNICITY AND SEX: SIGNIFICANCE OF *t*-VALUES

		A-B	A-MA	B-MA
Rape	All	.001	.001	.001
	Male	.001	.001	.001
	Female	.01	.001	.001
Fault	All	.001	.001	.01
	Male	.001	.001	.01
	Female	ns	ns	ns
Court	All	.01	.001	.001
	Male	.001	.001	ns
	Female	.01	.01	.001

Note: ns = not significant. The possible range of mean scores on Rape, Fault, and Court is 9 to 36. Low scores reflect definement of forced sexual encounters as rape, low assessment of female fault, and willingness to prosecute the assailant.

TABLE 29. Varimax Rotated Factor Structure of Attitudes About Sex Roles and Women's Liberation by Ethnic Group

| | | | | FACTORS | | | | | |
| | ANGLO | | | BLACK | | | MA | | |
ITEM	1	2	3	1	2	3	1	2	3
1. In marriage, the husband should make the major decisions.				58			42		
2. One of the most important things a mother can do for a daughter is prepare her for being a wife.				77					44
3. Secretarial work, nursing, and teaching are better jobs for women than engineering or business.				71					78
4. In marriage, the major responsibility of the wife is to keep her husband and children happy.				56					39
5. For women, looks or personality are more important than intelligence or education.				42	49		38		
6. Men are more intellectual than women.				40			39		

Notes: Only factor loadings of ≥ .30 have been included. To save space, the decimals were omitted throughout the table, and factor items are shown in abbreviated form; for the exact wording on each item in the interview schedule, see Appendix A.2. SR items were scored from 1 = strongly agree to 4 = strongly disagree; WL items (14-25) were scored from 1 = strongly disagree to 4 = strongly agree.

TABLE 29 (continued)

ITEM	ANGLO			BLACK			MA		
	1	2	3	1	2	3	1	2	3
7. Men are more aggressive/forceful than women.			40						
8. Women are more moral than men.			42	38		34			
9. Women are more sympathetic than men.			62	32					
10. Women are more artistically inclined than men.				49			34		
11. Women are more emotional than men.			60						
12. Men are better leaders than women.				57			61		
13. Men are more logical than women.				60	40		68		
14. Women should have as much sexual freedom as men.		66						60	
15. A woman has the right to go anywhere, do anything.	42	56				32		66	
16. Women should involve themselves more in politics and business.	54				31	33		41	
17. A woman has the right to put her own happiness ahead of that of her family.						61			
18. Women should receive equal pay for equal work.	31	32			54				

ITEM	ANGLO			BLACK			MA		
	1	2	3	1	2	3	1	2	3
19. A woman, whether married or not, has a right to decide whether to have a child.	31	44		38	32				
20. The ERA should be passed.	51				48				
21. A woman does not have to have a man around.	45								
22. Men and women are born with the same human nature.	30								
23. Taking care of the home and raising children is not as fulfilling/satisfying as a job or career.						37			
24. Women have been taken advantage of by men.	44				36				
25. There is almost no job a man can do that a woman cannot do just as well.	45					43			
Eigenvalue—Factor 1	4.65			4.34			2.81		
Variance explained	48.5%			42.4%			31.7%		
Eigenvalue—Factor 2	1.58			2.68			2.06		
Variance explained	16.5%			26.1%			23.2%		
Eigenvalue—Factor 3	0.93			1.32			1.58		
Variance explained	9.7%			12.9%			17.9%		
N	333			331			334		

FACTORS

TABLE 30. Varimax Rotated Factor Structure of Attitudes About Male-Female Sexuality and Rape by Ethnic Group

ITEM	ANGLO			BLACK			MA		
	1	2	3	1	2	3	1	2	3
1. Most rapes could be avoided if women did not provoke them or secretly want to be raped.			50	65	31		60		
2. Given the right situation, most men are capable of committing rape.	58			65			59		
3. A woman's past sexual history or reputation should have nothing to do with the question of rape.			−58			67			
4. Women are terrified of rape, but somewhere in the back of their minds there is a curiosity and exictement about rape.	36	45		63	38		43	47	
5. A woman cannot really be raped unless a weapon is used.		39		44	53			67	
6. Men can commit rape and get away with it.		−40				44		31	
7. Men sometimes have sex urges they can't control, especially when they see women dressed in sexy clothing.	58			58			53		

Notes: Some items appear here in slightly abbreviated form. For the exact wording, see Appendix A.3. Only factor loadings of ≥ .30 are included. To conserve space, decimals were omitted on factor loadings. Missing values were replaced by the group mean of each item. See Tables 17 and 18 for the number of missing values. Items were scored from 1 = strongly agree to 4 = strongly disagree.

FACTORS

ITEM	ANGLO			BLACK			MA		
	1	2	3	1	2	3	1	2	3
8. Men who commit rape are sick, emotionally disturbed people.	-43			-44		37			37
9. Men who commit rape usually hate women.	-50			38	39				83
10. Once a woman is raped, her reputation is ruined as far as men are concerned.				35	47		36		
11. Women should fight, resist a rapist rather than give in to him out of fear.			41		44				
12. Men are often falsely accused of rape.				32					
13. A woman cannot be raped by her husband.		38			48				
Eigenvalue—Factor 1 Variance explained	1.81	42.3%		3.41	70.8%		1.85	41.9%	
Eigenvalue—Factor 2 Variance explained	0.93	21.6%		0.75	15.5%		0.96	21.7%	
Eigenvalue—Factor 3 Variance explained	0.70	16.3%		0.66	13.7%		0.69	15.6%	
N	335			336			340		

STATISTICAL PROCEDURES FOR ANALYZING PUBLIC ATTITUDE DATA

APPENDIX D

D.1 Multiple Regression Analysis

A multiple regression analysis was used to test the relationship between the measures of Attitudes About Rape (R, F, and C Scores) and the fourteen selected independent variables. Twenty-seven regression equations were run on the data (see Tables 31–39). A stepwise inclusion procedure was utilized in conjunction with a preestablished hierarchy among two or (in some cases) three subsets of variables (Nie, et al., 1975, pp. 344–47). Where other dependent variables were entered into the regression equation to partial out their interdependence, these were entered first, followed by the demographic variables. After the demographic variables were entered, the stepwise inclusion procedure took over, entering the sex- and race-related variables in terms of their ability to explain the variance (from most to least powerful) in the dependent variables. The rationale for the combined stepwise-hierarchical procedure was dictated by several facts: (1) the interrelatedness of the dependent variables; (2) the evidence that demographic variables clearly influence certain attitudes; (3) beyond the zero-order correlation coefficients, there is neither theoretical nor empirical evidence to dictate the entry order of variables within the demographic and race-sex subsets.

It should be pointed out that the hierarchical inclusion procedure does *not* prevent other variables from entering the regression equation ahead of the demographic variables (entered first) if others are more powerful; it simply ensures their first consideration (Nie, et al., 1975, pp. 345–46). In addition, one or more variables could be (and frequently were) excluded from the regression equation if the criteria set by the parameters of the equation were not met. (Parameters were set as $n=8$, $F=2.0$, $T=.30$.)

D.2 Missing Data

The amount of data missing (no response or "don't know") was not great proportionate to that collected. However, whenever possible, such data were replaced by some systematic method of estimation. For example, where items were part of a composite or index measure, missing data were replaced with the mean of the valid items comprising that score or index on a case-by-case basis where at least one (but not more than half) of the items was missing. On the Rape, Fault, and Court measures, approximately 11 percent of the data was replaced in this manner, and on the Sex Role-Women's Liberation indices, just under 7 percent was replaced. There was, of course, considerable variation by sample, with Mexican Americans generally having the most missing data.

Other missing data (for example, the beliefs about male-female sexuality items and the various minority-related measures) had to be replaced with the group (sample) mean on that item. Missing data on these items were generally low, as was the case with the demographic variables except for income. A rather large number of Black respondents either refused to give their income or said they did not know the income of their spouse (if he/she worked). In approximately 19 percent of the cases (all samples combined), we estimated total family income via a procedure borrowed from the Bureau of the Census ("Methodology and Scores of Socioeconomic Status," Working Paper No. 15, Washington, D.C., 1963). The number of valid cases (N) shown in Tables 31–39 in this Appendix reflects the maximum missing data involved in any statistical procedure because every case with one item missing (where we had been unable to replace it) was dropped from the regression analysis.

D.3 Glossary of Statistical Terms

Beta and F Ratios for Beta. Beta weights are standardized measures of the independent variable's impact on the dependent variable. For research which involves variables measured in noncomparable units (for example, dollars and years), Betas transform the data into comparable units. Betas provide a measure of the strength of association between independent and dependent variables, and the sign of Beta indicates the direction of the association. Partial Betas are examined in these data in order to determine the association between independent and dependent variables with the other variables already in the equation or controlled. The F test for partial Betas is used as a means of determining those variables which, with other variables taken into account, have the strongest independent effect on the dependent variable. The variables found significant by testing the partial Betas may then be taken as the best predictors of Attitudes About Rape.

R^2 Change and F Ratios for R^2 Change. Semipartial (also called part) correlation coefficients (R^2 Change) are a measure of the correlation of the dependent variable and the residual of a particular independent variable (the effects of other independent variables partialled out). Squared semipartial coefficients are a measure of the absolute increment of explained variance (R^2) because of the addition of a particular independent variable to the equation which already contains other independent variables. Whether the incremental change in R^2 is significant to the overall explained variance in the dependent variable can be tested by use of the F ratio.

Explained variance (R^2). This is the proportion of variance in the dependent variable which is explained by each independent variable or by all in combination (cumulatively). If all the variance in a dependent variable were explained by a set of independent variables (which rarely, if ever, happens), the column labeled R^2 would add up to 1.00, indicating that 100 percent of the variance is explained.

Overall F. Testing the significance of the overall or table F simply means that one or more of the regression coefficients is statistically significant—that is, one or more of the independent variables (alone or in combination) is significantly linked with the dependent variable. The overall F test does not indicate which coefficient is significant.

Subset F. The subset F, as used in Tables 31–33 and 37–39 (this appendix), simply tests the significance of the proportional reduction of unexplained variance with the effects of dependent variables (in this case R and F Scores) partialled out of both independent and dependent variables. The subset F is based on the square of partial correlation coefficients used as a measure of the correlation of the residuals of independent *and* dependent variables. In effect, we can then test the significance of other variables in a regression equation, having partialled out the effects of inter-related dependent variables.

TABLE 31. Regression of Selected Demographic and Sex-Race Related Variables on Rape Scores for Anglos

INDEPENDENT VARIABLES	BETA	F RATIOS FOR BETA	R^2 CHANGE	F RATIOS FOR R^2 CHANGE	R^2
ANGLOS—ALL (N = 326)					
F Score	.315	42.07***	.170	78.31***	.170
Education	.087	3.14	.024	10.88***	.194
Age	.068	2.00	.016	7.49**	.210
MF3	.199	15.47***	.054	24.83***	.264
MF2	.182	14.08***	.034	15.66***	.298
Intergroup	.090	3.56	.007	3.13	.304
Discrimination	.083	2.92	.006	2.92	.311

Overall F = 20.48*** (*df* = 7/318) Subset F = 8.99*** (*df* = 6/318)

INDEPENDENT VARIABLES	BETA	F RATIOS FOR BETA	R^2 CHANGE	F RATIOS FOR R^2 CHANGE	R^2
ANGLOS—MALE (N = 160)					
F Score	.238	11.31***	.115	24.80***	.115
Education	.039	.28	.022	4.70*	.137
Age	.073	1.09	.015	3.27	.152
MF3	.222	9.41**	.066	14.31***	.218
MF2	.179	6.38*	.043	9.24**	.261
Discrimination	.153	4.51*	.017	3.84*	.278
Intergroup	.143	3.91*	.018	3.91*	.296

Overall F = 9.15*** (*df* = 7/152) Subset F = 5.20*** (*df* = 6/152)

INDEPENDENT VARIABLES	BETA	F RATIOS FOR BETA	R^2 CHANGE	F RATIOS FOR R^2 CHANGE	R^2
ANGLOS—FEMALE (N = 166)					
F Score	.365	29.33***	.212	51.50***	.212
Education	.086	1.58	.032	7.74**	.244
Age	.046	.44	.019	4.51*	.263
MF3	.165	4.97*	.039	9.54**	.302
MF2	.158	5.45*	.026	6.29**	.328
SR2	.143	4.23*	.017	4.23*	.345

Overall F = 13.97*** (*df* = 6/159) Subset F = 5.38*** (*df* = 5/159)

Notes: MF2 = Skepticism
MF3 = Female Responsibility
SR2 = Freedom-Equality
Subset F ratios were computed for partial correlations. They test the significance of the proportional reduction of unexplained variance with the effects of Fault (F) Scores partialled out of both independent and dependent variables.

*$p \leq .05$ **$p \leq .01$ ***$p \leq .001$

TABLE 32. Regression of Selected Demographic and Sex-Race Related Variables on Rape Scores for Blacks

INDEPENDENT VARIABLE	BETA	F RATIOS FOR BETA	R² CHANGE	F RATIOS FOR R² CHANGE	R²
		BLACKS—ALL (N = 289)			
F Score	.439	77.03***	.241	102.26***	.241
Income	.100	4.16*	.009	3.72	.250
MF3	.177	12.29***	.044	18.89***	.295
SR2	.147	8.81**	.024	10.02**	.318
Discrimination	.115	5.33*	.013	5.34*	.331

Overall F = 27.99*** (df = 5/283) Subset F = 8.36*** (df = 4/283)

INDEPENDENT VARIABLE	BETA	F RATIOS FOR BETA	R² CHANGE	F RATIOS FOR R² CHANGE	R²
		BLACKS—MALE (N = 142)			
F Score	.471	45.99***	.258	57.12***	.258
SR2	.239	11.49***	.068	15.13***	.326
Discrimination	.180	6.94**	.036	7.94**	.362
Intergroup	−.126	3.26	.010	2.25	.373
Age	−.117	2.78	.013	2.78	.385

Overall F = 17.04*** (df = 5/136) Subset F = 5.83*** (df = 4/136)

INDEPENDENT VARIABLE	BETA	F RATIOS FOR BETA	R² CHANGE	F RATIOS FOR R² CHANGE	R²
		BLACKS—FEMALE (N = 147)			
F Score	.392	28.75***	.192	38.41***	.192
Income	.140	3.65	.024	4.81*	.216
MF3	.203	7.32**	.060	12.09***	.276
SR3	.133	3.14	.016	3.14	.292

Overall F = 14.62*** (df = 4/142) Subset F = 5.86*** (df = 3/142)

Notes: MF3 = Victim-Defined Rape
SR2 = Modified Liberation
SR3 = Liberation

Subset F ratios were computed for partial correlations. They test the significance of the proportional reduction of unexplained variance with the effects of Fault (F) Scores partialled out of both independent and dependent variables. The minus sign (−) denotes relationships that were not in the predicted direction.

*p ≤ .05   **p ≤ .01   ***p ≤ .001

TABLE 33. Regression of Selected Demographic and Sex-Race Related Variables on Rape Scores for Mexican Americans

INDEPENDENT VARIABLES	BETA	F RATIOS FOR BETA	R² CHANGE	F RATIOS FOR R² CHANGE	R²
MEXICAN AMERICANS—ALL (N = 311)					
F Score	.370	54.21***	.148	60.80***	.148
Religion	.092	3.45	.016	6.40*	.163
MF2	.153	7.98**	.051	21.16***	.215
SR3	.153	7.85**	.014	5.62*	.228
MF3	.150	8.95**	.015	6.30*	.244
Sex	.109	3.84*	.006	2.49	.250
Age	−.170	6.70**	.008	3.18	.258
Education	.141	3.89*	.010	4.02*	.268

Overall F = 11.74*** (df = 8/302) Subset F = 6.05*** (df = 7/302)

INDEPENDENT VARIABLES	BETA	F RATIOS FOR BETA	R² CHANGE	F RATIOS FOR R² CHANGE	R²
MEXICAN AMERICANS—MALE (N = 152)					
F Score	.427	38.45***	.196	42.16***	.196
Income	.208	8.32**	.034	7.36**	.231
Age	−.109	2.19	.015	3.16	.245
MF2	.201	7.91**	.047	10.02**	.292
SR1	−.104	2.05	.014	2.92	.306
Intergroup	.135	3.38	.012	2.61	.318
MF3	.110	2.44	.011	2.44	.329

Overall F = 10.10*** (df = 7/144) Subset F = 3.97*** (df = 6/144)

INDEPENDENT VARIABLES	BETA	F RATIOS FOR BETA	R² CHANGE	F RATIOS FOR R² CHANGE	R²
MEXICAN AMERICANS—FEMALE (N = 159)					
F Score	.327	21.24***	.118	24.95***	.118
Religion	.173	6.14*	.040	8.44**	.159
SR2	.162	4.44*	.063	13.13***	.221
MF2	.113	2.28	.026	5.41*	.247
Discrimination	−.128	3.34	.016	3.34	.262
MF3	.144	4.13*	.015	3.17	.278

Overall F = 7.41*** (df = 6/152) Subset F = 5.49*** (df = 5/152)

Notes: MF2 = Rape Wish   SR2 = Equality
       MF3 = Sick Rapist   SR3 = Female Role
       SR1 = Male Role

Subset F ratios were computed for partial correlations. They test the significance of the proportional reduction of unexplained variance with the effects of Fault (F) Scores partialled out of both independent and dependent variables. The minus sign (−) denotes relationships that were not in the predicted direction.

$*p \leq .05$ $**p \leq .01$ $***p \leq .001$

TABLE 34. Regression of Selected Demographic and Sex-Race Related Variables on Fault Scores for Anglos

INDEPENDENT VARIABLES	BETA	F RATIOS FOR BETA	R^2 CHANGE	F RATIOS FOR R^2 CHANGE	R^2
ANGLOS—ALL (N = 326)					
Sex	−.224	16.66***	.028	10.17**	.028
Age	.047	.72	.013	4.98*	.041
MF3	.197	13.04***	.054	19.84***	.095
MF1	.159	8.42**	.020	7.59**	.115
SR1	.142	6.51*	.018	6.51*	.133

Overall F = 9.82*** (*df* = 5/320)

INDEPENDENT VARIABLES	BETA	F RATIOS FOR BETA	R^2 CHANGE	F RATIOS FOR R^2 CHANGE	R^2
ANGLOS—MALE (N = 160)					
MF3	.163	4.28*	.041	6.93*	.041
Intergroup	.156	4.13*	.022	3.77	.063
SR2	.152	3.74	.022	3.74	.085

Overall F = 4.82** (*df* = 3/156)

INDEPENDENT VARIABLES	BETA	F RATIOS FOR BETA	R^2 CHANGE	F RATIOS FOR R^2 CHANGE	R^2
ANGLOS—FEMALE (N = 166)					
Age	−.015	.03	.020	3.70	.020
MF3	.213	7.03**	.066	12.31***	.085
MF1	.178	5.70*	.025	4.60*	.110
SR1	.190	5.50*	.029	5.50*	.140

Overall F = 6.53*** (*df* = 4/161)

Notes: MF1 = Male-Female Sexuality
MF3 = Female Responsibility
SR1 = Liberation
SR2 = Freedom-Equality
The minus sign (−) denotes relationships that were not in the predicted direction.
*$p \leq .05$ **$p \leq .01$ ***$p \leq .001$

TABLE 35. Regression of Selected Demographic and Sex-Race Related Variables on Fault Scores for Blacks

INDEPENDENT VARIABLES	BETA	F RATIOS FOR BETA	R^2 CHANGE	F RATIOS FOR R^2 CHANGE	R^2
BLACKS—ALL (N = 289)					
Age	−.159	7.26**	.018	5.73*	.018
Sex	−.097	1.62	.009	2.93	.027
Income	.060	1.11	.009	3.01	.036
MF1	.166	6.13*	.029	9.34**	.066
MF3	.159	5.68*	.028	8.85**	.093
SR2	.127	4.70*	.014	4.46*	.107
SR1	.136	4.48*	.010	3.05	.117
Victimization	−.123	4.27*	.010	3.36	.127

Overall F = 5.10*** (*df* = 8/280)

INDEPENDENT VARIABLES	BETA	F RATIOS FOR BETA	R^2 CHANGE	F RATIOS FOR R^2 CHANGE	R^2
BLACKS—MALE (N = 142)					
Age	−.128	2.60	.019	3.23	.019
MF1	.160	3.21	.050	8.66**	.069
MF3	.147	2.89	.070	12.07***	.139
Victimization	−.185	5.55*	.024	4.20*	.164
SR3	.146	3.19	.021	3.54	.184
SR1	.178	4.22*	.018	3.12	.202
SR2	.157	3.27	.019	3.27	.221

Overall F = 5.44*** (*df* = 7/134)

INDEPENDENT VARIABLES	BETA	F RATIOS FOR BETA	R^2 CHANGE	F RATIOS FOR R^2 CHANGE	R^2
BLACKS—FEMALE (N = 147)					
Income	.280	12.00***	.066	10.43**	.066
Age	−.139	2.98	.019	2.98	.085

Overall F = 6.70** (*df* = 2/144)

Notes: MF1 = Sexual Conflict
MF3 = Victim-Defined Rape
SR1 = Traditionality
SR2 = Modified Liberation
SR3 = Liberation
The minus sign (−) denotes relationships that were not in the predicted direction.
*$p \le .05$ **$p \le .01$ ***$p \le .001$

TABLE 36. Regression of Selected Demographic and Sex-Race Related Variables on Fault Scores for Mexican Americans

INDEPENDENT VARIABLES	BETA	F RATIOS FOR BETA	R^2 CHANGE	F RATIOS FOR R^2 CHANGE	R^2
MEXICAN AMERICANS—ALL (N = 311)					
SR3	.196	10.77**	.024	7.83**	.024
MF2	−.141	5.39*	.016	5.32*	.040
SR2	.082	2.16	.008	2.73	.049
Discrimination	−.100	3.08	.007	2.20	.055
Intergroup	.091	2.47	.008	2.47	.063

Overall F = 4.11*** (*df* = 5/305)

MEXICAN AMERICANS—MALE (N = 152)					
Religion	.171	4.88*	.031	5.20*	.031
SR3	.239	9.06**	.036	5.95*	.067
SR2	.196	6.12	.039	6.49*	.105
Victimization	.123	2.53	.015	2.53	.121

Overall F = 5.04*** (*df* = 4/147)

MEXICAN AMERICANS—FEMALE (N = 159)					
Religion	−.122	2.36	.019	3.14	.019
SR3	.194	5.63*	.020	3.37	.039
MF2	−.145	3.06	.015	2.42	.054
Intergroup	.116	2.16	.013	2.16	.067

Overall F = 2.77* (*df* = 4/154)

Notes: MF2 = Rape Wish
    SR2 = Equality
    SR3 = Female Role
The minus sign (−) denotes relationships that were not in the predicted direction.
    *$p \leq .05$ **$p \leq .01$ ***$p \leq .001$

TABLE 37. Regression of Selected Demographic and Sex-Race Related Variables on Court Scores for Anglos

INDEPENDENT VARIABLES	BETA	F RATIOS FOR BETA	R² CHANGE	F RATIOS FOR R² CHANGE	R²
ANGLOS—ALL (N = 326)					
R Score	.761	523.63***	.683	750.69***	.683
F Score	.123	13.04***	.017	19.24***	.701
Sex	−.077	5.55*	.003	3.05	.703
Victimization	.066	4.51*	.004	3.96*	.707
MF1	.048	2.23	.002	2.23	.709

Overall F = 155.96*** (df = 5/320) Subset F = 2.98* (df = 3/320)

INDEPENDENT VARIABLES	BETA	F RATIOS FOR BETA	R² CHANGE	F RATIOS FOR R² CHANGE	R²
ANGLOS—MALE (N = 160)					
R Score	.756	221.89***	.635	295.58***	.635
F Score	.122	6.03*	.010	4.81***	.646
Education	.134	6.98**	.007	3.20	.653
Income	−.102	4.26*	.008	3.65	.661
Intergroup	.098	4.06*	.009	4.06*	.669

Overall F = 62.33*** (df = 5/154) Subset F = 3.40* (df = 3/154)

INDEPENDENT VARIABLES	BETA	F RATIOS FOR BETA	R² CHANGE	F RATIOS FOR R² CHANGE	R²
ANGLOS—FEMALE (N = 166)					
R Score	.763	277.96***	.717	445.09***	.717
F Score	.144	10.07**	.017	10.61**	.734
Intergroup	−.069	2.86	.004	2.24	.737
Victimization	.067	2.61	.004	2.60	.742

Overall F = 155.44*** (df = 4/161) Subset F = .24 (df = 2/161)

Notes: MF1 = Male-Female Sexuality
Subset F ratios were computed for partial correlations. They test the signifcance of the proportional reduction of unexplained variance with the effects of Rape (R) and Fault (F) Scores partialled out of both independent and dependent variables. The minus sign (−) denotes relationships that were not in the predicted direction.

*p ≤ .05   **p ≤ .01   ***p ≤ .001

217

TABLE 38. Regression of Selected Demographic and Sex-Race Related Variables on Court Scores for Blacks

INDEPENDENT VARIABLES	BETA	F RATIOS FOR BETA	R^2 CHANGE	F RATIOS FOR R^2 CHANGE	R^2
BLACKS—ALL (N = 289)					
R Score	.627	242.84***	.450	298.30***	.450
Sex	.264	32.08***	.101	67.05***	.552
Income	−.086	4.72*	.008	5.07*	.559
Discrimination	.108	7.04**	.008	5.13*	.567
SR3	.085	3.24	.005	3.25	.572

Overall F = 75.64*** (df = 5/283) Subset F = 15.65*** (df = 4/283)

INDEPENDENT VARIABLES	BETA	F RATIOS FOR BETA	R^2 CHANGE	F RATIOS FOR R^2 CHANGE	R^2
BLACKS—MALE (N = 142)					
R Score	.707	129.59***	.595	231.38***	.595
F Score	.090	2.15	.014	5.39*	.609
Age	.111	4.37*	.010	3.74	.618
SR3	−.154	7.65**	.018	6.88**	.636
Discrimination	.117	4.51*	.011	4.43*	.647
Intergroup	.079	2.11	.005	2.11	.653

Overall F = 42.27*** (df = 6/135) Subset F = 3.80** (df = 4/135)

INDEPENDENT VARIABLES	BETA	F RATIOS FOR BETA	R^2 CHANGE	F RATIOS FOR R^2 CHANGE	R^2
BLACKS—FEMALE (N = 147)					
R Score	.697	83.03***	.251	58.08***	.251
F Score	.228	9.08**	.057	13.10***	.308
Income	−.179	6.10*	.023	5.31*	.331
Age	.115	2.89	.011	2.56	.342
SR3	−.168	6.02*	.034	7.76**	.376
Discrimination	.118	3.08	.013	3.11	.389
MF2	.095	2.00	.009	2.00	.398

Overall F = 13.13*** (df = 7/139) Subset F = 3.61** (df = 5/139)

Notes: SR3 = Liberation
MF2 = Blame-Skepticism

Subset F ratios were computed for partial correlations. They test the significance of the proportional reduction of unexplained variance with the effects of Rape (R) and Fault (F) Scores partialled out of both independent and dependent variables. The minus sign (−) denotes relationships that were not in the predicted direction.

*$p \leq .05$ **$p \leq .01$ ***$p \leq .001$

TABLE 39. Regression of Selected Demographic and Sex-Race Related Variables on Court Scores for Mexican Americans

INDEPENDENT VARIABLES	BETA	F RATIOS FOR BETA	R^2 CHANGE	F RATIOS FOR R^2 CHANGE	R^2
MEXICAN AMERICANS—ALL (N = 311)					
R Score	.620	205.98***	.481	338.66***	.481
F Score	.078	3.47	.005	3.18	.485
Sex	.181	19.37***	.023	16.49***	.509
Education	−.084	4.56*	.010	7.08**	.519
Religion	−.068	3.17	.005	3.26	.523
SR3	.160	14.59***	.033	23.04***	.556
SR2	−.103	6.60*	.011	8.04**	.568
MF2	.076	3.24	.005	3.23	.573

Overall F = 50.50*** (*df* = 8/302) Subset F = 8.51*** (*df* = 6/302)

INDEPENDENT VARIABLES	BETA	F RATIOS FOR BETA	R^2 CHANGE	F RATIOS FOR R^2 CHANGE	R^2
MEXICAN AMERICANS—MALE (N = 152)					
R Score	.698	184.65***	.577	237.34***	.577
Education	−.087	3.08	.010	4.11*	.587
MF2	.126	4.72*	.040	16.52***	.627
MF1	.097	2.64	.013	5.44*	.640
SR3	−.088	2.14	.005	2.14	.645

Overall F = 53.12*** (*df* = 5/146) Subset F = 5.91*** (*df* = 4/146)

INDEPENDENT VARIABLES	BETA	F RATIOS FOR BETA	R^2 CHANGE	F RATIOS FOR R^2 CHANGE	R^2
MEXICAN AMERICANS—FEMALE (N = 159)					
R Score	.539	71.24***	.408	123.67***	.408
F Score	.170	7.63**	.025	7.51**	.433
Income	−.089	1.95	.019	5.87*	.452
Age	−.115	3.25	.007	2.22	.460
SR3	.161	7.06**	.029	8.62**	.488
Intergroup	−.104	3.17	.010	3.17	.498

Overall F = 25.18*** (*df* = 6/152) Subset F = 4.40** (*df* = 4/152)

Notes: SR2 = Equality   MF1 = Male-Female Sexuality
        SR3 = Female Role   MF2 = Rape Wish
Subset F ratios were computed for partial correlations. They test the significance of the proportional reduction of unexplained variance with the effects of Rape (R) and Fault (F) Scores partialled out of both independent and dependent variables. The minus sign (−) denotes relationships that were not in the predicted direction.

     *$p \leq .05$ **$p \leq .01$ ***$p \leq .001$

REFERENCES

Abarbanel, Gail. 1976. Helping victims of rape. *Social Work* 21: 478–82.

Agopian, Michael W.; Duncan Chappell; and Gilbert Geis. 1974. Interracial forcible rape in a North American city: an analysis of sixty-three cases. In *Victimology*, eds. Israel Drapkin and Emilio Viano, pp. 93–102. Lexington, Mass.: D. C. Heath.

Amir, Menachem. 1971. *Patterns of Forcible Rape*. Chicago: University of Chicago Press.

Barrera, Mario; Carlos Muñoz; and Charles Ornelas. 1974. The barrio as an internal colony. In *La Causa Politica: A Chicano Politics Reader*, ed. F. Chris Garcia, pp. 281–301. Notre Dame, Ind.: University of Notre Dame Press.

Bart, Pauline. 1975. Rape doesn't end with a kiss (unpublished paper).

BenDor, Jan. 1976. Justice after rape: legal reform in Michigan. In *Sexual Assault: The Victim and the Rapist*, eds. Marcia J. Walker and Stanley L. Brodsky, pp. 149–60. Lexington, Mass.: D. C. Heath.

Bird, Caroline. 1969. *Born Female*. New York: Pocket Books.

Blauner, Robert. 1972. *Racial Oppression in America*. New York: Harper and Row.

Bode, Janet. 1978. *Fighting Back*. New York: Macmillan Publishing Company.

Bohmer, Carol. 1977. Judicial attitudes toward rape victims. In *Forcible Rape: The Crime, the Victim and the Offender*, eds. Duncan Chappell, Robley Geis, and Gilbert Geis, pp. 161–69. New York: Columbia University Press.

Brodyaga, Lisa; Margaret Gates; Susan Singer; Marna Tucker; and Richardson White. 1975. *Rape and Its Victims: A Report for Citizens, Health Facilities, and Criminal Justice Agencies*. Washington, D.C.: National Institute of Law Enforcement and Criminal Justice, Law Enforcement Assistance Administration, U.S. Department of Justice.

Brown, Lee P. 1977. Causes of crime. In *Black Crime: A Police View*, ed. Herrington J. Bryce, pp. 37–65. Washington, D.C.: Law Enforcement Assistance Administration, U.S. Department of Justice.

Brownmiller, Susan. 1975. *Against Our Will: Men, Women and Rape*. New York: Bantam Books.

Burgess, Ann Wolbert; and Lynda Lytle Holmstrom. 1974a. *Rape: Victims of Crisis*. Bowie, Md.: Robert J. Brady.

————. 1974b. Crisis and counseling requests of rape victims. *Nursing Research* 23: 196–202.

————. 1974c. Rape trauma syndrome. *American Journal of Psychiatry* 131: 981–86.

————. 1976a. Coping behavior of the rape victim. *American Journal of Psychiatry* 133: 413–18.

————. 1976b. Rape: its effect on task performance at varying stages in the life cycle. In *Sexual Assault: The Victim and the Rapist*, eds. Marcia J. Walker and Stanley L. Brodsky, pp. 23–33. Lexington, Mass.: D.C. Heath.

Calhoun, Lawrence G.; James W. Selby; and H. Elizabeth King. 1976. *Dealing with Crisis.* Englewood Cliffs, N.J.: Prentice-Hall.

Calhoun, Lawrence G.; James W. Selby; and Louise J. Warring. 1976. Social perception of the victim's causal role in rape: an exploratory examination of four factors. *Human Relations* 29: 517–26.

Carmichael, Stokely; and Charles V. Hamilton. 1967. *Black Power: The Politics of Liberation in America.* New York: Random House (Vintage Books).

Cash, W. J. 1941. *The Mind of the South.* New York: Alfred A. Knopf.

Chappell, Duncan; Gilbert Geis; and Faith Fogarty. 1974. Forcible rape: bibliography. *The Journal of Criminal Law and Criminology* 65: 248–63.

Chappell, Duncan. 1976. Forcible rape and the criminal justice system: surveying present practices and projecting future trends. In *Sexual Assault: The Victim and the Rapist,* eds. Marcia J. Walker and Stanley L. Brodsky, pp. 9–22. Lexington, Mass.: D. C. Heath.

Chappell, Duncan; Robley Geis; and Gilbert Geis, eds. 1977. *Forcible Rape: The Crime, the Victim and the Offender.* New York: Columbia University Press.

Chappell, Duncan; Gilbert Geis; Stephen Schafer; and Larry Siegel. 1977. A comparative study of forcible rape offenses known to the police in Boston and Los Angeles. In *Forcible Rape: The Crime, the Victim and the Offender,* eds. Duncan Chappell, Robley Geis, and Gilbert Geis, pp. 227–44. New York: Columbia University Press.

Chappell, Duncan; and Susan Singer. 1977. Rape in New York City: a study of material in the police files and its meaning. In *Forcible Rape: The Crime, the Victim and the Offender,* eds. Duncan Chappell, Robley Geis, and Gilbert Geis, pp. 245–71. New York: Columbia University Press.

Chodorow, Nancy. 1972. Being and doing: a cross-cultural examination of the socialization of males and females. In *Women in Sexist Society,* eds. Vivian Gornick and Barbara K. Moran, pp. 259–91. New York: New American Library.

Clark, Lorenne; and Debra Lewis. 1977. *Rape: The Price of Coercive Sexuality.* Toronto, Canada: The Women's Press.

Clark, Terri Patrice. 1976. Primary health care: counseling victims of rape. *American Journal of Nursing* 76: 1964–66.

Cleaver, Eldridge. 1968. *Soul on Ice.* New York: Dell Publishing.

Cohen, Murray L.; Ralph Garofalo; Richard B. Boucher; and Theoharis Seghorn. 1971. The psychology of rapists. *Seminar in Psychiatry* 3: 307–27.

Connell, Noreen; and Cassandra Wilson. 1974. *Rape: The First Sourcebook for Women.* New York: New American Library.

Cotera, Martha P. 1976. *Diosa y Hembra: The History and Heritage of Chicanas in the U.S.* Austin, Tex.: Statehouse Printing.

Curtis, Lynn A. 1975. *Violence, Race and Culture.* Lexington, Mass.: D. C. Heath.

————. 1976. Rape, race and culture: some speculation in search of a theory. In *Sexual Assault: The Victim and the Rapist,* eds. Marcia J. Walker and Stanley L. Brodsky, pp. 117–34. Lexington, Mass.: D. C. Heath.

Day, Beth. 1977. The hidden fear. In *The Black Male in America,* eds. Doris Y. Wilkinson and Ronald L. Taylor, pp. 193–206. Chicago: Nelson-Hall.

Del Drago, Maria. 1975. The pride of Inez Garcia. *MS* 3: 54, 84.

Dollard, John. 1957. *Caste and Class in a Southern Town.* Garden City, N.Y.: Doubleday Anchor Books.

Domhoff, G. William. 1967. *Who Rules America?* Englewood Cliffs, N.J.: Prentice-Hall.

DuBois, W.E.B. 1921. *Darkwater.* New York: Harcourt, Brace and Company.

Dye, Thomas R. 1976. *Who's Running America?* Englewood Cliffs, N.J.: Prentice-Hall.

Elmendorf, Mary. 1977. Mexico: the many worlds of women. In *Women: Roles and Status in Eight Countries,* eds. Janet Zollinger Giele and Audrey Chapman Smock, pp. 127-72. New York: John Wiley.

Fanon, Frantz. 1967. *Black Skin, White Masks.* New York: Grove Press.

_____. 1968. *The Wretched of the Earth.* New York: Grove Press.

Farris, Buford E.; and Norval Glenn. 1976. Fatalism and familism among Anglos and Mexican Americans in San Antonio. *Sociology and Social Research* 60: 393-402.

Federal Bureau of Investigation, U.S. Department of Justice. 1980. *Uniform Crime Reports for the United States.* Washington, D.C.: U.S. Government Printing Office.

Feild, Hubert S.; and Nona J. Barnett. 1977. Forcible rape: an updated bibliography. *The Journal of Criminal Law and Criminology* 68: 146-59.

Feild, Hubert S. 1978. Attitudes toward rape: a comparative analysis of police, rapists, crisis counselors and citizens. *Journal of Personality and Social Psychology* 36: 156-79.

Fisher, Gary; and Ephraim Rivlin. 1971. Psychological needs of rapists. *British Journal of Criminology* 11: 182-85.

Fox, Sandra Sutherland; and Donald J. Scherl. 1972. Crisis intervention with victims of rape. *Social Work* 17: 37-42.

Friedan, Betty. 1964. *The Feminine Mystique.* New York: Dell Publishing.

Gager, Nancy; and Cathleen Schurr. 1976. *Sexual Assault: Confronting Rape in America.* New York: Grosset and Dunlap.

Gebhard, Paul H.; John H. Gagnon; and Wardell B. Pomeroy. 1965. *Sexual Offenders: An Analysis of Types.* New York: Harper and Row.

Golan, Naomi. 1978. *Treatment in Crisis Situations.* New York: Free Press.

Greer, Germaine. 1970. *The Female Eunuch.* New York: McGraw-Hill.

Griffin, Susan. 1971. Rape: the all American crime. *Ramparts* 10: 26-35.

Groth, Nicholas A.; and Ann Wolbert Burgess. 1977. Rape: a sexual deviation. *American Journal of Orthopsychiatry* 47: 400-406.

Guttmacher, Manfred; and Henry Weihofen. 1952. *Psychiatry and the Law.* New York: W.W. Norton.

Hacker, Helen Mayer. 1951. Women as a minority group. *Social Forces* 30: 60-69.

Halpern, Howard A. 1973. Crisis: a definitional study. *Community Mental Health Journal* 9: 342-49.

Harris Survey. October, 1977. Rape act of violence. New York: Louis Harris and Associates.

Hernton, Calvin. 1977. The Negro male. In *The Black Male in America,* eds. Doris Y. Wilkinson and Ronald L. Taylor, pp. 244-64. Chicago: Nelson-Hall.

Holmstrom, Lynda Lytle; and Ann Wolbert Burgess. 1978. *The Victim of Rape: Institutional Reactions.* New York: John Wiley.

Horos, Carol V. 1974. *Rape*. New Canaan, Conn.: Tobey Publishing.

Hunter, Floyd. 1959. *Top Leadership USA*. Chapel Hill, N.C.: University of North Carolina Press.

Iscoe, Ira; Martha Williams; and Jerry Harvey. 1964. Age, intelligence and sex as variables in the conformity behavior of Negro and White children. *Child Development* 35: 451-60.

Jones, Cathaleen; and Elliot Aronson. 1973. Attribution of fault to a rape victim as a function of respectability of the victim. *Journal of Personality and Social Psychology* 26: 415-19.

Kammeyer, Kenneth. 1966. Birth order and the feminine sex role among college women. *American Sociological Review* 31: 508-15.

Katz, Sedelle; and Mary Ann Mazur. 1979. *Understanding the Rape Victim*. New York: John Wiley and Sons.

Kemmer, Elizabeth Jane. 1977. *Rape and Rape-Related Issues: An Annotated Bibliography*. New York: Garland Publishing.

Klemmack, Susan H.; and David L. Klemmack. 1976. The social definition of rape. In *Sexual Assault: The Victim and the Rapist*, eds. Marcia J. Walker and Stanley L. Brodsky, pp. 135-47. Lexington, Mass.: D. C. Heath.

Kopp, Sheldon B. 1962. The character structure of sex offenders. *American Journal of Psychotherapy* 16: 64-70.

Ladner, Joyce. 1971. *Tomorrow's Tomorrow: The Black Woman*. Garden City, N.Y.: Doubleday.

Largen, Mary Ann. 1976. History of women's movement in changing attitudes, laws, and treatment toward rape victims. In *Sexual Assault: The Victim and the Rapist*, eds. Marcia J. Walker and Stanley L. Brodsky, pp. 69-73. Lexington, Mass.: D. C. Heath.

Liebow, Elliot. 1966. *Tally's Corner*. Boston: Little, Brown and Company.

McCahill, Thomas W.; Linda C. Meyer; and Arthur M. Fischman. 1979. *The Aftermath of Rape*. Lexington, Mass.: Lexington Books.

McCombie, Sharon L. 1976. Characteristics of rape victims seen in crisis intervention. *Smith College Studies* 46: 137-58.

McCombie, Sharon L.; Ellen Bassuk; Roberta Savitz; and Susan Fell. 1976. Development of a medical center rape crisis intervention program. *American Journal of Psychiatry* 133: 418-19.

McDermott, Joan M. 1979. *Rape Victimization in 26 American Cities*. Washington, D.C.: Law Enforcement Assistance Administration, National Criminal Justice Information and Statistics Service.

MacDonald, John M. 1971. *Rape Offenders and Their Victims*. Springfield, Ill.: Charles C. Thomas.

Machado, Manuel A., Jr. 1978. *Listen Chicano! An Informal History of the Mexican American*. Chicago: Nelson-Hall.

MacKellar, Jean. 1975. *Rape: The Bait and the Trap*. New York: Crown Publishers.

Mann, Coramae Richey; and Lance H. Selva. 1978. Sexualized racism: the impact of the myth of Black sexuality. Paper presented at the annual meeting of the Southwestern Sociological Association, April 1978, at Houston, Texas.

————. 1979. The sexualization of racism: the Black as rapist and white justice. *Western Journal of Black Studies* 3: 168-77.

Mason, Karen Oppenheim, with Daniel R. Denison and Anita J. Schacht. 1975. *Sex-Role Attitude Items and Scales from U.S. Sample Surveys.* Rockville, Md.: National Institute of Mental Health.

Medea, Andra; and Kathleen Thompson. 1974. *Against Rape.* New York: Farrar, Straus and Giroux.

Millett, Kate. 1969. *Sexual Politics.* New York: Avon.

Mills, C. Wright. 1956. *The Power Elite.* New York: Oxford University Press.

Mirandé, Alfredo; and Evangelina Enríquez. 1979. *La Chicana.* Chicago: University of Chicago Press.

Moore, Joan, with Harry Pachon. 1976. *Mexican Americans.* 2d ed. Englewood Cliffs, N.J.: Prentice-Hall.

Moquin, Wayne; and Charles Van Doren, eds. 1971. *A Documentary History of the Mexican Americans.* New York: Praeger.

Murillo, Nathan. 1976. The Mexican American family. In *Chicanos: Social and Psychological Perspectives,* ed. Carol A. Hernandez, pp. 15–26. St. Louis: C. V. Mosby.

Myrdal, Gunnar. 1964. *An American Dilemma.* Vol. 2. New York: McGraw-Hill.

Nass, Deanna R. 1977. *The Rape Victim.* Dubuque, Iowa: Kendall/Hunt.

Nie, Norman H.; Hadlai C. Hull; Jean G. Jenkins; Karin Steinbrenner; and Dale H. Bent. 1975. *Statistical Package for the Social Sciences.* 2d ed. New York: McGraw-Hill.

Nieto, Consuelo. 1974. Chicanas and the women's rights movement. *Civil Rights Digest* 6: 36–42.

Nieto-Gomez, Anna. 1974. Colonial women in Mexico. *Regeneracion* 2: 18–19.

————. 1976. Heritage of la hembra. In *Female Psychology: The Emerging Self,* ed. Sue Cox, pp. 226–36. Chicago: Science Research Associates.

Notman, Mulkah T.; and Carol C. Nadelson. 1976. The rape victim: psychodynamic considerations. *American Journal of Psychiatry* 133: 408–13.

Pacht, Asher; Seymour Halleck; and John C. Ehrmann. 1962. Diagnosis and treatment of the sex offender: nine year study. *American Journal of Psychiatry* 118: 802–8.

Peñalosa, Fernando. 1968. Mexican family roles. *Journal of Marriage and the Family* 30: 680–89.

Rainwater, Lee. 1970. *Behind Ghetto Walls: Negro Families in a Federal Slum.* Chicago: Aldine.

Rawick, George P. 1972. *From Sundown to Sunup: The Making of the Black Community.* Westport, Conn.; Greenwood Press.

Reynolds, Janice M. 1974. Rape as social control. *Catalyst* 8: 62–67.

Rose, Vicki McNickle. 1977a. Rape as a social problem: a byproduct of the feminist movement. *Social Problems* 25: 75–90.

————. 1977b. The rise of the rape problem. In *This Land of Promises: The Rise and Fall of Social Problems in America,* eds. Armand L. Mauss and Julie Camille Wolfe, pp. 167–96. Philadelphia: J. B. Lippincott.

Rossi, Peter; Emily Waite; Christine E. Bose; and Richard E. Berk. 1974. The seriousness of crime: normative structure and individual differences. *American Sociological Review* 39: 224–37.

226   *References*

Russell, Diana E.H. 1975. *The Politics of Rape: The Victim's Perspective.* New York: Stein and Day.

Scanzoni, John. 1972. *Sexual Bargaining: Power Politics in the American Marriage.* Englewood Cliffs, N.J.: Prentice-Hall.

Schlegel, Alice. 1977. Toward a theory of sexual stratification. In *Sexual Stratification,* ed. Alice Schlegel, pp. 1–40. New York: Columbia University Press.

Schram, Donna. 1978. *Forcible Rape.* Washington, D.C.: National Institute of Law Enforcement and Criminal Justice, Law Enforcement Assistance Administration.

Schultz, Leroy G., ed. 1975. *Rape Victimology.* Springfield, Ill.: Charles C. Thomas.

Selby, James W.; Lawrence G. Calhoun; and Thomas A. Brock. 1977. Sex differences in the social perception of rape victims. *Personality and Social Psychology Bulletin* 3: 412–15.

Stack, Carol B. 1974. *All Our Kin.* New York: Harper and Row.

Stampp, Kenneth M. 1956. *The Peculiar Institution.* New York: Random House (Vintage Books).

Staples, Robert. 1973. *The Black Woman in America.* Chicago: Nelson-Hall.

Stember, Charles H. 1976. *Sexual Racism.* New York: Harper and Row.

Stevens, Evelyn P. 1973. Marianismo: the other face of machismo in Latin America. In *Female and Male in Latin America,* ed. Ann Pescatello, pp. 89–101. Philadelphia: University of Pittsburgh Press.

Sutherland, Sandra; and Donald Scherl. 1970. Patterns of response among victims of rape. *American Journal of Orthopsychiatry* 40: 503–11.

Terry, Robert. 1974. The white male club. *Civil Rights Digest* 6: 66–77.

United States Commission on Civil Rights. 1970. *Mexican Americans and the Administration of Justice in the Southwest.* Washington, D.C.: U.S. Commission on Civil Rights.

Valentine, Bettylou. 1978. *Hustling and Other Hard Work.* New York: The Free Press.

Walker, Marcia J.; and Stanley L. Brodsky, eds. 1976. *Sexual Assault: The Victim and the Rapist.* Lexington, Mass.: D.C. Heath.

Walster, Elaine. 1966. Assignment of responsibility for an accident. *Journal of Personality and Social Psychology* 3: 73–79.

Weis, Kurt; and Sandra S. Borges. 1973. Victimology and rape: the case of the legitimate victim. *Issues in Criminology* 8: 71–115.

Williams, Joyce E. 1973. *Black Community Control: A Study of Transition in a Texas Ghetto.* New York: Praeger.

Wood, Jim. 1976. *The Rape of Inez Garcia.* New York: G. P. Putnam's Sons.

Yankelovich, Daniel. 1974. *The New Morality.* New York: McGraw-Hill.

INDEX

ABOUT THE AUTHORS

JOYCE E. WILLIAMS is Associate Professor of Sociology at Texas Woman's University in Denton, Texas. She is the author of *Black Community Control: A Study of Transition in a Texas Ghetto.*

KAREN A. HOLMES is Assistant Professor of Social Work at the University of Houston, Central Campus, Houston, Texas. Her articles have appeared in *Health and Social Work, Victimology, Social Casework,* and other journals.